The Sack Race

THE SACK RACE

THE STORY OF FOOTBALL'S GAFFERS

CHRIS GREEN

MAINSTREAM
PUBLISHING

EDINBURGH AND LONDON

First published in Great Britain in 2002 by
MAINSTREAM PUBLISHING COMPANY (EDINBURGH) LTD
7 Albany Street
Edinburgh EH1 3UG

ISBN 1 84018 588 0

A catalogue record for this book is available from the British Library

Typeset in Apollo, Century Gothic and Garamond
Printed and bound in Great Britain by
Creative Print and Design Wales

Contents

Acknowledgements		7
Preface		9
CHAPTER ONE	Season 2001: A Managerial Idiocy	13
CHAPTER TWO	The Gaffer's Lot: The Manager's Job Under the Microscope	28
CHAPTER THREE	Cometh the Hour, Cometh the Gaffer: How Britain's Football Bosses Bloomed	43
CHAPTER FOUR	The Vision Thing: The Gaffer in Football's 'Golden Age'	60
CHAPTER FIVE	The 1960s: The Sacking Spree Starts	75
CHAPTER SIX	A Change at the Top: Do Sackings Work?	88
CHAPTER SEVEN	Jobs for the Boys: The Case for Qualified Football Managers	104
CHAPTER EIGHT	Money Matters: The Wheeling, Dealing World of Football's Bosses	119
CHAPTER NINE	Blame it on the Boardroom	134
CHAPTER TEN	Fit to Manage? Health, Wealth and Heart Attacks Among Britain's Football Bosses	150
CHAPTER ELEVEN	Tough at the Top, Harder at the Bottom	164
CHAPTER TWELVE	From a 'Turnip' to a Swede: International Management and the Continental Coaching Invasion	178
CHAPTER THIRTEEN	Gearing Up the Gaffers of Tomorrow	195
CHAPTER FOURTEEN	I Will Survive: Does the Gaffer Have a Future?	210
Bibliography		220
Sources		222
Index		224

Acknowledgements

The biggest problem when writing a book about a profession like football management is time. Football managers, at all levels of the game, don't usually have any. I have torn my hair out (and, believe me, I don't have much to spare!) trying to obtain interviews, being agonisingly close to prising managers away from the demands of their job . . . and failing. So, I would like to give a hearty thanks to all the football folks (too many to list, I fear) who have spared the time to be interviewed for this book. Gaffers, take a bow!

I would like to pass on special thanks to Stuart Clarke for the wonderful photos, Andrew and Ben Cullis, especially for the loan of family photos, Janet and Dan Bergara, Hugh Hornby at the National Football Museum in Preston (if you haven't been, go visit), David Barber at the FA library, John Barnwell and the staff at the League Managers Association, John Stevens of Sports Coach UK, the folk at Callowbrook Swifts FC, Dr Dorian Dugmore and his trusty assistant at the Wellness Centre, Damian Watson, the staff at the *Birmingham Post and Mail*, my journalistic colleague, David Conn, who has been a constant source of encouragement . . . and anyone else I have pestered to death!

Finally, extra special thanks to my wife, Teresa, not only for her help and support but also her love, and for putting up with me during the period I have been writing this book. Oh, and our cat, Mia, who has watched me write virtually every word without feeling the need to help.

Preface

In April 1979, John Barnwell, the manager of Wolverhampton Wanderers, nearly lost his life in a late-night car crash. A car wing mirror stuck in his head. A millimeter either side and he could have died. Was it the result of tiredness? We'll never know the exact cause, for Barnwell can't recall anything of the three months following the crash, but he blames the long hours of football management and, in this case, his unnecessary decision to drive across the Midlands from a charity function so he could be at the training ground early the following morning.

After surviving a tricky operation, Barnwell ignored the recommended recuperation time. 'We need you back, John,' a director told him. Within weeks, despite thumping headaches and having to wear 'a silly woolly hat' to work, Barnwell negotiated the two biggest transfers in British football history at the time. He took Wolves to a victorious League Cup final later in the season. John Barnwell was the toast of the town. Two years later he resigned after refusing to sign a new contract as Wolves, careering into debt due to ground redevelopments, attempted to sell their star striker, Andy Gray, behind Barnwell's back.

Eighteen years earlier, Stan Cullis – who guided Wolves to a trio of Football League championships, a couple of FA Cup final wins and had captained them (and England between the wars) had been sacked shortly after keeling over his desk through worry at the club's poor start to the season. A man who lived and breathed football, who was known as the 'passionate puritan', a deeply religious man whose motto, written on the walls of the Molineux dressing-rooms, was 'there is no substitute for hard work', was unceremoniously sacked and asked to return his club keys immediately and pay the advance telephone rental to the club.

Welcome to the ruthless world of football management where the normal rules of business and morality need not apply. Wolverhampton Wanderers span into decline after both these dismissals – almost terminally following Barnwell's exit – but they are not unique in the way they have treated some of their managers.

In six seasons at Stockport County, Danny Bergara made millions of pounds for the club by developing players and selling them on. He took them from the old Fourth Division into the new Second Division. After a row about a small expenses bill he was slapped around, threatened and then sacked by the club chairman.

These are just a few of the tales of managerial conflict included in this book, in which I seek to explain the harsh reality of the gaffer's job and its often crushing after-effects.

The Sack Race is the real story of football management, far removed from the sanitised biographies of rich, famous and successful managers. Yes, they are here too, but only in the context of football management as a whole, alongside less notable, though no less passionate or articulate, names. *The Sack Race* looks at how this breed of football bosses emerged, at how their job developed as a mixed, fundamentally flawed, myriad of two separate functions – administrator on one hand, coach on the other – with the people asked to straddle these jobs often not qualified to do either. Many still aren't. Managers struggle to shake off the yoke of this legacy.

Their continental coaching counterparts, who have come into British football in increasing numbers over the past decade, carry none of this baggage. European players and coaches have introduced standards of professionalism that have never been seen in this country before. Coaching is seen as a profession on the continent, not just something you fancy doing when your playing days are over and because you're a mate of the chairman.

For too long British football management wallowed in a dark age where the myths of the magic sponge, munching steak and chips three hours before kick off, running off injuries and the spurious theory that denying players the chance to train with a ball would somehow make them 'want it' more on matchdays, reigned supreme. Even drinking water during rigorous training sessions was banned because football's mythology said it was bad for you.

The Sack Race is also about the future of coaching and management, a debate the game must have if the current wave of sackings described 'as an embarrassment to our industry' by one interviewee for this book is to cease. British football gets the managers it deserves. Too many are unqualified, ill-prepared, wrongly appointed, operating under unacceptable working conditions, prematurely sacked and berated in the media. When there are complaints, many justify managers' poor working conditions by arguing that they are well paid (and obviously those at the top earn huge salaries). It may be suggested that they aren't good enough for the clubs they are managing, that if they don't like the heat they should get out of the kitchen (to go where, precisely?).

But the blame should not simply be directed at managers. What about the system that educates coaches and managers, the directors who hire and fire them, the fans and the media, the prevailing climate that constantly demands fall guys at clubs perceived as failing?

There are huge efforts being made to improve the training of managers and coaches so they have the skills to cope with the modern demands of football management. At many of the top clubs, there are admirable attempts being made to ease the manager's workload, to re-examine the previously held boss's brief. The old-style gaffers who were left to deal with transfers, contracts and agents are on the way out, and a good job too. Their freedom to dabble in murky financial waters underpinned the Bungs Inquiry of the 1990s. Why did the game have a culture where some managers were doling out or receiving brown paper envelopes? Because their clubs allowed them to.

Football management should be a dream job. Imagine having the chance of assembling a team of professional players, who can combine their respective skills and become a winning team? It is said so often by football's gaffers that it really is the next best thing to playing. Management is like a drug to many of them. There are endless tales of masterstroke decisions that have swung matches, or memorable mottoes and team talks. Alec Stock, the former Fulham, QPR and

Luton manager always sent his teams out with a final message: 'Remember, chaps, we always play with a bit of style and a bit of class.' Gary Megson sent his West Brom side, who were on the brink of promotion in April 2002, out for the second half of a game with Crystal Palace with the words: 'You're going out as First Division players, come back as Premiership players.' These are moments of inspiration. If only it was always so simple.

For many, football management turns into a nightmare. It can lead to serious health problems, reduce managers to workaholics, alcoholics or nervous wrecks and, ultimately, to bitter and beaten men. A job which should bring joy, and so often does, should not be this way. It has to change.

Oh, and I never did find a convincing reason why football managers are ubiquitously called 'The Gaffer'.

– CHAPTER ONE –

Season 2001:
A Managerial Idiocy

THAT WAS THE SEASON THAT WAS. THERE WAS A MEMORABLE championship race, with Arsenal, as in 1998, ultimately achieving the Premier League and FA Cup Double. England reached the World Cup quarter-finals, beating old enemies Germany and Argentina en route – Germany 5–1 in the qualifiers and Argentina 1–0 in the so-called 'Group of Death' in Japan – but losing to skilful, swanky Brazil.

Gérard Houllier's heart attack served as a timely early season reminder of the pressures involved in football management. It wasn't, after all, Sir Alex Ferguson's final season in football, and, for once, Man Utd didn't win the Premiership. The Football League's longest-serving managers, Dario Gradi and Dave Bassett, passed their 1,000th games in charge . . . and then promptly saw their respective clubs get relegated.

Domestically, it was a depressing picture. The season ended with huge financial questions hanging over the game. Ten Football League clubs were in administration in the summer of 2002, with many of them citing an anticipated loss of future revenue in the wake of the collapse of ITV Digital as a reason. The Football League took the unusual step of encouraging fans to protest directly to ITV Digital's parent companies, Granada and Carlton, as part of a longer-term strategy, as they see it, to get the companies to pay a greater slice of the money owed for the remaining two years on their agreement than has been on offer.

If English football needed a wake-up call that all was not well with the state of football management, season 2001–02 provided it. More managers lost their jobs then than any previous season. Including the close season (making the timescale from May 2001 to May 2002), 63 English Premier/Football League managers moved on: more than two-thirds. The figure reached 70 within weeks of the end of the season – the sacking cycle was moving on. Going into season 2002–03, only 11 managers have been in charge of their clubs for five years or more.

The average managerial tenure, previously at an appallingly low 18 months, plummeted to an even more pitiful 15 months. This is a worrying statistic for any industry, particularly one where loyalty to the gaffer is legendarily weak.

'I simply don't know why it is,' says Steve Coppell, who left Brentford at the end of the 2001–02 season. The former chief executive of the League Managers Association (LMA), and Bungs Inquiry panellist, added: 'Most chairmen don't run their private businesses the way they run football clubs. If they did, they wouldn't have made any money in the first place.' It's a widely held view, and one that is difficult to disagree with.

The situation is clear. In the face of any semblance of a crisis, English football clubs give their managers the boot. A closer look at the statistics makes even grimmer reading. Not only did the dismissals come in record numbers but they came earlier in the season, too. Paul Bracewell quit Halifax before the end of August and six further managers had lost their jobs by the end of September, including notable names like Peter Taylor at Leicester City (the first big Premiership casualty of the season) and Gordon Strachan, who had been under fire for months at relegated Coventry City. These managers were given less time than the length of the pre-season build-up. Mind you, two managers didn't even make the starting line; Andy King was sacked by Swindon and Ian Atkins resigned from Carlisle United.

Then came October – traditionally a quiet month for managerial manoeuvres. Not in 2001. Ten managers were dismissed in this month alone, including more big names: Jim Smith, after six years in charge at Derby, Stuart Gray, who had only been appointed at Southampton in March (so had only been given six months to prove himself, three during the close season), Trevor Francis after five years at Birmingham, and Peter Shreeves, who had battled manfully against the financial odds at Sheffield Wednesday. A further ten had gone by

Christmas, with Scotland's Craig Brown also leaving his post.

In November, former England defender Mark Wright left Oxford United amid a row about racist remarks made to an official. At first sight this looked like a rare moral stance in football taken by the club's Asian owner, Firoz Kassam. Wright was fined £1,750 by the Football Association (FA) for making an offensive remark to a black referee and resigned hours before an internal club disciplinary hearing. But the appointment of Ian Atkins, only a few weeks earlier, as director of football had muddied the waters. As Wright left, Atkins moved seamlessly into office.

Managers were so incensed by the unprecedented spate of dismissals there was talk of revolt in the air. A knighted former shipyard trade union leader, now residing at Old Trafford, reportedly urged his colleagues to down tools – or at least boycott those clubs unprepared to honour the contracts of the managers they'd sacked. The prospect of placard-waving managers huddled around burning oil drums at the gates of club training grounds did not materialise. Sir Alex Ferguson's idea was immediately given short shrift by the LMA chief executive, John Barnwell. With the prospects of a Professional Footballers' Association (PFA) strike looking a distinct possibility, over a row about how much money the Players' Union should receive from the fresh TV deals negotiated in the summer of 2001, Ferguson's suggestion did not seem that fanciful. After all, the LMA receives only a fraction of the revenue that the PFA gets from the game's central funds (the LMA receives funds from the FA, Premiership and Sky TV) and one could hardly say their members are not key personnel.

'Nineteen sacked managers and we're not even into November,' fumed Sunderland's Peter Reid. 'We all go through lean spells . . . but it's up to everyone to keep their nerve.' Wolves' boss Dave Jones thought it was 'crazy – it's just one big merry-go-round'. Much-travelled Leicester boss Dave Bassett hurled the ball back in to the directors' court. 'I question a lot of the directors who make the changes. I'm not sure they are qualified in a lot of cases,' he said.

But the predominant reaction to the wave of dismissals was shrug-shouldered weariness. Sackings, we're told, are part of the inevitable pressures of the modern game, a consequence of the irritability of club chairmen, the volatility of PLCs and the ever-increasing expectations of the media and fans.

Yet these glib phrases don't stand up to scrutiny and fail to answer the fundamental question: why do we have such an appalling approach to football management in this country?

For starters, more managers lose their jobs lower down the ladder, where the only blue chips in sight are soggy ones left on the terraces several days after matches. The Stock Exchange can only ever be partly to blame at a very specific number of clubs, unless you include the pressure placed upon smaller clubs by the growing gap between rich and poor, which is undeniably significant, but largely irrelevant in terms of managerial loyalty.

Another common belief is that most managers are sacked. This is a reasonable assumption. Radio phone-ins are full of fans who reckon their manager has 'lost the plot', and call for his head. You can almost hear the grinding of the axe echoing through club corridors.

'You don't listen to them,' says Peter Taylor, who moved on to Brighton and won promotion to Division One in 2002 before unexpectedly leaving at the end of the season. 'If you did, you'd go mad.' There were even fickle Manchester United fans who phoned Radio Five Live's *Six-o-Six* programme in December demanding the Old Trafford board give Sir Alex Ferguson the boot – retirement or not.

Two-thirds of the managers who lost their jobs in 2001–02 were sacked, with the rest resigning, retiring or leaving by 'mutual consent' (which usually means that in exchange for keeping quiet, the club will settle up your contract pronto). Any group of employees leaving in such huge numbers in any other industry would be viewed with alarm. An immediate remedy would be sought. Action would be taken. British football does nothing.

At times, football seemed to have lost its moral compass in 2001–02, and at nowhere more than Elland Road. If any club walked across the road to find a manhole cover to fall down it was Leeds United. The club's management, in its broadest sense including the boardroom, was at the heart of it. The trial of Lee Bowyer and Jonathan Woodgate, who were defendants in a case where an Asian teenager, Sarfraz Najeib, had been chased and beaten up in Leeds city centre, ended in

December 2001. Woodgate was convicted of affray, for which he served 100 hours' community service. Bowyer was acquitted. But although Leeds fined both players – Woodgate two months' wages and Bowyer eventually four weeks' wages after initially being transfer-listed for refusing to pay – both were offered new contracts within a month of the trial verdicts.

If this wasn't deemed insensitive enough (although the media itself immediately forecasted, in some cases demanded, Bowyer's prompt return to Sven's England squad), the decision of David O'Leary and his publishers to call his book *Leeds United on Trial*, released in January 2002 (again, less than a month after the end of the Bowyer/Woodgate hearing) seemed at best opportunistic, at worst crass. Described in the blurb for his book as 'arguably the most charismatic football manager in Britain today', O'Leary promised 'the inside story of an astonishing year'. The main concern for many people wasn't the book's content so much as the timing of its publication, within a month of the trial ending. The title didn't help. It implied Leeds United somehow felt they had been put in the dock. In the week it was published O'Leary had an altercation with Cardiff City chairman Sam Hammam in the Ninian Park car park after Leeds' volatile exit from the FA Cup. His constant defence of serial red card collector Alan Smith became a bore.

It all fell apart for Leeds United – they slipped out of the UEFA Cup, the Premiership title race and the FA Cup. But it wasn't chairman Peter Ridsdale, O'Leary, Bowyer, Woodgate or Smith who were blamed by the fans. Instead they rounded on the club's quiet coach, Brian Kidd. To the fans he was, and always will be, a Manc, a former Manchester United player and coach, but a few people decided it had all gone wrong when Kidd arrived. In the sort of admirable stance that was long overdue, chairman, manager and players all stood by O'Leary's assistant.

In the summer of 2002 O'Leary was sacked. Both chairman Peter Ridsdale and O'Leary deny it had anything to do with his book, its content, timing or indeed anything to do with the so-called Bowyergate trial, although this was initially picked upon by the media. It has been suggested it boiled down to results and Leeds' relatively poor showing in 2001–02, and O'Leary's apparent unwillingness to part with his best players in order to balance the books. We may not know the real reason for some time.

While most of Leeds United's problems appeared to be off the pitch, fellow Yorkshire club Sheffield United's difficulties were most definitely on it during one mid (or mad) March home game. Their match against promotion-chasing West Bromwich Albion exploded into controversy in the space of a few second-half minutes. It became known as the 'Battle of Bramall' (United's ground is Bramall Lane).

United were already down to ten men, having had their goalkeeper Simon Tracey sent off early in the game, when West Brom went 2–0 up midway through the second half. United manager Neil Warnock decided to make an immediate double substitution, bringing on Cameroon striker Patrick Suffo and French midfielder Georges Santos. But within a couple of minutes both players were sent off, Santos for an horrendous tackle on Albion's Andy Johnson (apparent retribution for being elbowed in the face by Johnson, at the time a Nottingham Forest player, the previous season) and Suffo for head-butting visiting captain Derek McInnes in the inevitable ensuing mêlée.

Now down to eight men, United quickly conceded another goal to make it 3–0, but the game ended in farce with eight minutes left when United defender Robert Ullathorne went down injured and midfielder Michael Brown left the pitch with a groin injury. When a team has only six players the game has to be abandoned, so referee Eddie Wolstenholme had no option but to call a halt to the chaotic proceedings.

The resulting acrimony was not a good advert for English football. Neil Warnock is no stranger to controversy. Warned and fined for his touchline behaviour several times during the 2001–02 season, only weeks earlier he had allegedly told a magazine reporter that if he won the National Lottery he would buy Sheffield Wednesday's ground, Hillsborough, and burn it down. With his opposite number from West Brom, Gary Megson, making veiled accusations of 'someone' on the United bench ordering players to go down with fake injuries and/or get themselves sent off to get the game abandoned (and possibly replayed), Warnock appeared to be in hot water. Megson claimed he was so disgusted with what was going on he left the touchline to sit in the directors' box for the remainder of the game.

Warnock did little to dampen the flames when asked after the game what he thought should happen next. He replied 'Dunno,' which suggested he didn't necessarily think West Brom should be awarded the points. Although he later changed his mind, saying he thought the result should stand, he also appeared to offer an unconvincing reason for withdrawing Brown. Warnock claimed Brown had been carrying a groin injury for several weeks – so why had he started this largely meaningless match (meaningless for United at least; they were in mid-table)? If Brown had been carrying an injury for so long, why wasn't he substituted earlier, for example when Santos, a fellow midfielder, came on?

Warnock's enemies – he prides himself on being unpopular among fellow managers and the press – called for him to be sacked. There was also speculation that Sheffield United might be heavily punished by massive fines for the club and some of the individuals concerned. A ten-point deduction was mooted, which would have cast them into the relegation zone.

Five days later the Football League duly handed West Brom the three points but the FA, who are responsible for disciplinary matters, let the dust settle and a month later fined Sheffield United £10,000. Manager Warnock was cleared of a charge of improper conduct, but was found guilty of a minor charge involving the fourth official, for which he was fined £300. Player/coach Keith Curle was fined £500 for improper conduct and Suffo was handed a £3,000 fine for violent conduct. No action was taken against Gary Megson for his remarks about the unnamed United staff. In glorious irony, United beat two of West Brom's rivals in the week following the so-called Battle of Bramall and at the end of the season Curle, Suffo and Santos all left the club.

That victory for West Brom was the first in a sequence in which they won eight (and drew the other) in a nine-match unbeaten run-in. Megson's men pipped their near (but not so dear) neighbours Wolves to the second promotion spot in the First Division. It brought unbridled joy to their long-suffering fans. But party time in the Black Country didn't last long. No sooner had the champagne corks been popped than the club were in turmoil. Chairman Paul Thompson resigned ten days after the Baggies' final game of the season (see

Chapter Nine for more detail). The constant rows between Thompson and Megson went on for most of last season and were often fought out via the media. Their differences encapsulate an essential tension in British football management.

Thompson believes that, like any other form of business, decision-making within a football club should be a team concept, but that final decisions rest with the board. Although the football manager or first-team coach is the most important employee at the club, there are certain areas, like the scouting system or youth development, where the manager has an input but responsibility should remain outside his immediate control. Relieving the manager of these responsibilities seems to make sense when you look at the ludicrously wide duties of managers and the long hours worked by Britain's football bosses. Gary Megson does not agree.

Thompson took the unusual step of standing down after a brief meeting with Megson on 30 April 2002. Realising that Megson's stock was high with the supporters, he resigned rather than risk the fans' wrath by sacking a popular manager or trying to muddle along at loggerheads with him. He wrote to the club's season-ticket holders and to other Premiership chairmen explaining his actions and why he believes football management is failing and needs to change.

It is a compelling argument and supported by the shocking statistics highlighted earlier in this chapter. If the stalwarts of the football industry fail to recognise that change is needed then British football management has no chance of improving.

In less than his two and a half years as a football club chairman Paul Thompson was remarkably successful. He was clearly doing something right – he had an approach which achieved results. Gary Megson had managed four clubs in five years prior to joining West Brom, so has witnessed or been a victim of the game's notorious managerial instability. Together Thompson and Megson forged a formidable partnership.

It took Megson three months after Thompson left to sign a new contract with West Brom. This uncertainty was not what a club going into the Premiership would have wanted. Thompson's resignation (although, significantly, he has kept his 23 per cent shareholding) caused a boardroom split and a battle for the control of the club. A fan wrote on a supporters' website that 'good managers are hard to find, but good chairmen are almost impossible to find'. Last season West Brom had both. The tragic irony is that going into the Premier League, when the club needed both to be at their best, they faced having neither. Jokes flying around the West Midlands that West Brom will be in the Premiership for three seasons – autumn, winter and spring – could turn out to have a ring of truth.

The reasons behind the rising number of managerial resignations must be a cause of concern. Of course, some seek higher office at a bigger club, others retire and many jump before they are pushed. In the face of poor results (often regardless of the reasons) it is easier to walk away without the public ignominy of being sacked. But many more walk for seemingly nebulous reasons: 'the pressure', 'to spend more time with my family', to take early retirement or move upstairs into that new and often vague role, director of football.

Long-term statistics show that another fallacy – that there is simply some kind of managerial merry-go-round where the same group of managers swap seats when the music stops – isn't true. Of the 275 managers who lost their jobs in the five seasons prior to season 2001–02, only 34 are still managers and a further 63 are in other coaching roles, which leaves 178 who have left the game altogether. Two-thirds. Where have they gone? What are they doing? Does anyone care?

Not that we should view managers as martyrs or cowering victims. Although some managers have to wait months, maybe years, for compensation payments when they are sacked, many receive the sort of massive pay-offs when they leave clubs that most employees in other walks of life could only dream of. And this for usually cocking things up. Many drive smart cars and own huge houses, the trappings of wealth unimaginable to people from similar social and educational backgrounds. I've failed to get hold of other out-of-work managers who have been busy sunning themselves in far-off climes. Poor a lot of them ain't.

Football bosses are hardly a loyal breed, either to their clubs or their fellow managers. Enough managers leapt into the breach in 2001–02 with indecent haste when a managerial colleague was axed to raise questions over whether discussions took place while the previous incumbent was still in position. But that's football. Whether it is the fault of the directors or the managers, it is simply seen as 'just the way it is'. There is also too little loyalty shown by some managers to clubs, the fans, or the boards of directors who sometimes dig deep into their pockets when Mr Right (manager) comes along. Given the whiff of a chance to move to a seemingly more attractive post, although that is often difficult to define, most managers head for the door, regardless of where that leaves their former club.

The difficulty of walking out on a long-term contract was seen in 2001 when Steve Bruce left Crystal Palace for Birmingham City. Bruce was amazed to find that he couldn't simply walk out on his contractual obligation without any comeback. But Palace chairman Simon Jordan was made of sterner stuff. He won a High Court injunction which made Bruce serve a period of notice until a satisfactory compensation package was reached with his new employers, Birmingham City. Jordan said he was even prepared to make Bruce wait nine months if necessary. In the end, it took two months of legal wrangling for Bruce to complete his move to St Andrew's. It is not surprising that when he returned to Selhurst Park on Easter Monday with Birmingham he did not receive a hero's welcome.

In the sort of irony football frequently throws up, Palace then appointed Birmingham's former boss, Trevor Francis, as their new manager. Bruce, who at the time of writing has managed five clubs in four years, offered to quit management altogether if he didn't get Birmingham into the Premiership in five years. But at the end of the season Birmingham, and Bruce, were duly promoted via a penalty shootout in the play-off final.

Bruce and Francis weren't the only managers to swap seats in season 2001–02. When Micky Adams left Second Division Brighton & Hove Albion for Premiership Leicester City, albeit as Dave Bassett's No. 2 (although he took full charge towards the end of the season), Peter Taylor went in the opposite direction.

Taylor's topsy-turvy experience exemplifies much of the management folly. An England international player in the mid-'70s, he worked his way up from non-league football and even cut his teeth managing a Sunday-morning team. Taylor was made England Under-21 manager by his former Spurs team mate Glenn Hoddle in 1997. At the time Taylor was managing Conference side Dover Athletic, but had managed Southend and been a coach at Watford.

Taylor later balanced the England Under-21 job with guiding Gillingham to promotion to the First Division in his only season with the club. He moved on to Leicester City, and, with Steve McClaren, took charge of the senior England team for one game ahead of Sven-Goran Eriksson's appointment.

Then it all fell apart. Leicester's league form plummeted, they were knocked out of the FA Cup by Second Division Wycombe Wanderers, and a poor start to the 2001–02 season was too much. He was sacked in September 2001 and, to make matters worse, Taylor had relinquished his role with the England set-up in the summer. He lost the lot. So it was back to square one – to the Second Division, where he was two years ago with Gillingham. Like that small spider constantly weaving its web in the cave with Robert the Bruce, he went back to building up his career all over again. Taylor is acknowledged as one of the English game's better coaches. He was fast-tracked by Hoddle, but has now been dropped like a stone. Surely we should look after coaches better than this? At the end of the season Taylor quit Brighton, who he had steered to promotion from the Second Division, after a row about the funds available for First Division football.

Promisingly, last season also saw the launch of a new FA course for élite managers and coaches, the long-awaited UEFA Pro Licence course, a qualification every other major European country including Scotland has offered its top coaches for ages, and which is a pre-requisite to coaching in many countries across Europe. A select group of 11 invited managers took part in the inaugural course, uniquely comprising a 240-hour distance-learning package (see Chapter 13). More will follow year on year. It is a qualification our top managers should aspire towards, but, as yet, there is no mandate to take a single coaching badge in order to manage in the UK at present.

British football lags behind the rest of Europe and South America in this regard. A licence doesn't make you a good coach, not having one doesn't mean you can't do the job. But if football management is to achieve professional status, and professional respect, the system has to change. The UEFA Pro licence must be given greater significance, or it won't be worth the paper it is written on.

There are calls for mandatory coaching qualifications to be introduced into English football. UEFA are pushing for all Champions League club managers to have the Pro licence from 2003. There are many people, like the FA's technical head Howard Wilkinson, who see this as a good step, but there are significant elements within the English game who are resistant.

The arguments against seem flimsy. But who is going to compel clubs to act? Where will the exemption line be drawn? Will the FA really punish, say, Man Utd if Alex Ferguson doesn't put his 240 curricular hours in to get a Pro licence? Hardly. Lower down the game, the Football League are likely to object to mandatory qualifications. 'Anything that costs them money will be given short shrift,' I was told by a League spokesman. Coaching courses cost money. 'It isn't even an issue.'

Which means that the Football League's more notable names, like the manager of last season's First Division champions, Kevin Keegan at Manchester City, will be able to carry on unqualified. While the 11 managers and coaches selected for the UEFA Pro licence were beavering away at the start of the course in July 2001, David Platt, England's first full-time Under-21 manager, was taking up office after starting his UEFA A licence, the next level down.

Football managers routinely work in conditions that would be deemed unacceptable in other areas of employment. The lure of this glamour game and supporters' views that 'they would play for nothing' has allowed employment conditions to be routinely steamrollered. They work excessive hours and few have watertight job descriptions. Football managers didn't even have their own professional body – the LMA – until 1992.

The fact is that beneath the sackings and scandals, far away from the £1 million salaries of the Premiership bosses, there are managers habitually working double the number of maximum hours recommended in the EU's Working Time Directive. Most of the managers interviewed in this book cheerfully (and wearily) admit to working 80-plus hours a week, including the ubiquitous four to five nights a week on scouting missions.

Most lack the will, the imagination or the basic management skills to delegate and, perhaps more importantly, to trust others to do the routine work. They insist they have to be seen on the training ground at the crack of dawn the following morning. Why? Can't the assistant manager take a coaching session? Can't scouts be relied upon to report back? Can't the managers see that burning the candle at both ends is a recipe for disaster?

There are two important factors here. The first is that managers are so susceptible to the sack they actually want to make all the key decisions; that's why they need to see, for example, every potential signing for themselves. After all, it's their neck that is on the line. Secondly, the pressure is so enormous there are now legitimate concerns about the health of managers.

2001 also saw the start of a project called Fit to Manage, being carried out by the Wellness Centre in Stockport, a cardiology unit, funded by the LMA. It's a four-year rolling project which allows members to undergo regular health testing and monitoring. The aim is to predict and prevent stress levels reaching a critical stage. The heart attack suffered by Gérard Houllier at half-time during a Liverpool v. Leeds game in October 2001, and other victims like Joe Kinnear, Graeme Souness, Barry Fry and, fatally, Jock Stein, hang over the sport.

A *Tonight With Trevor McDonald* programme screened in January 2002 monitoring blood pressure levels of Bolton's Sam Allardyce and Leicester's Dave Bassett during a tense relegation encounter, revealed the sorts of stress and tension experienced by managers during games. There is more on this work in Chapter Ten.

Temporarily, Gérard Houllier's heart attack led to many people (not least of all in my profession) to pause and think about the pressures heaped on football managers and the goldfish-bowl existence they work in. It didn't last.

Soon the headlines were screaming for more sackings. Why? So that more pressure can be applied to the next poor sucker? What does that do for continuity at a football club? How exactly does sacking the manager necessarily push the club forward? Nationally, how does the game breed better managers when so many are routinely hammered into the ground week in, week out? And what happens to those who can't 'stand the heat'?

On the international front, salvation appeared to be found in an unusual place – at the head of English football, with England coach,

Sven-Goran Eriksson, who brought a breath of fresh air to football management in the crazy season that was 2001–02. Eriksson's appointment was criticised by many quarters of the game, including LMA chief executive John Barnwell, who insisted that any number of Englishmen could have done the job. The answer was Germany 1 England 5, a performance like no other in a generation, one which rang alarm bells around the world. Here was a coach (not a manager note, and definitely not someone you'd call 'Gaffer'), who didn't beat his chest to inspire his side, who didn't swear and shout himself hoarse or put faith in mystics. Here was a well-qualified, intelligent coach who was capable of taking an arbitrary look at the players and coaches available to him, and handling them in a manner which got the best out of them.

Significantly, there was no cultural or historical baggage applied to his selections – no silent bias (he can't be a good player, he plays for club X). Sven also had no history of antagonism with managers he would require to release players for international duty. He was something of a blank piece of paper for the press. They knew little about him, apart from his remarkable career managing some of Europe's biggest clubs.

The press reaction to Sven has been largely favourable so far, although England's failure to match Brazil in terms of technical skill and the manner of their defeat – an inability to fight back when losing – led to the first real doubts about Eriksson's ability.

But the national game had needed leaders capable of handling affairs on the world stage, and they aren't to be found readily in the domestic game, which is why FA chief executive Adam Crozier should be applauded for making this bold choice. So what does this say about our national game? Lots. It says that in 2001 there wasn't a credible candidate for the England manager's job. When Sven moves on, let's hope there are more options.

Even Scotland – which has produced more than its share of top managers – looked overseas last season. In February 2002, Berti Vogts became Scotland's national team coach. He did not wave a magic wand. His first game in charge was a 5–0 thrashing in France. Unlike England, Scotland has a legacy of nurturing world-class coaches by the score – 42 Scots bosses have taken the UEFA Pro licence, for example. Coaches from all over the world (including England) head to Largs (the home of the SFA coaching centre) to take their coaching qualifications. It carries weight. It means something. But they don't stay. Or don't, or won't, return. After Brown, Scotland felt the need to look abroad and chose a coach with a proven track record. Now they need the players . . .

One of the genuinely welcomed appointments of 2001–02 was David Moyes, a product of Largs, who moved from Preston North End to Everton in March 2002. Moyes is a fully qualified coach with a UEFA Pro licence, and a keen-eyed gaffer who is hungry for success. He is not a 'big-name Charlie' looking to earn a few bob before retiring; he has been tipped for the top.

A novel *Big Brother*-style idea of allowing the fans to have an input in selecting the team almost materialised in 2001–02. A Channel 4 series called *You're the Manager* was planned for a spring screening. Fans at Nationwide Conference club Stevenage Borough would influence team selection by voting a limited number of players in or out of the team. It had to happen. But the six-week experiment was rejected by the League's committee. Ironically, Borough's real boss, Paul Fairclough, quit a few weeks later.

Season 2001–02 also saw the release of a comedy film about football management. *Mike Bassett Football Manager*, with Ricky Tomlinson cast in the lead role, was 90 minutes of as many managerial clichés as possible. Tomlinson was a mix of many a manager, from Graham Taylor and Barry Fry to Barry Williams (Sutton United's poetry-quoting boss who oversaw the non-Leaguers' 1988 FA Cup victory over holders Coventry City) and more. Bradley Walsh played a Phil Neal 'yes, boss'-type sidekick, and another character resembled Lawrie McMenemy. It was all too close for comfort.

But where does British football's confused jargon come from? The media, the terraces (remember them) or the game itself? Our attitudes to football management are emblematic of the problems weighing down British society and culture, raising issues about the role of sport in our society, about our historical baggage (we're forever playing catch-up and resistant to change) and uneasy employer/employee relations.

Football is the most highly professionalised and passionate sport in the country, yet it treats the people who teach, coach and manage it as expendable pawns. There's too little loyalty shown and there isn't an atmosphere to inspire the best of sporting ethics to prevail. Season 2001–02 showed the best and worst of the manager's lot.

– CHAPTER TWO –

The Gaffer's Lot: The Manager's Job Under the Microscope

People still phone me and call me gaffer or boss. They can call
me anything they like as long as they win. But if you say to
footballers you can call me anything you like they would still
call me the gaffer, because that's the way football is.

Ray Graydon

THE GAFFER. IN FOOTBALL, IT IS THE HIGHEST TERM OF ESTEEM, THE
ultimate accolade, bestowed upon the man in charge. The manager, the
gaffer, the boss. A youth or reserve manager or coaches will never be
called 'gaffer'. Neither will an academy director, chief executive or
director of football, not even the chairman, no matter how 'hands on',
not even if he is bankrolling the whole show, will be recognised by this
title. Even ex-gaffers are called 'gaffer' by footballers. Football folk
litter their conversations with phrases like: 'So I said "gaffer" . . .'

In other forms of industry 'the gaffer' is slang for the man in charge,
usually a foreman or chargehand. These days, people only call their
boss a gaffer in jest. It carries echoes of Ealing comedies, warm beer
and industrial heritage – days when workers tugged their forelocks,
but only to trusty old gaffers who knew their trade. No self-respecting
overalled worker would ever call a smart-arsed yuppie a gaffer. It just
doesn't work. Gaffers ruled ok. People in charge of boats are called old
gaffers. Film and TV lighting engineers are called gaffers. Dictionaries
define gaffers as paternalistic figures, often old men, respected for their
wisdom and seniority, even Godfathers, though don't, as they say in

modern parlance, go there. Did Ruud van Nistelrooy have to kiss 'Don' Ferguson's hand when he arrived at Old Trafford. 'Some day, Ruud, I may call upon you to do me a favour . . .'

Today the only people who call their bosses gaffers with any hint of sincerity are footballers, sometimes even foreign footballers for whom the phase has no significance. They may be huge wage earners, the sort of people who don't have to call anybody anything if they don't fancy it, players who negotiate six-figure weekly salaries and image rights. Bet Beckham calls Fergie 'the gaffer' all the time.

In how many other industries do workers earn multiples more than their bosses? Despite the job's legendary insecurity, football managers are called gaffers, although statistically a gaffer isn't likely to be your gaffer for long (less than 18 months on average), so why grovel to him? And what is the gaffer's lot? I mean, what does he actually do? Quite often the gaffer's role is blurred because, frankly, the aims of his job are unclear. If you were to stop a football manager in full 'let's all gel together and take each game as it comes' flow, ask him what his job is and where it's written down, I bet he would struggle to tell you.

Historically, managers have always had some kind of nebulous role – partly administrative, partly coaching. Yes, we all know football managers deal with team affairs and that the analogy of a corner-shop manager compared to a supermarket manager holds true – it is no good trying to claim that Sir Alex Ferguson deals with the same minutiae as the boss of a non-league club – but there are similar shades of grey. At the top level, the modern manager's role is now primarily that of a senior coach, especially at clubs who employ chief executives or directors of football to deal with transfer and contracts negotiations. But British football's gaffers still carry the historic guilt of their predecessors on their shoulders.

Many refuse to go home after the coaching is done, after there are no more team affairs to be handled, after the media have disappeared. Their continental counterparts – who earn much more respect in their communities because they are perceived as professionals (a point to be covered later in the book) – have no compunction about sunning themselves on the veranda or beach in the afternoon. British football managers cherish the work ethic. Most work ludicrously long, often needless, hours.

The manager's duties have never been clearly defined. Small wonder so many football managers become dyed in the wool dabblers, enmeshed in areas of the business they have no right (or experience or expertise) to deal with, like complex financial deals involving the transfer of players, wages and contracts. 'Only a lunatic would enjoy this side of the job,' says Howard Wilkinson, the former Sheffield Wednesday and Leeds United manager, now the FA's technical director. It is not something Wilkinson ever felt comfortable doing. Others are not so reticent. In his autobiography *Big Ron*, Ron Atkinson recalls, as manager of West Brom, agreeing a fee with Real Madrid for the sale of Laurie Cunningham by writing figures on a supermarket carrier bag at his home until they reached a suitable figure. Albion's chairman, Bert Millichip, a solicitor by trade who was nicknamed 'Bert the Inert' during his later chairmanship of the FA, sat in an adjoining room while these ad hoc negotiations took place.

The problem for some managers is that their precise role often isn't laid out in the terms and conditions of their employment. Nowadays they can consult their lawyers and/or the League Managers Association to get a contract hammered out with clear demarcations of duties. The clubs actually want it in writing. Chairmen, chief executives and directors of football will usually handle contracts and transfer negotiations, freeing up the gaffer to do what most of them want to do – coach the team. Scratch beneath the surface, though, and you'll find gaffers who have never seen a job description or taken a medical to get their job (regardless of the huge sums lavished on players). There are some who didn't want to work to a contract – they trusted the club! The most vulnerable gaffer is the one who wants, *really* wants, his first job.

When Bruce Rioch captained Scotland in the 1978 World Cup he couldn't have imagined that just four years later he would be scrubbing the baths at Torquay United. Rioch played 24 times for his country and enjoyed a notable playing career with Luton, Aston Villa, Derby (twice), Everton and a short spell in America with Seattle, before joining the Devon club as an understudy to the much-travelled Frank O'Farrell. O'Farrell was a wise old gaffer, a former manager of Leicester City and, briefly, Manchester United. He was one of the celebrated members of the so-called West Ham Academy – a group of players who, in the 1950s, used to discuss in-depth tactics in Cassettari's café on the Barking Road near Upton Park. Rioch says the hours he spent watching, listening and learning the rudiments of management from the soon-to-retire O'Farrell were 'invaluable'. His subsequent managerial career has included Middlesbrough, Millwall, Bolton, Arsenal, Norwich and Wigan – but he started on his hands and knees at Torquay.

'I was manager, coach, physiotherapist, kit man, cleaned the dressing-rooms, washed the baths, did the laundry,' Rioch recalls. 'I did it because I didn't want the chairman seeing it dirty. It was a difficult time for the club and we didn't want him to think it was falling apart. We wanted a pride in the place.'

This unqualified multi-skilling was never questioned by the club's hierarchy. 'I was at Tranmere one day and Joe Mercer came to make a presentation. He said to me: "Bruce, you'd be far better up here watching the game. You get a better view." I picked up the bucket and sponge and said: "Joe, it's a long way to run on from up there." I was trainer as well.' Rioch looks back on it with a smile, but also with shame. 'It was wrong, but I did it because it was necessary. A football club should know better that to let someone do that. Me running on, unqualified, with a bucket and sponge? It isn't right and it should have been recognised by the club. But it was overlooked.'

This sort of behaviour raised few eyebrows because, in Britain at least, the football industry has been allowed to run its own unregulated course. Rioch recalls telling his former boss at Luton Town, the late Alec Stock – a wise old managerial sage whom Bruce calls 'dear old Alec' – the extent of his duties at Torquay. 'He replied: "Steady on, old chap, you're bringing tears to my eyes." It was as if to say "Don't give me all that, I've seen it all before."'

When Rioch later managed Middlesbrough in the mid-1980s, when the gates of their former home, Ayresome Park, were locked as the club lurched into liquidation, the memories of Torquay came flooding back. 'My assistant was Colin Todd, the former England international defender, who has had his own career in management. We were changing in a little cubicle in a gymnasium amongst the vaulting horses and so forth. It was pitch black. Toddy said, "This is terrible."

I replied, "This is better than Torquay." It was progress of sorts. That sort of experience builds up resistance. You don't want your players seeing you upset or getting down. You have to project a positive attitude among your players or else it can fall apart.'

Rioch had no idea his first tentative steps in management would be taken in such reduced circumstances. It is the way so many managers start, and later they can't give up the hands-on approach when they move to more prominent posts. When playing for Aston Villa in his early 20s, Rioch would join club coach, Ron Wylie, on scouting missions to pick up tips from managerial greats like Bill Shankly. 'When you look to sign a player for Liverpool what are you looking for, Mr Shankly?' 'Well, son, I'm looking for a player who can play 42 games a season.' It stayed with Rioch. When signing players, even with today's squad systems, he still questions why a player has missed several games a season. 'Is he injury prone? Does he drop in form? It's a good guide.'

As for actually doing the job, Rioch has never forgotten the advice he received from O'Farrell. 'He brought me into the inner sanctum of the manager's office. I used to listen to him on the telephone dealing with managers, negotiating transfer fees. He would come up with some wonderful sayings like "You don't set out to be unpopular, but on the way you make unpopular decisions".'

Man-management is arguably the toughest and most important part of the gaffer's brief, in particular having to deliver bad news. 'One of the hardest parts of managing is telling young players you're releasing them. Frank told me to tell them the way you would want to hear it yourself, not to make it too long, and always be honest. I have a standard line: "I'm afraid I am going to be the bearer of bad news today. I'm going to release you from your contract." You've told the player what is going to happen, then you carry on with the details. It's better than spending time chatting with a player who is wondering what is going to happen to his future.'

'They're sad moments – really sad moments. I don't think anyone can enjoy seeing a 17-year-old youngster crying his eyes out in front of them. The mature professionals don't feel the same disappointment, but tears often flow with the young boys. They've set their hearts on being a footballer and it's a massive blow for them.'

Other managers have to find out the hard way. It is a profession akin to ski jumping – the only way to find out exactly what it is like is to hurtle down the slope. Ian Atkins, now director of football at Oxford United, always wanted to be a football manager. Throughout a nomadic playing career with eight clubs, which included winning a First Division championship medal with Everton in 1985, he would travel back to manage his mates' Sunday-morning team in his home town of Birmingham. When he returned to Birmingham City as a player, he coached the youth team at non-league Moor Green in his spare time, developing players like Ian Taylor (now Aston Villa), Dave Busst (the Coventry defender whose career was ended by a horrific leg injury) and Stewart Talbot, who moved on to Port Vale and Rotherham. But he was totally unprepared for the grim reality of being a gaffer when he was appointed player/manager of Colchester United at the age of 33 in 1990.

'Five weeks after becoming a manager I had to tell one of the players that his dad had committed suicide by setting fire to himself. It is the hardest thing I have ever had to do. I had to tell him because his sister had been on the phone. Welcome to the wonderful world of football management.'

Atkins had no interpersonal skills to fall back on. In most industries, managers are trained to handle their staff, taught how to dole out bad news. Not football. You're thrown into the deep end and it's hoped, rather than expected, that you can swim. 'I was shell-shocked. How do you tell a player, a person, that their father has killed himself? The player was my first signing, which made it all the more significant, in a way.'

Colchester had just been relegated from the Football League. The club had sacked their previous manager, Mick Mills, at the end of the previous season and for several weeks the playing side of the club had been ignored. 'It was one hell of a grounding. It was six weeks before the season started and we had no fixtures, no kit, no balls or training bibs and only a few players. It took months to get the team sorted out. It was a difficult spell with a difficult chairman. When he took them over he said he wanted them in the First Division in five years. A year later they were in the Vauxhall Conference.'

Atkins nearly resigned after his opening game, a tricky away fixture. 'The chairman came into the dressing-room criticising the team, so the next day I quit. I'd had enough. I was trying to get the thing going but what help was I getting? Some of the other directors came round and said "No, no, don't leave." I was playing as well. Everything calmed down and I stayed. I stuck to my guns and to what I thought was right. It stood me in good stead.'

Atkins' managerial career could have run into the sidings. Less hardy souls would, indeed, have quit. Instead, Atkins has become a renowned lower-league grafting gaffer. If you want someone who can wheel and deal, who can juggle a tight budget, who has a track record of scrimping and saving, of bringing players in cheaply, Atkins is your man. He managed Doncaster during a period when the club was in financial difficulty and Nothampton Town when they were brought back from the brink of extinction. At Chester City he worked for an owner, Terry Smith, who insisted on calling himself the manager (Atkins was director of football). He moved to Carlisle United during a season when the chairman, Michael Knighton, was struck off from being a director and his 23-year-old son, Mark, took over as chairman. There was very little money available because Knighton Snr was trying to sell the club. Atkins is now director of football at Oxford United.

You might think Rioch and Atkins had an unusually tough introduction to football management at lower-league clubs, where the money is legendarily tight. But the same happens further up the scale. In fact, most managers only get jobs when things are going wrong. They have little time to learn. Football's lack of continuity means background staff are rarely promoted from within. New gaffers usually bring their mates with them. It is often a clean sweep of the coaching staff when a manager is sacked.

Steve Coppell was identified as management material early in his career. The Manchester United and England winger had been chairman of the PFA and was a rare university graduate playing full-time football. When injury brought his playing career to a premature close, he had to decide what to do next. Like so many players, he went into management simply as a means of staying in the game. He was offered the manager's job at Second Division Crystal Palace in 1984 and accepted it.

'My first year in management was very much skin of the teeth,' he recalls. 'I was very fortunate. We finished seventh from bottom on the last weekend and that was the highest position we had been in all season. It was touch and go all season. I wouldn't wish that year on anybody because the learning curve was too steep.

'I took over a club who had been struggling at the bottom of the league for two years. There were massive financial restrictions at that time, I couldn't really do anything in the transfer market. At varying stages of the season I knew the players were looking to me to give them something that would help them win football games and, to be honest, I didn't have anything to offer. It was grit and determination that won us matches rather than design. It was a massive experience. I learned more in that year than in the rest of my managerial career put together.'

Coppell survived, and later thrived. He eventually took Palace into the (old) First Division and to an FA Cup final. But he could have sunk without trace. I guess that's football, but it seems no way to prepare people for this demanding job.

When a manager's brief can involve anything from running the youth set-up to scouting and spotting players, signing them, coaching them, dealing with transfers, deciding how much to pay them and running various administrative aspects of the club, let alone some of the things Bruce Rioch ended up doing at Torquay, he has to be a remarkable character. At larger clubs, the manager has to be a team leader – not just of players but also of his coaching staff and network of scouts and talent spotters. Managers need to have extraordinary leaderships skills. They also need to learn to delegate, to trust the opinions of those they employ. Too many don't. Most managers watch three to five games a week on top of their own club matches. This is exhausting, energy-sapping, involving endless hours on motorways travelling to and from games late at night, particularly when their control-freak tendencies demand that they be on the training ground early the next morning.

In 20 years of management Bruce Rioch has only ever signed one player without seeing him first. 'When you're spending someone else's money you'd better at least look at him. When you're sat around the boardroom and they ask "How many times have you seen him play?"

and you say "None, I'm going on the word of a chief scout," or the press ask the same question, they'll want to know why.

'I've only signed one player without seeing him play. It was Jon Goodman, when I was at Millwall. I was in Aberystwyth and my assistants Ian Evans and Bob Pearson had been to Bromley to see him play. They said: "I think you'd better sign him now or someone else might take him," and I asked, "How much is it going to cost?" They said "£20,000." I said: "Is he worth it?" "Yes." So I told them to do the deal.'

No football gaffer will get it right all the time. The best ones simply make the fewest mistakes. When Bruce Rioch was managing Middlesbrough in 1986 and the club were in liquidation he had to release 20 of the club's 34 professionals. Only one found another professional club. Rioch got it right. The remaining 14 formed the backbone of a side that would win successive promotions.

Most managers are not trained decision-makers. Coaching courses help, but the majority of managers learn, like Rioch, Atkins and Coppell, from hard experience. Football management, as Rioch found out at Torquay, can mean doing the lot – but without a defined brief, how can a manager hope to succeed? Rioch didn't even see a job description until he joined Arsenal – the fifth club he managed. He is not alone. 'It's one of those things you don't get in football,' says former Ajax and Liverpool midfielder Jan Molby, who is manager of Hull City. 'If I did have one, it wouldn't mean anything.'

We met while Molby was managing Third Division Kidderminster Harriers. He resigned a few weeks later. 'I am in charge of football matters, but who decides what that is? Obviously the first team, reserves and youth team, contract negotiations, in and out, and organising the coaching side of things. But that is a narrow brief and most managers will do other things on top.' Molby, like most of the managers interviewed for this book, did not have to take a medical to get a managerial job in football. 'I should be surprised but I'm not,' he says when he learns how common that is, 'because I know that's how football works. These are things that need to come in.'

So what distinguishes a manager from a coach? What credentials make a manager a true leader of men, the sort of person footballers are supposed to be prepared to run through brick walls for? Former

Walsall manager, Ray Graydon, a respected coach, one of the many managerial victims to get the dreaded sack in season 2001–02 and now boss at Bristol Rovers, says it's all down to decision-making:

'The gaffer is the guy who picks the team. You're the man in charge. You've got to make the decisions. Coaches don't. Gaffers have to make the tough decisions. I enjoy being a boss, having the final say, but I also enjoy being on the training ground working with the players rather than dealing with contracts or whatever. I can do both.'

The ability to inspire is paramount. The game is packed with stories of homespun psychology, the sort of natural man-management skills that would turn marker-pen-waving, flip-chart-filling business trainers green with envy. Bruce Rioch recalls his playing days at Luton Town, where Alec Stock would prowl the dressing-room before matches constantly quizzing his players and perking them up with his inspirational idiosyncrasies. 'Well?' he once asked Bruce, when he was tying his bootlaces. When he looked up, Stock had gone. 'I thought: "Well what? What does he want from me?" Then it clicked – he was keeping my mind alert.'

Stock would also pin signs around the wall. 'The winners are in this dressing-room', 'Don't walk through this door if you don't think you can win', and Rioch's favourite, 'Remember chaps, we always play with a bit of style and a bit of class'. 'Imagine going out with those words ringing in your ears,' laughs Rioch. Stock was the nostalgic football man Paul Whitehouse based his 'Ron Manager' character on for BBC2's *The Fast Show*. Jumpers for goalposts. Marvellous.

And then there was Cloughie. Brian Clough, the master of the message, Ol' Big-head, the media man's dream. Clough did not bother with elaborate tactics or team talks. 'Just find a red shirt,' he would say to the Nottingham Forest players prior to games. In other words, keep possession. While we have the ball, they can't score, we can. Frank Clark, who would succeed Clough after his remarkable 18-year reign at Nottingham Forest, remembers what Clough was like when he joined the club in their late 1970s heyday from Newcastle United. Clough, like Rioch, Atkins and co, began his managerial career the hard way at Fourth Division Hartlepool, where he even trained to drive the team coach, though he never actually did.

'If it is possible to be a born leader, Clough was it,' says Clark. 'He got the maximum from every player. I'm not sure how he did it, but there was a fine line between fear and healthy respect. I was a mature, experienced player who had played 500–600 games for Newcastle already. He knew what he was doing, he had an innate sense of what was right. He wasn't a great tactician. He didn't fill our heads with in-depth theory, he stuck to a rigid 4-4-2 system. But he had an aura about him. He knew what he was doing.

'He would do the unexpected. He never studied psychology, he just knew what worked. I remember when we went to play Liverpool in the second leg of a European Cup tie. We were going along the M62 when he told the driver to stop on the hard shoulder and made everybody have a bottle of beer. If you mentioned that today, people would be horrified. He did it to ease the tension – he hated seeing the players uptight. He believed you can't play if you aren't relaxed.

'The night before a League Cup final against Southampton, we had already eaten but he got everyone together, ordered two dozen bottles of champagne and made us all stay there and listen to him and Peter Taylor telling stories while we drank the champagne. Most managers wouldn't even dream of that. We won the final, of course. When you were expecting a bollocking you didn't get one, and when you weren't, that was inevitably when you got one. He kept you on your toes. He was a master at it.'

Clough's approach is not to be copied – other managers rightly prefer to be more studious. David Moyes, another managerial name to move clubs in 2002, this time through genuine promotion from First Division Preston North End to Premiership Everton, uses a psychologist. One of the new breed of managers, Moyes is comfortable working alongside sports science professionals. In the 2000–01 play-off semi-finals against Birmingham City, Moyes deployed his own psychology. He had seen footage of Manchester United's last-gasp Champions League win over Bayern Munich in 1999, which showed the respective benches when United equalised in the last minute of the game. The Bayern bench was down, United were buoyed – they immediately scored a second goal in injury time.

'It showed the difference a goal could make,' says Moyes. 'We trailed Birmingham 1–0 after the first leg. All we needed was a goal to get right back into it.' Moyes was right, Preston equalised. But then

Birmingham scored. Preston, though, levelled in the last minute (just like United in the Champions League final) to take the tie to penalties. Again, Moyes had done his research. 'I had studied every penalty Birmingham had taken in the League Cup final a couple of months earlier and noted which way their goalkeeper preferred to dive and where their players put their penalties.' This information was fed to Preston 'keeper David Lucas, while Moyes' opposite number, Trevor Francis, was busy complaining about which end of the pitch the penalties should be taken from and filling his own players' minds with doubt. Moyes had given his players the confidence they needed. Preston won the shootout 4–2.

Bruce Rioch used similar psychology in the First Division play-off final in 1995. He was manager of Bolton Wanderers, who trailed Reading 2–0 at half-time. Reading had also had a penalty saved. Bolton were on the ropes. Three goals for victory seemed an insurmountable task. 'I knew I had to be positive,' recalls Rioch. 'I went straight onto the pitch to tell the referee I was making a substitution. I was going to play with four strikers. In the dressing-room I told the players, "We need a goal and then we're back in it." If you say "we need two or three", that's no good. That's miles away for them. Just one. They went on to score four. It was an emotional rollercoaster because the prize was a place in the Premiership. We were elated, Reading were deflated. It showed how your life can swing in 45 minutes.'

A football manager's career does indeed rest on such decisions. But the whole job is under intense scrutiny. Every player he spots and signs is pored over by the press and supporters, and his ability to motivate the players is frequently questioned in lean times. Rioch's experience helped. What few managers are prepared to do, are capable of doing, or are given time to do, is plan long term.

When Howard Wilkinson left Sheffield Wednesday to go to Leeds United in 1988, that is precisely what he did. It was more like Wilkinson interviewing Leeds than vice versa. He needed to satisfy himself that their aims and objectives were achievable and realistic before taking the job. Wilkinson is a rarity in football – a player who gave up the professional game to study for a PE degree. Whilst studying, he worked as an assistant to Jim Smith at Boston United, and when Smith moved on, Wilkinson was able to put the academic theory he had encountered into practice. 'I could steal a march on others. The first year I was there we did physiology of exercise. I immediately latched onto this and said: "Hang on, we can do this with football." I'd look at different sports like basketball and hockey, read books and look at different training techniques, and introduce them into our sessions.'

Wilkinson was a success at Boston, managed the England semi-professional team, became a regional FA coach and managed the England Under-21s. His first taste of Football League management came at Notts County, whom he took into, and kept in, the (old) First Division. He repeated the trick with Sheffield Wednesday. Then came the chance to manage Leeds United, who were struggling at the foot of Division Two at the time. 'At Sheffield Wednesday I started to have views about the wider aspects of the club including finance, policy and strategy. When I went to Leeds the interview lasted three weeks. At the end of that period we agreed on the strategy, the policy and the aims, and that's what I started to work towards.' Wilkinson took Leeds up at the first time of asking and delivered the First Division championship two years later. He also laid the foundations of the club's successful youth policy, which has helped his successors.

Now the FA's technical director, Wilkinson is known for his methodical approach to coaching. He is no media smoothie, nor is he particularly suited to high-profile management, but in terms of preparation, in common with long-lasting managers such as Sir Alex Ferguson at Manchester United and Dario Gradi at Crewe, he has shown the importance of planning for the future. 'I see myself as a coach who managed. Leeds taught me it was becoming increasingly more difficult to manage.'

John Barnwell, chief executive of the LMA, supports Wilkinson's view. 'The manager now has more responsibility and less control. The modern manager has two phenomena which make his job more difficult: the new owners of football clubs, shareholders, buy into football clubs not as a badge of honour but to make money, so they're more demanding. Players' agents continually destabilise players to make themselves more money. The manager is in between all the time. If a manager drops a player, he suddenly wants a move, he downs tools, with money being the motivator. So the manager cannot control players in the manner he once did.'

When Graham Taylor went into management 30 years ago at Lincoln City there were few such problems. When it came to the media, he would do a weekly interview with a sports reporter from the local paper and an occasional update over the phone. Now, stepping back into management at Aston Villa after a short period of retirement, Taylor – no stranger now to the media and a victim of some of its excesses during his period as England manager – is inundated with requests. My interview was squeezed between a scouting trip to Denmark and watching a game in London. He was putting the finishing touches to the £5 million signing of striker Peter Crouch.

Taylor adopted a holistic approach to the gaffer's lot. At Lincoln City and Watford he deliberately set out to weld the clubs to the local community. 'It was very important to me when I started at Lincoln to let the supporters know that we represented them every Saturday.

'I thought it was important to get to know one another. I thought that they came to see us work on a Saturday, so what would be the problem if we went to see them during the week? I organised visits and trips to the places our supporters worked and built up good relationships.

'I continued that when I went to Watford. Because we were doing things off the pitch as well as on it, they took an interest in their football club, even if they weren't supporters, particularly if the club was doing well. It was important to get the footballers to appreciate that their performances meant a lot of things to a lot of people. I've carried that philosophy to all the football clubs that I've worked with.'

At Watford, where Taylor took the club from the Fourth to the First Division, he showed what is possible if a gaffer can get not just the club but the community behind him. But times are changing, and with them the gaffer's lot.

'With all the hype that the game has now and all the money that has come into it, it is more difficult now to convince players that they do have a role to play in terms of relationships with supporters. I don't think I could ever repeat the ten years I had at Watford where a town and the football club came together. Unless you were part of that I think it's very hard to understand exactly the wonderful feelings you get when a relationship between the football club and the town is so solid and supportive of one another.'

Taylor was like an old-style pre-war football gaffer – he ran Lincoln and Watford from top to bottom. The difference was that in those days the gaffer wasn't particularly responsible, in the way that Taylor was, for results and performances on the pitch. Indeed, the gaffer had no coaching duties at all. Curiously, his modern-day successor has often been expected to be both coach and administrator – an impossible task.

– CHAPTER THREE –

Cometh the Hour, Cometh the Gaffer: How Britain's Football Bosses Bloomed

The place of sport and coaching in our culture is different to most other European nations . . . We have this traditional British colonial influence where sport in schools was supposed to be character building and about participation rather than practice.

Howard Wilkinson, FA technical director

THERE IS A COMMON BELIEF THAT FOOTBALL MANAGERS ALWAYS existed, that leather- or sheepskin-coated men always bellowed orders from dugouts, from the very inception of the game. Not so.

In China, in the first century AD, where one of the first forms of football originated (an ancient Chinese text likens the round ball and square goal to the shape of yin and yang), it is unimaginable that a white-eyed old master sat cross legged saying: 'Grasshopper, you have done well. The boys done good today but as ancient prophet says . . . I will not talk about championships. We must take each game as it comes.'

Maybe there was the odd touchline ban handed out in the Middle Ages to the organisers of rough and wild forms of street football, which were repeatedly banned. While marauding young men were racing up and down their towns' high streets risking life and limb in pursuit of a bag of wind, there was probably another old windbag holding court in the pubs of Ashbourne and Atherstone, urging his team mates to 'keep their shape' in the annual Shrove Tuesday match:

'If we keep it tight early doors by stringing 200 along the back and push up from mid-town, I'm sure we can nick a goal at some stage.'

Alas, coaching and tactics were never high on the agenda as football emerged and developed into a formalised professional sport in the nineteenth century. It was only when the public schools – the upper- and middle-class boys of Harrow, Eton, Westminster, Winchester, Charterhouse and Rugby – actively sought to iron out their many and varied rules of what was, in essence, a similar game played at their respective schools, that football began its move from a folk custom into a recognised, regulated sport in the early part of the century.

It is a sobering thought that football's first gaffers – the people who actually ran the games, who devised and shaped their rules and tactics – may have been cruel adolescent bullies, those senior pupils who were effectively left to run the school to their own devices by teachers who trod in fear of insurrection which could sometimes only be quelled by the police or even the local militia (whither OFSTED in those days?). Never mind Sir Alex Ferguson's supposed 'hairdryer treatment'; these sons of toffs would dole out far harsher penalties than a haranguing from a stony-faced Glaswegian. Those fags who failed to hack and shin-kick their opponents to order weren't merely substituted or transfer-listed to other schools, but were mercilessly flogged, beaten and subjected to all kinds of degrading treatment.

It is hard to imagine that the sport played, coached, watched and, yes, loved, by so many worldwide – the sport that truly is the people's game – emerged from this limited social context. Certainly, the mores, values, beliefs and idiosyncrasies of the public schools led to the game's formalised development.

Mythically, in 1823, a cheeky blighter at Rugby School called William Webb Ellis, picked up the ball and ran with it. Everyone cheered. 'Hurrah for Webb Ellis – he's invented a new game. Hey, lads, let's name it after our school. Let's head for the town to sup ale and sing songs. On the way home, to show we're real men, we can bare our bums at passers-by. Bet they'll think that's really funny.' Or maybe not. While the slowcoaches who wanted to pick the ball up and trample all over each other went one way, those who preferred to kick, chase and carefully manoeuvre it with their feet went the other. The first rules of football were drawn up in 1848, the Football Association was formed in 1863 and the FA Cup began in 1873.

The public school old boys saw football as their game, played on their terms, to their rules and with their ethics. Sport, and therefore football, was all about laudable aims: taking part, the benefits of physical exercise, promoting a fair chance and a sporting goal.

But working-class communities, particularly those in urban industrial towns and cities, would soon seize the sport from them. There was widespread concern that the failure of Victorian factory owners to grant their workers any rest days (let alone weekends) or holidays (except for an hour on Sunday mornings) might get them down a tad. Maybe some time off would allow them to recharge their batteries? Hell, they might even enjoy it! The Factory Act of 1847 reduced the working day to ten hours, which allowed for more leisure time. Better organise some wholesome activities for them, mind. Bear-baiting, bull-baiting, cock-fighting, bare-knuckle fighting, endless bouts of drinking and the many other unseemly pastimes that were part of early nineteenth-century life somehow didn't fit the bill. Fresh air and physical exercise were better, especially that sport the bosses used to play at school – football.

The ex-public schoolboys who became merchants, industrialists, clergymen or just plain old wealthy patriarchs, then, would sell the folk custom of football back to the working classes, but on their terms and with their rules. As part of the establishment of leisure time, and ultimately leisure industries, with infamous missionary zeal they would sponsor matches, organise factory and church teams, and generally help provide the time and space for football to flourish. They would help found and fund the first professional football clubs. These truly were football's first gaffers – and that is precisely what many would have been called. They were, after all, the factory owners, the employers, the guy you bowed to in church.

Football was slowly eased away from the southern middle-class public schoolboy teams: 'Thanks for the game, lads – mind if we take the ball home?' The old boy tactics, such as they were, had been based upon dogged individualism, with near-constant attempts to dribble the ball around the pitch until it was lost and someone else tried to do much the same. Like a veritable bunch of nineteenth-century sporting proto-Thatcherites, they espoused and expressed their individuality to the last – head down, no turning back, there's no such thing as teamwork. There was no 'gelling together as a unit', very little teamwork or elaborate patterns of play. That would all come later. Their football was based on the benefits of participation, where a firm handshake could rub balm over the previous 90 minutes' hacking and clogging. The slide towards what the Brazilian legend Pelé would famously dub 'the beautiful game' did not develop until team tactics were introduced.

The biggest indication that the game had taken hold successfully among England's working-class communities came when Blackburn Olympic became the first northern working-class team to win the FA Cup in 1883. Heck, they even had supporters who travelled down to London to see them beat Old Etonians by 1–0. Their team of tradesmen (including weavers, spinners and foundry workers) had taken time off work to train in the week running up to the final. Like many a northern team since, they went to Blackpool to improve their strength on the energy-sapping but stamina-building sands, and to imbibe the bracing sea air. Their training schedule and diet consisted of sherry and raw eggs first thing, followed by a brisk walk and then a breakfast of porridge and haddock. Morning training preceded mutton for lunch, tea was more porridge and a pint of milk, with oysters for supper.

Two years later professionalism was legalised, ending a ridiculous situation where players were openly being recruited but paid under the table. The clubs of the English industrial towns and cities had already started attracting the more committed Scots players to be found north of the border. In 1888 the Football League was formed by 12 clubs, but the public school old boy teams would have nothing to do with this vulgar professionalism and the inevitable commercialism that sprang from clubs enclosing their grounds and charging spectators for admission.

Full-time footballers were free to train all day in order to hone and practise their skills, be it dribbling, passing, tackling, shooting or saving. They were specialists. Division of labour was nothing new to the mainly working-class stock of professional players. It was part of the fabric of their lives – the industries they or their family and friends worked in were based upon this method of work. It made sense. Being a cog in a wheel wasn't the slap in the face it seemed to the old boy amateurs. Setting out systems of play and dividing the tasks made them football tradesmen, whether they were goalkeepers, backs, wingers or forwards. This was teamwork. They could move the ball quickly, they were interdependent upon each other, the game could be spread across the pitch to allow the players the time and space to display their skills. These were the essential ingredients that made football an absorbing game to play and watch.

A football match could be, and still can be, balletic. Its moves are observable and appreciable. It has skills worth watching, worth paying money to see, worth supporting, worth cheering. Its artisans could be from the same street as you – this was unlikely to be the case with other sports such as cricket, where county teams comprised largely of upper- or middle-class amateurs with the odd professional run-around thrown in. Footballers were, and would continue to be, representatives of their communities.

Professional football became organised essentially around its economics. Football managers did precisely what their job title suggested – they managed football clubs. They did not coach the players, they did not don tracksuits or woolly jumpers with whistles around their necks on wobbly bicycles, they did not devise tactics or discuss intricate moves. A trainer, or more probably the team captain, did that. Instead the manager – truly the gaffer of the football factory – wore a suit and ran the administrative affairs of the club from top to bottom. Sometimes he had a secretary, sometimes he didn't. Sometimes he did both jobs. Look through the club histories and you will find that most clubs, even well into the twentieth century, had secretary-managers. Some, like Tranmere Rovers, had secretary-managers up until the late 1960s.

David Sheepshanks, the current Ipswich Town chairman, likens the running of clubs well into the 1970s as 'amateur structures in a professional setting'. Sheepshanks recalls that even the late, great Alf Ramsey, who managed Ipswich Town between 1955–63 before becoming England manager, was a secretary-manager. 'We had a manager, a trainer, and a secretariat who did everything else. It was only in Bobby Robson's era at Ipswich (1969–82) that we brought in commercial staff, and only in the past ten years that we had staff like a public relations officer and a chief executive. The way football developed led to the football manager having a wide brief.'

West Bromwich Albion had one of the most remarkable administrators in football history. Fred Everiss joined the club as a 17-year-old clerk in 1900 but within two years became secretary-manager, a position he held for an incredible 46 years, until 1948. His son, Alan, would follow him as Albion secretary. West Brom have had 25 managers in the last 54 years, but then the role has changed somewhat.

At that time the manager had ultimate responsibility for the club, and that meant the team, so he selected the players. He would certainly be responsible for buying and selling them and deciding how much they would be paid, but he was not employed for his coaching or tactical nous. He might have come from the professional classes, he would certainly be a leader (mind you, it's debatable what notice West Brom's players would have taken of a perceived 19-year-old whippersnapper), but the manager was predominantly a pen pusher.

Eventually, the football manager would make the slow crawl from his office to the training ground, but would retain an awkward legacy of both roles. This duality has muddied the waters for many a manager to this day, and has often been the root of disputes between player and manager. 'If you've just told a player he's going to be paid, say, £10 less than he's expected, how can you turn round and motivate him on the training ground ten minutes later?', a former First Division footballer, now manager, told me. 'The managers who were pros know what they will think: "Bollocks to you, why should I run myself into the ground for you?" It's wrong, but it happens. I know – I've been there and heard it and felt it myself. It's one of the reasons I never get involved in politics, religion or player contracts.'

Tommy Docherty, a legendary post-war manager who cheerfully describes himself as having had more clubs than Jack Nicklaus and is steeped in British managerial culture, discovered the fault in this approach when he went to coach (not manage, notably) abroad:

'Like most things in this country, we're 50 years behind the times. I coached at Porto in Portugal in 1970 and you were the coach. They signed the players. You told them the player you required and if they could afford him they went and got him for you. They did all the players' contracts, so as coach you didn't deal with any contracts at all – which is a great idea because that meant you never fell out with a player about the terms of his contract, over money or a signing-on fee. If there was any fallout it was between him and the financial director.'

For all their apparent forelock-tugging subservience – the gaffer etc. – there were disputes between players and management from the very start of professional football. The late-nineteenth century saw a huge rise in trade unionism and the popularity of the labour movement. Footballers were plucked from the same working-class stock as trade unionists, their bosses were often the same patrician factory owners. Then, as now, the football manager wasn't their employer, he was a hapless go-between. No sooner was a Players' Union formed (in 1897, though it wasn't recognised by the FA or Football League for ten years) but a 'cap', a maximum wage, was introduced to keep the clubs on an even keel. There were fears that a few big city clubs would simply pay their players more and they would retain control of the game. Sound familiar?

The game was taking shape at all levels in a myriad of ways: the development of professional and amateur leagues, constant rule changes, county FA administrations, a separate English Schools FA; but this expansion grew without a strategy for the training and preparation of coaches. Astonishingly, the FA didn't have a coaching department until after World War Two, some 60 years after the game had been professionalised. And then its first incumbent, the visionary Walter Winterbottom, had to share the job with managing the senior national team. Prior to World War Two, the FA's secretary, Stanley Rous, wrote in an introduction for the FA's first ever coaching manual, published in the late 1930s:

> Coaches, teachers, trainers and players have for some time shown a desire for a reference book on Association Football and this manual has been prepared in the hope that it may fill that need.

There is something quite awful in an admission from the FA – the world game's oldest, most august body – that it only 'hoped' to fill what must have been a gaping need. The FA, not for the first or last time in its history, had failed to lead. Rous also acknowledges the English game had begun to slip behind many other countries in the world at a time when it showed no particular interest in competing against those same nations. England did not enter the World Cup until 1950 and was only a member of FIFA for a short four-year period between the wars: 'In countries where Association Football has been extensively developed, much time and thought has been expended on the training and coaching necessary to achieve physical fitness without which the essential technique is lacking.'

It wasn't just that the game lacked coaches – especially ones who had any real insight or knowledge, or physical education qualification – but that players were often allowed to devise their own training programmes, to make up their own industry practice if you like. For the best part of half a century it wasn't even considered to be a potential impediment to enhancing the quality of the game. Like many other aspects of football that were to remain familiar custom and practice for most of the twentieth century in Britain, things were done the way they were because that was how they had always been done.

An insight into the mindset of British football and the running of clubs can be gleaned from the various volumes of a splendid piece of social history called *Association Football and the Men Who Made It*, published in 1905, with contributions from several leading lights of the day. William ('Billy') Isaiah Bassett was West Bromwich Albion chairman for 32 years, a former England winger who played in three FA Cup finals during a 16-year career. Described as 'not a giant in stature but a giant in the game', he would become an FA councillor and international selector. In a section entitled 'The Club Secretary and His Duties', Bassett insists 'the secretary should be the mainstay of the club and its manager'. His responsibilities are clearly defined: 'He has a directorate who are really interested, a trainer who has well-defined responsibilities and plenty of advisers, scouts and agents. But the junior secretary is usually left to his own devices.'

The captain's role is one we would more readily recognise as that of a coach: 'The fitness of the men should occupy a captain's thoughts as well as their actual play . . . he should keep in touch with his players, train a little, go for runs or riding when possible and for practice if it is deemed likely to produce better results at the weekend.'

Writing in a later volume dedicated to team management, John Cameron, the Scottish manager of Tottenham Hotspur between 1899–1906, believed the manager should be 'the mouthpiece of his board'. His attributes would severely test many modern-day managers: 'A present-day football manager or secretary must not only know everything there is to know about football . . . but must also possess an extensive knowledge of the practice of joint stock companies.'

As for his duties:

> They are many and varied in their scope. They range from calling and addressing meetings of shareholders, and signing dividend warrants . . . to supervising more or less trivial arrangements on the football ground. He must use a great deal of tact in his negotiations. He must always be at the disposal of his board of directors, who frequently require information . . . he must keep his heavy correspondence up to date and see that the players obey their training orders and dwell together in peace and unity (and) . . . he must be on the alert for promising talent . . .

Notably, his management of the players as opposed to, say, his club managerial duties are latter concerns. Cameron describes the trainer as 'the father of the team': 'Addressing the players' smallest wants, dressing their injuries, rubbing them down, hardening their muscles and freely giving advice on a thousand matters. The occupation of a trainer is a busy one. Solely upon his efforts and shared judgement the appearance on the field of a popular player sometimes depends.'

So you have managers and secretaries, or manager-secretaries, with broadly similar jobs, a trainer who watches over the training, who deals with injuries and reports back to the manager or secretary-manager, and a club captain who puts the men through their paces. What is missing is any description of training or structured coaching, or any mention of a coaching culture among clubs. Indeed, there is no mention in the four heavy volumes of *Football And The Men Who Made It* of the training of coaches.

In another weighty tome of its time, *The Book of Football* published in 1906, Billy Bassett talks about the actual training and players' weekly routine at West Brom. 'The average man had a dim and imperfect idea of the way in which a footballer fits himself for his work . . . personally I do not mind admitting that I am no believer in this organised system of training.' You can see why Bassett felt at home at the FA, can't you? Too much training, argues Bassett, only dulls the players' appetite for the game. 'I say it is practically impossible for these men to be as enthusiastic as we were and this constant attendance at the grounds is, in my opinion, the cause of all the stereotypical listless and automatic play we get.'

So what sort of energy-sapping routine were the players expected to endure? What kind of punishing schedule was harming the game, in the view of a player who had only hung his boots up seven years earlier? And what should replace it?

> Monday: nothing; Tuesday: the trainer takes the players for a good walk in the country five or six miles at a fair pace . . . this is a form of training I cordially approve of. Should the morning not be conducive to pleasant walking then the trainer should offer alternative exercise like skipping vigorously, it makes for increased agility and improves the wind.

The rest of the week is little more taxing. There is talk of players throwing Indian clubs around, punching the ball for half an hour – why? 'This is one of the most fluent and interesting exercises ever devised.' The running exercises sound fairly straightforward too: 'Most of the players will run around the ground a few times or many according to the amount of exercise each is deemed to require. There is sprinting but there is danger of overdoing this kind of training. Men who indulge in it are likely to have breakdowns.'

West Bromwich Albion were a successful club around this time, in the First or Second Division, so there is little to suggest that their training schedules would have been markedly different to those of their opponents. Bassett was clearly a top player and a respected figure. His views would be somewhat typical of the wider thought in the game at the time. Absent from the training schedule thus far, you may have noticed, is any mention of the ball: 'Once a week, and once a week only, the men should have ball practice. So far as I have been able to see, the men simply kick in.' Now Bassett breaks ranks: he can't quite see the point of eight attackers 'kicking in' toward a goalkeeper and two hopelessly overworked defenders: 'You can see them dribbling deliberately, passing deliberately and stopping the ball dead, and then they shoot. That is to say they do precisely what they would never do in a match. I cannot see that this is beneficial.'

The Baggies' players were taken to Droitwich Brine Baths in Worcestershire for a once-a-week salt bath and rubdown to relieve their aching muscles. In some respects this seems a quite sophisticated form of therapy compared to the rest of their schedule.

It may seem unfair to challenge late nineteenth/early twentieth-century sporting regimes the best part of 100 years later, and I don't intend to poke undue fun at Billy Bassett and his generation of footballers or administrators, but we can see football training and coaching folklore starting to take root, especially the myths football became saddled with, even arguably wallowed in, until fairly recently. The big problem was, and fundamentally still is in many respects, a dogged attitude that professional footballers know best. But what exactly was their professional standing? Where did their expertise lie? It was based on playing the game, not having built up a body of knowledge tested via the taking of professional qualifications or having any knowledge of, say, physical education. In other words, they merely played the game, and then they coached what they knew.

This is where the myth of the mystical powers of the 'magic' sponge comes from. This treatment may be administered, of course, by anyone although certainly not a qualified physician. It's where the single two-hour-a-day training session (which is still largely de rigueur, and sits quite comfortably among today's well-heeled footballers) originated. Then there is the least credible myth of them all, intimated by Billy Bassett's advocacy of once-a-week ball practice, that if you somehow starve the players of the ball they will 'want it' more on matchdays. Even at clubs like Arsenal, former players like John Barnwell, now chief executive of the LMA, insist this belief was well in place up until the 1960s, ignoring the somewhat more overwhelming logic that the more the players actually played with the ball the more proficient they might actually become.

The great Stanley Matthews, the so-called Wizard of Dribble, one of England's finest ever players (and ambassadors), whose sublime skills were matched only by his incredible fitness and longevity (Matthews played until he was 50, a career spanning some 35 years), would train on his own every afternoon at Stoke City. The fact that Matthews' immense ability owed so much to practice could hardly have evaded the attention of his team mates – yet few, it seems, felt the urge to accompany him. Instead football's impenetrable training day schedule stayed in place.

'You were an oddball, even in the 1960s, if you trained twice a day,' recalls Howard Wilkinson, the FA's technical director since 1996. Wilkinson is an astute scholar of the game and coaching in British sport. 'The place of sport and coaching in our culture is different to most other European nations and other world nations. In Germany, Italy and France you went to school to be educated physically. Physical education in those countries is about educating the physical side of your life. If you wanted to play a sport you went to a club and the club employed specialist coaches and the coach was a professional. He was on a par with a doctor, a teacher or lawyer and his training regime was strict.

'We only started to adopt this after the war when a lot of English sports-minded people like Walter Winterbottom and Geoff Dyson, who had observed overseas coaching, went back into PE colleges and led the *Chariots of Fire*-type thing. They said: "Look, there are some scientific principles involved here to do with physiology, psychology and so on." It has been a difficult process because we're fighting 300 years of culture here, going right back to Eton. That's the fundamental reason we've got this cultural attitude to sport and they've got theirs in Europe.'

The point is that professional footballers, in common with the other, relatively few, full-time sportsmen in the country, did not have specialist qualified coaches. They were trained by their own kith and kin. And ex-pros all too often passed on tried and trusted regimes. They did not, by and large, consult sports professionals in other disciplines, or sports science academics who might have been able to assist them. The clubs did not think about paying these people to come into the game: outsiders rarely penetrated the walls of British professional football. Small wonder new training methods, standards of coaching, physiological and psychological advice, diet and fitness regimes that might have actually improved the performance of footballers were slow to creep in.

'You are a prisoner of your own experience,' says Howard Wilkinson, who recalls his early playing days at Sheffield Wednesday in the early 1960s, when players munched on steak and chips followed by bread-and-butter pudding a mere three hours before kick-off, a routine which would have been rejected by many amateur sportsmen. Not in football – the pros knew best.

Dennis Mortimer, the former Aston Villa captain and now a PFA regional coach, supports Wilkinson's view. 'We haven't grown up with a coaching culture in this country. We've got a lot of coaches who just take players out, warm them up, put them into some kind of drill routine, do some running and play a small-sided game – you'll probably find there's very little actual coaching going on. Coaching done properly can give players loads of information about what they are capable of achieving.' Mortimer recalls tough pre-season training at Coventry City and Aston Villa in the 1970s. 'There was no sports science knowledge at all. In the middle of summer we would work hard for two hours but never drink water, so we weren't rehydrating. We were told it wasn't good for you. Nowadays the recommendation is that you drink at least one cup of water for every 15 minutes of exercise and the players have isotonic drinks to replenish the carbohydrates in their system. The game was too introverted. It was insular. We weren't looking outside the game to find out what was going on.'

It had always been this way. British football had dismissed fanciful ideas of outsiders and foreigners. While the rest of the world pushed the sport on tactically, technically and physically, the national game sat with its collective hands over its ears, shouting and stamping its feet so it couldn't see or hear what was going on. Football had not developed with coaching in mind, it had soon shifted its attention to commercialism, and in between the wars in particular, the English FA (though, even now, they don't like to be called the English FA, just *the* FA) adopted a policy of splendid isolation.

Football has been described as Britain's most durable export. To quote a well-worn phrase, football was a game we gave to the world, and they developed it. From the mid-nineteenth century, when it barely had rules, football was exported around the world by its disciples – schoolboys, soldiers, tradesmen and ex-patriots – and they took part of their culture with them. Holland, Spain, Italy and Germany all had football associations before the end of the nineteenth century. Soccer also took hold in South America, in Uruguay before most other countries on the continent, but failed to grow at the same rate in Africa, Australasia and North America, despite the more obvious social and cultural links.

The developments in South America and on the continent of Europe were largely ignored in Britain. The world governing body, FIFA, was formed in 1904, but the British nations didn't want to join for the first year, and when they did, they could not understand FIFA's reluctance to recognise them as separate nations. By 1911 FIFA gave way, allowing England, Scotland, Wales and Northern Ireland to have individual voting rights. After World War One, Britain, unlike its Allies, would not play against their former foes of Germany and Austria. They withdrew from FIFA for six years, and rejoined briefly for four years between 1924–28, only to draw up the barricades until after World War Two.

When Uruguay hosted the first World Cup in 1930 the British nations gave a curt 'no' in response to the invitation to participate. The game abroad was adopting differing tactics and a different ethos in playing the game. Many of Britain's more enlightened coaches, like Jimmy Hogan, who coached in several European countries, realised the English game was using primitive training methods.

A savage critique of both pre- and post-World War Two British football is supplied by former Austrian goalkeeper and notable soccer journalist, Willy Meisl, in *Soccer Revolution*, published in 1955. Meisl, whose brother Hugo had been one of the great European coaches of his generation (described in the book as 'the Pitt, Disraeli, Bismarck and Napoleon of Austrian Soccer' – there's brotherly love for you), insists 'British fans were never told enough about the development of soccer abroad to have had the chance to foresee England's decline after the war'. Meisl paints a bleak picture of British football in the inter-war years, where 'pace and punch had pushed out cleverness and craft, brain given way to brawn, speed had taken the place of precision and money had all but killed genius'.

The root problem, as Meisl saw it, lay in British conservatism. By the 1920s the game became defence oriented, and as fewer goals were scored the turnstiles clicked slower. The answer wasn't to look to improve the technical skill of the game but to change the offside rule so that more goals were scored. The old rule dictated that an attacker was offside when he was between three defenders and the goal; this was reduced to two. The British nations, having returned to FIFA, pushed this rule change through the 22-country body and promptly left. 'The directors triumphed,' says Meisl, 'for a time. Defenders learned to play to the new rule and all but killed the game.'

The dominant English manager of the day – indeed other than perhaps Major Frank Buckley (the 1930s Wolves manager) the only pre-World War Two manager football fans will probably know – was Herbert Chapman, the legendary Huddersfield Town and Arsenal manager. Chapman (a great friend of Meisl's masterly managerial brother Hugo) was a tactical genius. Although he been banned from football for a year following an illegal payment scam along with several club officials at Leeds City, he returned to management to lead Huddersfield Town to successive First Division championships in 1924 and 1925 (his predecessor, Cecil Potter, guided them to a third), before joining Arsenal. He brought the Football League championship to Highbury three times – plus the FA Cup – and set Arsenal on a remarkable course of success throughout the 1930s. Without Chapman it is doubtful Arsenal would have emerged as the huge club they are today. His bust still stands proudly in the foyer of Highbury's marbled entrance. According to Meisl, Chapman was a 'natural showman as well as a football general' who brought David Jack and Alex James to Arsenal, and moved Cliff Basten from inside-left onto the wing. He also introduced the stopper by withdrawing the centre-half into the heart of defence, which meant the full-backs moved outwards to block the wingers, and the half-backs dropped deeper. 'At Highbury, and soon throughout Great Britain, the third back was the pivot on which the entire defence hinged.' The message was safety first: 'If we manage to keep the opponents from scoring we have one point at least. If we manage to score a goal we have two points.'

It was a method that would serve the Gunners well in the post-war era under Bertie Mee and Don Howe, and later George Graham. But Meisl, who believes Chapman (who died in 1934) would have been shrewd enough to have utilised more subtle tactics, feels that changing the laws to accommodate the defensive measures sent out a wider message: 'I am out to spoil, I am destructive, craftsmanship is needed to create constructive play.' And there simply wasn't enough craftsmanship around. The game and its environment did not encourage it. There weren't the coaches to teach or preach it, or the pitches to allow it to prosper. 'British soccer had become barren of ideas, crammed inside a plaster cast of Chapman's Arsenal, but lacking Chapman's stars,' concludes Meisl.

Technically, the attacking players should have felt comfortable enough, before the original offside laws were altered, to hold the ball for a fraction longer in order to spring the offside traps that were being set, but they lacked the technical ability seen elsewhere in world football. This could have been taught if a developed coaching structure had been put in place. Instead the focus had been on speed and strength, the core values the self-taught pros had passed down the line. Ill-prepared, needlessly muddy pitches (which blighted the game until well into the 1980s) didn't help. Hoofing the ball was the preferred, safe first option.

As British football withdrew into its shell, the game was growing elsewhere. The signs weren't visible domestically because England didn't play competitive matches outside of the Home Internationals and had never lost to a foreign nation – until they were beaten 5–3 by Spain in Madrid in 1929. They didn't enter the World Cup until 1950, some 20 years after it was first staged, when a true test of their international standing revealed that English football was far from the best in the world.

The future of the mighty Manchester United could all have been so different had one particular Scottish inside-forward not found the barrack-room lawyers of the Manchester City dressing-room too intimidating. Matt Busby was a talented half-back, a boy from

Bellshill, a mining village near Glasgow, and a sensitive soul.

Busby joined Manchester City at the age of 18. Manchester legend (he had played for both City and United) Billy Meredith was Busby's first coach, and Ernest Magnall was City's manager. Magnall was a typical manager of the era, an administrator rather than a coach, and had overseen the building of Old Trafford in 1910 and Maine Road for City a decade later. He was rarely seen on the training ground. As Eamon Dunphy, in his biography *A Strange Kind of Glory* notes, 'Busby couldn't settle into the harsh world of professional football . . . the game and the clubs run by players. Coaches and managers didn't get involved more than necessary . . .' Dunphy suggests the problem lay in the club structures. Directors were 'idiots or autocrats', managers merely their representatives. 'Occasionally an autocrat like Chapman or Magnall would come along . . . and enforce his will . . . but it was rare . . . the manager with strong views had better make it work and quick.'

Manchester City almost sold Busby in 1930 but their poorer neighbours, United, couldn't afford the £150 fee. He switched to wing-half from inside-forward and improved, winning a Scottish cap and an FA Cup-winner's medal, both in 1934. He later moved to Liverpool for £8,000. Busby's experience as a junior player was to stay with him. He vowed that if he ever became a manager he would respect players as individuals. He was to become the ultimate visionary gaffer of the post-war era – English football's Golden Age.

– CHAPTER FOUR –

The Vision Thing: The Gaffer in Football's 'Golden Age'

> You never saw the manager. And you didn't have coaches, you
> had trainers. They were what it said – they trained you, they
> ran you around the pitch. You only saw the manager once or
> twice a week.
>
> John Barnwell

THE ROLE OF THE BRITISH FOOTBALL MANAGER CHANGED IN THE
post-war era. He was to move out of his office, take off his shirt and
tie and slip on a tracksuit. Coaching came of age. As a result, the gaffer
became more visibly linked to the direct success or failure of the team,
and was therefore more susceptible to the sack.

Soccer's so-called Golden Age of the 1950s, when that green oblong
at the heart of football communities brought relief to the grey days of
austerity, saw record crowds and a plethora of cigarette-card stars
whose names effortlessly tripped off the tongue: Matthews, Finney,
Milburn, Lofthouse, Lawton, Mortensen, Wright et al. It was also the
start of an era when giant gaffers stalked British football – Busby,
Cullis, Shankly, Nicholson, Ramsey, Mee, Mercer, Revie, Stein and
later Clough, Allison, Sexton, Docherty and Robson.

So what finally prised the manager away from his desk and his
secretarial duties? How was he crowbarred down the corridor onto
the training ground? What seismic shift happened after the war to
distinguish that period from the deeply introspective inter-war years,
when British football pulled up its collective drawbridge to any
outside influence?

First, the seeds of a coaching culture were planted under the influence of FA head coach, Walter Winterbottom. Second, many of the soon-to-emerge post-war gaffers had sharpened their leadership skills and broadened their horizons during wartime service. Third, change *had* to happen – British football was proven to no longer be the best in the world. Its national team didn't enter the World Cup until 1950 – some 20 years after it was first staged – when a true test of their international standing revealed that English football was far from the best in the world. The nation sampled World Cup defeat (humiliation even, at the hands of the United States in 1950), and were beaten by the Hungarians, those Magnificent Magyars, who trounced England home and away in 1953–54. You couldn't argue with these results – something had to change. Also, Busby's Babes and Cullis's Wolves had reached their hands across the water to pit their wits against European club opposition. There were a number of genies that weren't going to glide back into their bottles.

In 1946, FA secretary Stanley Rous (later Sir Stanley, a future leader of FIFA) had finally had enough of his cumbersome committees. He had wanted to establish a director of coaching at the FA for some time, someone who could develop a coaching structure throughout all levels of game. He also wanted to appoint an England team manager. The blazers did not like either scheme. Some, amazingly, though they had friends among the pro game too, rejected the very idea of coaching per se as they thought it stifled natural talent. Others believed a department for coaching would be too expensive. As for an England manager, well, they had rather liked the perk of being called upon occasionally to select the side. It was fun. A committee of nine would select eleven players. Not that some of these time-servers were well-versed students of the professional game, or had any distinct knowledge. They often had to rely on the advice of club trainers, or, in these pre-TV days, opt for players they had seen in their particular neck of the woods. To say the least, it wasn't ideal. Selection meetings would last several hours.

As a result the England side had little consistency. Stanley Matthews, despite his legendary Wizard of Dribble status, was a frequent victim of the committees. He was in and out of the England team and only made 54 appearances in a 22-year international career.

He later said: 'I have travelled the globe and walked in parks in just about every country in the world but I have never seen a statue to a committee.'

Worse still, England players met only on matchdays, or maybe the evening before a game. A trainer, appointed on a rota basis, would look after them. On foreign tours they had the captain to represent them, but he did not sit around a table with the great and the good. The folly of this policy was seen when, without the sort of advanced objection a manager would surely have made, the England team were ordered to Sieg Heil prior to the now-infamous German international match in Berlin in 1938. A manager might have remonstrated with the FA and the Foreign Office, who had ordered the Nazi salute, but when thrust upon the irate players at the last minute, it was too late. This would be one of the most shameful images associated with British sport. After six years of war against this particular foe, and the horrors of the Holocaust still fresh in the mind, there was little public appetite for such bumbling authority.

Rous decided on a compromise. The two jobs – a new head coach and an England manager of the senior side, Under-23s and the youth team – could be done by one person. Two for the price of one – you can't say fairer than that. But who would head this new department? What sort of person had the credentials to manage these two important, though disparate, briefs? The FA plumped for Walter Winterbottom, a man with a foot in both the professional game (he had played for Manchester United until injury ended his career) and education (he was a lecturer at Carnegie College in Leeds). He was 33 years old and undoubtedly destined for a bright career in higher education.

Like many a post-war manager, such as Sergeant-majors Cullis and Busby, Winterbottom had proved his leadership skills during the war. He had been a wing commander in charge of physical training in the Air Ministry. He had studied coaching practice around the world and in other sports. He understood there were scientific principles that could improve sports performance. He was a passionate advocate of coaching and the need for trained qualified coaches.

The FA Coaching Manual drawn up in 1936, with Rous's proviso that 'Englishmen do not take kindly to the grind of training and are too often inclined to take to their sport too carelessly', had been compiled by a committee with representatives from the English Schools FA, Oxford and Cambridge Universities, a couple of county FAs, the army, a public school and a Fourth Division club. The lecturers who acted as joint editors, included representatives from the Corinthians, the Old Merchant Taylors, Carnegie Physical Training College (Winterbottom) and the West Riding FA. It is safe to say the professional game felt under-represented. For all their tiring 'we're the professionals, we know best' mantra, surely they did have something to contribute?

The divide between the perceived professionals (no matter how amateurish their approach) and amateurs/academics (what the heck did they know about playing professional football?) hampered the FA Coaching Department from day one. It has remained a cause of division. Indeed, not until the fairly recent appointment of Howard Wilkinson in 1996 did the professional game truly feel they had 'one of their own' leading the FA's technical department. Winterbottom had to wrestle not only with this problem, but also with what has been dubbed 'the second most important job in the country', managing the English national football team. Although press reaction to results wasn't as scathing as it is today, there was plenty for Winterbottom's detractors to moan about in his early years in the job.

The technical deficiencies of British football were exposed via a series of results against foreign opposition. A forewarning came immediately after the war, in 1945, when Moscow Dynamo, effectively the Russian national team, made a goodwill tour of the UK. Huge crowds flocked to see them play: 82,000 squeezed into Stamford Bridge, 45,000 were at Cardiff City and 90,000 at Glasgow Rangers. It wasn't the results of the matches that mattered, it was the quality and style of the Muscovites' play, a neat, passing game which British clubs, by and large, had failed to cultivate.

Although Winterbottom's reign got off to a decent enough start in terms of results, the major challenge came when England entered their first World Cup in Brazil in 1950. England were back in FIFA, and were fancied as one of the tournament's favourites. They were certainly expected to pass through their group stage with ease. Not so. An opening win over Chile was followed by a humiliating defeat against the USA. An English team of great players including Mannion, Finney, Mortensen and Wright went down 1–0. They then lost their final group game to Spain by a similar scoreline and were dumped out of the tournament. The World Cup was won by Uruguay, a passionate South American football nation, but a country with a population of just two million people.

England could no longer claim to be the world leaders they had assumed themselves to be in the pre-war era, a point that was emphatically driven home three years later when Olympic champions Hungary became the first continental country to beat England on their own soil. There was no mistaking the magnitude of this defeat at Wembley, or the cultural imbalance it represented. England's 6–3 home defeat was followed by a 7–1 drubbing in Budapest six months later.

Tom Finney, who missed the Wembley match through injury, was watching from the stand: 'The Hungarians came out 20 minutes before the game to warm up. It was totally unheard of in English football. I mean, you just came out five minutes before kick-off and had a kick around, the referee blew his whistle and you were off. I focused on Puskas and was amazed at the things he was doing with the ball – it was exhibition stuff. Then they went back inside and had a proper warm-up.'

Puskas' first goal of two is still one of the most frequently shown pieces of 1950s soccer footage. He draws the ball back to evade Billy Wright's lurching challenge and in a swift movement rifles the ball into the English net. It summed up the difference in class. Nandor Hidegkuti, the Hungarian deep-lying centre-forward (a position unheard of in British football), scored three at Wembley.

In the 1954 World Cup, England would at least progress past the two-game group stage, but were beaten 4–2 by Uruguay. Scotland, meanwhile, had finished bottom of their group, losing both their games, including a 7–0 thumping by the Uruguayans.

Faced with this failure, even Winterbottom's detractors, who had hated his schoolmasterly use of dressing-room diagrams, had to listen now. The Hungarians had humbled the whole of the English game and its shambolic approach. They had exposed its physical and technical inadequacies. Maybe there was something to be gleaned from this coaching idea after all.

Winterbottom was supported by friends from afar. For all the post-war record crowds, the star players and the big-name managers, Austrian goalkeeper and journalist Willy Meisl, who had panned the insularity of inter-war British football in *Soccer Revolution*, had not noted much change up to the time of the Hungarian defeats. Now living in England, Meisl, who was to predict the eventual rise of Total Football (popularised by the Dutch national team in the 1970s) painted a dour view of the game in Britain. It was dominated by outmoded routines: players rarely warmed up sufficiently before matches, they wore unsuitable short-sleeved shirts on the coldest of days and games were played on quagmire pitches or dangerous icy surfaces; indeed, despite the huge crowds and revenue raised, the pitches were inadequately maintained. It was symbolic, argued Meisl, of British football's attitude.

There was official resistance to the introduction of substitutions, which meant players, who were determined not to let their team mates down, too often played on with career-threatening injuries, sometimes making them worse. Not a single second of injury-time was added, and as a result the public were being short-changed. The game was in a negative mindset. When 33 people died and over 400 were injured in a crush prior to a cup tie at Bolton Wanderers' Burnden Park ground in 1946, the game was played on.

Winterbottom started his coaching brief with a blank piece of paper. Coaches had to be educated and educators had to be recruited. He would design a range of coaching courses and establish a network for delivery to players and managers at professional clubs, and via county FAs to teachers and other students of the game. He may have had his critics, but he also had his disciples. Many of the players who took his initial Preliminary badge, and then the more detailed Advanced badge, would form the basis for England's first coaching culture.

'He was a massive influence,' recalls Jimmy Armfield, the former England full-back, BBC radio commentator and current coaching adviser to both the FA and PFA, whose career began at Blackpool in 1952. 'It was more on subsequent generations than our own. Our generation were fortunate because we saw him in action. He was the first man to ever put down the skeleton of a coaching course, which was followed all over the world.'

Many notable names would emerge from Winterbottom's circle, such as his England assistants, Bill Nicholson and Jimmy Adamson (a suggested successor to Winterbottom as England manager when he relinquished the role in 1963), future England managers Alf Ramsey, Ron Greenwood and Bobby Robson, and coaches Don Howe and Malcolm Allison. Their day would come, but not yet. The old-style manager and his modus operandi were not dead. 'You learned to play by learning to play,' recalls Jimmy Armfield. 'No one ever told me how to play football. I had very little coaching. I had a little bit of regular training with our reserve team trainer, heading and volleying and that sort of thing, but no tactical training. I had to learn the hard way.'

Trainers, though, were not medical men or physiotherapists. It was another aspect of British football that belied its professional status. Tom Finney recalls the crude approach to injuries in the so-called Golden Age. 'Invariably an ex-player would be the trainer, who had picked up what he knew from when he played. An infra-red lamp was used to cure everything. I remember I had a broken jaw but we didn't know at the time. I went up for a collision and I was out for the count. I woke up with the trainer slapping my face. He didn't know that I had broken my jaw and, of course, I shot up like a cork. But I went back on the field and he said "You'll be all right, run it off." After the game I went to hospital and spent the night there. There were no substitutes in our day.'

The English FA may have rejoined FIFA, but they were firmly against European competition for domestic clubs. They certainly weren't prepared to delay or postpone fixtures for clubs who did seek to pit their skills against Europe's finest, and are still reluctant to persuade their leagues to reschedule domestic matches. It wasn't until the 1990s that fixtures were suspended for national team players. The introduction of floodlights in the 1950s made midweek matches possible and this gave European matches a shot in the arm. Teams could fly to the continent and still make it back for their weekend Football League fixtures. English football had clubs with ambitious managers whose eyes were set on European domination. The way they shaped their clubs would have a profound influence on the image of post-war gaffer.

Matt Busby and Stan Cullis were a new breed of boss – they were close friends but markedly different men. Their respective clubs, Manchester United and Wolverhampton Wanderers, were the giants of 1950s domestic football. United won the First Division championship five times under Busby (three times in the '50s) and were runners-up on seven occasions in his twenty-four years in charge at Old Trafford. Wolves lifted the title three times under Cullis and were runners-up on a similar number of times in his 16-year reign at Molineux. Both teams won the FA Cup twice under these managerial greats.

Football clubs had always had patrician owners (and in many cases still do). They were about to get paternalistic managers – symbolic fathers of their clubs. Cullis took up the reins at Molineux when his playing career ended in 1948, Busby joined Manchester United as manager four years earlier. The clubs were their families, their sons were the players, the wider community were aunts, uncles, nephews, nieces and neighbours. They established a seemingly impenetrable belief that the club was theirs – and yours. You, the townsfolk, would obviously want the best for these protégés – and, boy, could they play. If you were a chairman or director you'd better have a good reason to try to chop down one of these giant managerial oaks. Their teams played in their fashion. Busby, for example, favoured a schooled science, a natural but structured style of play. Cullis had a more forceful approach. Long balls, tireless running, few frills and fancies, an ethos drilled into the players on the training ground.

Cullis was a one-club man. He had prospered under the rigid regime of Major Frank Buckley, Wolves' manager throughout the 1930s. He was Wolves captain at the age of 20 and England's youngest-ever skipper at the age of 22. He only won 12 England caps but lost what would have been his best years to the war. A tough-tackling centre-half, he prospered under Buckley and had achieved success through hard work and discipline. Matt Busby, a half-back, had not liked the harsh dressing-room culture and vowed to change things if he got the chance. He played for Manchester City, where he had taken time to settle, and Liverpool towards the end of his playing days. He earned a single Scottish cap, but was generally felt to have underachieved.

There were symbolic links to industrial pride and regional identity. Cullis wrote 'There is no substitute for hard work' on the dressing-room walls and was nicknamed the Iron Manager, a tag that rang a bell with the Black Country's foundry workers and metalbashers, with their beer caddies to help them build up a sweat for their white heat work. Busby encapsulated a kind of King Cotton Mancunian cool in this metropolis of the north. He was not a man to readily display his emotions, unlike Cullis who would kick and head every ball from his position in the stands, and would endlessly elbow and kick anyone unfortunate to sit nearby. Even his own son. 'If a corner came over he would lean on you as if to head it away – and that was watching a neutral match,' recalls Stan's son, Andrew. 'I've sat next to him and been kicked to pieces. He was lost in football. When I was older I got left behind at Blackburn because he forgot I was there.'

No matter how much he might have symbolically fathered his Wolves team, Cullis was so absorbed with football he frequently forgot to tell his real family where he was going or what he was doing. 'He was very busy and not around a lot,' says Andrew. 'One day we were sat down to tea and Mum said "I wonder where your dad is." We watched the TV, and there he was getting on a plane to Russia.'

Cullis would be cruelly discarded in time, eventually becoming one of the game's tragic managerial figures, but in the 1950s this was unimaginable. His players had a love–hate respect for him. They trained twice a day, which was unheard of at the time. Cullis described telling a fellow manager about this training regime: 'I might as well have told him I was about to set the boardroom on fire.'

The 'passionate puritan', as John Arlott once described Cullis, never swore but was brutally honest when assessing football talent. 'He very rarely watched me but when I was nine years old I played for an Under-11s team,' recalls Andrew Cullis. 'I scored three goals and was feeling really good about myself. After the game he said, "No, Andrew, you'll never make it." If you did that now you'd have the social services after you, wouldn't you?'

Tactically, Cullis didn't want to emulate England's masters; he wanted to take them down a peg or two. Wolves went some way to avenging the Hungarian hammerings of 1953–54 a year later, when they beat Honved – a side containing many of the formidable Magyars including Puskas – 3–2 at Molineux. Cullis invited the press to come and see his exhausted but victorious players after the match. 'There they are – the champions of the world,' he proclaimed.

Wolves had been 2–0 down at half-time, but fitness, hard work and a specially watered pitch (in mid-winter!) sapped Honved's players' strength as the game wore on. Cullis's players used clubs to build up body strength and their sprinting speed was regularly tested by an international runner, Frank Morris. Cullis's remarks hailed the start of the European Cup. Europe's top clubs wanted to deny his claims.

For all the magic of the Molineux nights, when Wolves invited foreign opposition to the Black Country, they would not win the European Cup, or fare particularly well in their two attempts to win it. Cullis's long ball game, for all its speed and excitement, was based on the crude tactics of the infamous Wing Commander Charles Reep. Mathematically, Reep argued, most goals were scored from a few passes. There was logic, therefore, in getting the ball as deep into the opposition penalty area as quickly and often as possible. Cullis studied this theory closely. His players did not elaborate, his half-backs did not dwell on the ball or shuffle it around the middle of the pitch. They played the 'W' formation – long balls, often played first time, whacked out to wingers whose delivery to onrushing fowards was fast, furious, exciting to watch and successful. Wolves didn't just win things, they scored at will. This was not the Wimbledon-esque tactics of the 1980s, it was not reliant on thrusting elbows into defenders' faces, the ball wasn't blasted down the middle of the pitch, but neither was it sophisticated football that was winning trophies all around the world.

At Old Trafford, Matt Busby assembled successive sides that would offer a bit more guile. Manchester United might have (indeed some argue, would have) lifted the European Cup in 1958 – and memorably would do so with another Busby team ten years later – but the dreams of the Busby Babes were to end on a frozen runway in Munich.

It is hard to imagine the Manchester United Matt Busby inherited after the war. Their ground had been bombed, the club had bounced between the top two divisions with regularity. Young fans will find it difficult to comprehend that just 3,900 fans rolled up to their final league game in 1931 when they were relegated from the First Division.

They had only one gate over 10,000 in the entire season, for the visit of neighbours Manchester City.

Although United had won two championships, in 1907–08 and 1910–11, that was too long ago for anyone to imagine in 1945 that the club would embark on a succession of championships and become such a major force in the game. It would be like making the same expectations of Bradford, Barnsley or Birmingham City today. United had been kept afloat thanks largely to the inter-war efforts of secretary Louis Rocca, secretary-manager Walter Crickmer, and the club's owner, clothing merchant James Gibson. Under Gibson, the club set up the Manchester United Junior Athletic Club (MUJAC) in 1936, a pioneering youth scheme. Although many other clubs would improve their scouting networks in the post-war era, United stole an important march that was to bear fruit.

During the war, Busby was a Company Sergeant-major in the army. Like many well-known footballers he played his share of services soccer. He 'guested' for Reading, Aldershot and Hibernian and managed army teams including players like Joe Mercer, Cliff Britton and Frank Swift. Arthur Rowe, who later became Spurs boss, was his second in command. The army was also where Busby met his eventual assistant at Manchester United, Jimmy Murphy, who had been a Welsh international. After the war he took over the failing Manchester United, where he refused to tolerate any of the pre-war dressing-room bullying he had experienced. He would rebuild the club along family lines. Busby was its head. The players were his sons; they would literally be called his 'babes' by the press when he tossed them into the first team in huge numbers. They swept all before them. The kindly uncle, Jimmy Murphy, spotted and schooled them, arguably having more direct influence than Busby. This was a different approach to that at Wolves. Players were encouraged to express themselves, and not just the (iron) will of their manager.

Busby delivered unprecedented success to United fans – the FA Cup in 1948 and a trio of championships in the 1950s. Busby's Babes included Duncan Edwards, Bobby Charlton, Dennis Viollet, Bill Foulkes, David Pegg, Eddie Colman, Albert Scanlon and Wilf McGuinness. It would come to a halt in February 1958 at Munich, where a flight from Belgrade, where United had just beaten Red Star

3–0, stopped to refuel. Busby was desperate to get back – he ordered the players to help clear snow off the plane so the repeated attempts to take off could continue. The pilot failed. Those killed included players Duncan Edwards, Roger Byrne, David Pegg, Tommy Taylor, Eddie Colman, Mark Jones, Billy Whelan and Geoff Bent, and eight journalists. Busby punctured his left lung and was in an oxygen tent for weeks. He was given the last rites twice. Andrew Cullis recalls how he found out about the Munich disaster. 'I can visualise it very clearly. I was on my way home from school, I had my satchel with me, and before I reached the house my sister met me and said "Uncle Matt has been hurt, we must pray for him." I knew some of the other managers but I don't recall calling any of them "uncle". We were very close.' Busby would recover and return to management. Stan Cullis would be cut down in the 1960s, but other major bosses of their ilk would emerge.

In 1959, Bill Shankly took over at Liverpool and transformed them into one of the world's best-known clubs. He knew the impact the exaggerated irony of his beliefs would have on Merseyside, a region noted for its self-deprecating Scouse wit. Why else, in a city known for high unemployment and in the wake of the hammering Britain's main cities had taken during the war, would anyone, no matter how obsessed with the game, say 'Football isn't a matter of life and death – it's more important than that'?

Shankly, in another of his memorable, though this time totally accurate, one-liners, said: 'I was made for Liverpool and Liverpool was made for me.' When gasping defenders trailed in the wake of crimson-shirted Liverpool attackers, whose tenacity had been shaped on the playing fields of Melwood, it wasn't the supposed 12th extra man of the roaring Kop that disheartened them, it was the face of Shankly, and the unshakeable faith this granite-featured Scot had in Liverpool. Wanted: players to keep a clean sheet when all others are failing – only the hard-hearted need apply.

The likes of Busby, Cullis and Shankly raised the profile of the gaffer to new heights, to standards others would struggle to follow. In Busby's case, Manchester United spread from being a local or regional club into a national and international one, establishing a massive fan base that has made them the richest club in the world. Busby has his critics who question the harsh treatment of players (especially those who were injured at Munich and ushered through the side door), but United undeniably prospered from his legend.

Yet this breed of boss wasn't necessarily the technically astute, tactical coach Winterbottom sought to develop. Instead, they were survivors of the pre-war era, British football's dark ages. Winterbottom wanted men who could bring it into the light.

Frank O'Farrell did not come from a classic football background. As a boy growing up in Cork in the Republic of Ireland, he had always wanted to be an engine driver. Many small boys did. Instead Frank achieved what lots of others dreamed of – he became a professional footballer. He moved from Cork United to West Ham United in 1948 and spent eight years with the Hammers before moving on to Preston North End for three years and then into management. He played nine times for his country but is best known for the tempestuous time as manager of Manchester United in the early 1970s. In the immediate post-war era the life of a professional footballer was markedly different from what it is today. There were no agents, players were fixed to a maximum wage which was pitched slightly above that of the average working man. For a young boy from Cork, the bombsites of the East End were a forbidding place.

West Ham were not necessarily a club to lift the spirits. They had mostly been a Second Division club of little notoriety. Football was to be enjoyed not endured in this part of London; there wasn't much appetite for the dogged grinding out of results. Fans wanted to be entertained, they wanted their team to play good football – they still do. It was as important as winning. Almost. From this unlikely setting sprang the fountain of English football's first coaching intelligentsia.

'We had a young manager, Ted Fenton, who asked us how we thought we had played, where we went wrong and what we were doing,' recalls Frank O'Farrell. 'We were encouraged to talk.

'It wasn't like that at other clubs. Billy Wright once told me that the players at Wolves – even experienced internationals – would quake in their boots, some literally shaking with fear when they heard Stan Cullis walking down the corridor. They'd dive into the toilet to avoid him. It wasn't like that at West Ham. We were able to express ourselves. We weren't particularly successful, but in those days so much of the East End had been ruined by the war – there were more important things in life than football.'

The tactical debate Walter Winterbottom's courses sought to instigate filled the Upton Park dressing-room, and West Ham had plenty of players willing to offer their opinions. Several would go on to be well-known managers. A brave new West Ham would also emerge, a club which would achieve success in the 1960s and provide three notable players for England's 1966 World Cup-winning team: Bobby Moore, Geoff Hurst and Martin Peters. A club which not only developed its own players but an internal coaching structure with, notably, fewer managerial changes than most clubs.

Back in the grey days of the mid-'50s, the discussion would spread beyond Upton Park. 'Most of us were in digs, we didn't have cars, weren't married, so we used to eat in cafés after training.' Cassetarri's on the Barking Road was their favourite haunt. 'We would talk tactics and push the salt and pepper pots and the cutlery around the table,' says O'Farrell. Around the table at were Dave Sexton, Noel Cantwell, O'Farrell, John Bond, Malcolm Musgrove and Jimmy Andrews. They became known as the West Ham Academy.

Their leader was Malcolm Allison, an outspoken defender, who had joined West Ham from Charlton, and had done some of his National Service in Austria. He had seen a lot of continental football first hand. His blinkers were off – he believed the British game was too limited in its outlook, and wasn't afraid to say so.

'Malcom always led the discussions,' recalls Frank O'Farrell. 'He wanted us to train with the ball a lot more – you hardly saw the ball in training at most clubs – and he introduced weight training.' Among Allison's seemingly bizarre, though no doubt practical, steps was to cut shirts so they fitted better. He also persuaded the club to obtain lighter boots. 'Anything which made the players feel more comfortable,' says O'Farrell.

Fenton let Allison take the coaching sessions and he was a particular influence on a young defender who would replace him in the West Ham team, Bobby Moore. Sadly, though, Allison did not benefit as a player from the changes he made. He contracted tuberculosis in West Ham's 1957–58 promotion season and had to have a lung removed. Allison drifted into non-league football, then became a soccer coach, oddly, at Cambridge University and in Canada before returning to England with Bath City, Plymouth Argyle and, famously, at Manchester City with Joe Mercer (who, and this is how old football circles revolve, was Stan Cullis's boyhood friend in Ellesmere Port).

'There was a new style of management at West Ham – and that's where the coaching you see today really started,' insists O'Farrell, who is keen to praise the 'gentlemanly' influence of Walter Winterbottom. 'The theory was that players must be happy with the tactics they are playing. It certainly whetted my appetite for coaching and management.'

These new-style managers, like Winterbottom, directly took coaching sessions and were as readily seen in tracksuits as lounge suits. When Winterbottom left the FA in 1963, it took two men to replace him. Allen Wade, a former Notts County player and Loughborough University teacher, took on the coaching brief, while Alf Ramsey became England manager. Winterbottom remained one of English football's most revered figures, his success barely quantifiable in terms of achievement, but 'massive' (to use Jimmy Armfield's word) in terms of the things he instigated. He was later knighted and his contribution was rightly acknowledged by many of the game's great and good when he passed away in February 2002. 'I wouldn't be here today if it wasn't for Walter,' said Bobby Robson. Jimmy Hill described him as 'inspirational and innovative'.

Curiously, football management moved in a new direction in the socially liberated 1960s. The training ground gaffer would have less job security – but would carry the yoke of his former duties, making him a cumbersome target for his employers if (or more often when) he failed. The easily disposable football manager was about to be born. The sack race was about to start.

– CHAPTER FIVE –

The 1960s:
The Sacking Spree Starts

When I first started playing managers didn't get sacked. There was never any question of our manager at Blackpool, Joe Smith, who had been there since 1935, being sacked.

Jimmy Armfield

My housemaster at school said, 'Cullis, what has happened to your father?' I replied, 'He's been sacked.' 'Oh, seems to happen a lot nowadays.'

Andrew Cullis

ON AN UNUSUALLY COLD MAY MORNING IN 2001 A GROUP OF grey-haired old men filed into the pews down one side of St Peter's Church in the centre of Wolverhampton. This was a memorial service for the late Stan Cullis, who had died a month earlier. They were the Wolves stars of the 1950s. Cullis was their former manager.

Despite being in a house of God, Wolves ran the show as if it were their home ground a short walk away. Sections of the church had been taped off, with prime seats reserved for club directors and officials. Stewards rather than ushers showed members of the congregation to their seats. The club's current players, one of them casually chewing gum, filed in at the back. Outside, curious onlookers stood in respect with their old gold and black scarves draped over them. One fan had travelled from Germany, another from East Anglia; they wanted to pay their last respects to Wolves' greatest-ever manager. The congregation, and the selection of music like 'You'll Never Walk Alone' and 'The

Happy Wanderer', emphasised the unity that can exist between a football club and the community.

It seemed hugely appropriate that Cullis, the 'passionate puritan', a strictly moral man whose own son Andrew is now a vicar, would be remembered in this way. Andrew Cullis, Bert Williams, the former Wolves goalkeeper who is chairman of the Wolves Former Players Association, Aston Villa chairman Doug Ellis (who, like Cullis, is from Ellesmere Port), Wolves owner Jack Hayward, and Jim Holden (author of *The Iron Manager*, an excellent biography of Cullis) all did readings. It was a moving occasion.

The congregation were strangely asked to pray for, among others, the club's sponsors. Though it wasn't quite the 'disgrace' one Wolves employee suggested outside, it sounded inappropriate. Andrew Cullis insists the family didn't have any input into that part of the service. 'I had a fleeting thought: "This is a sign of the times. This is where we've got to," nothing more than that.'

This was, after all, 'A Celebration Of The Life Of Stan Cullis 1916–2001'. For 30 of those years Stan gave unswerving loyalty to Wolverhampton Wanderers, the club he played for, captained and managed. Yet no amount of dewy-eyed reminiscences of the heady days of the 1950s when Cullis's warriors lifted a trio of championships, two FA Cups, and the magic of those floodlit nights against foreign opposition, or even Stan's notable playing career, could quite erase the memory of his dismissal some 35 years earlier. Not even the efforts of Sir Jack Hayward, who sought to bring Cullis back into the fold by naming one of the new stands in his honour in the early 1990s (and ensuring Stan was a welcome guest), could quite take away the bitter taste of his callous sacking. For to the left of the Stan Cullis Stand towers the two-tier John Ireland Stand, which all but crippled the club when it was built in 1981, a memorial to the secondhand car salesman and former Wolves chairman who cut Stan Cullis down. His sacking sent shockwaves through football and a whisper along the football boardrooms of Britain. If you could sack Stan Cullis and get away with it, anyone was fair game.

It is hard to emphasise enough how heartless it was for Wolves to dismiss Stan Cullis in September 1964. After a poor start to the 1964–65 season, Wolves were anchored to the foot of the First

Division. Cullis keeled over at his desk through ill-health and worry. Andrew believes it was a minor stroke. His father always took defeat particularly badly. It hurt. His doctor ordered Stan to take a few weeks off to relax. On the morning of his return, John Ireland, who had been club chairman for a year, strode in and, without enquiring about his health, ordered Stan to resign. When he refused, he was sacked. Cullis was then asked if he could take charge of the team one final time that evening. Amazingly he agreed. Wolves beat West Ham 4–3. Within days, he was ordered to hand back his club keys via a letter with his name as manager blanked out on it, and asked to pay back the advance line rental on his telephone. Manchester United manager Matt Busby wrote to Stan saying his dismissal had 'knocked him sick of human nature. How people could do such a thing after you giving them your life's blood?' Stanley Matthews urged him not to 'let the actions of some very small people get you down'.

It was a public relations disaster for Wolves. They issued a terse one-line statement on his dismissal, and then dedicated just six lines in the next club programme to the matter. They were understandably pilloried in the press. Gates dipped as fans stayed away in droves. Hundreds wrote to the local paper, the *Wolverhampton Express & Star*, to complain. Nationally, it was front-page news.

'For three days we were literally marooned in our house,' recalls Andrew Cullis, who was 16 years old at the time. 'There were TV crews camped outside our house and they were climbing up trees to take pictures. My mum wouldn't let us go outside.'

Not that sacking Cullis worked. Wolves were relegated the same season. Although they bounced back a couple of years later – ironically under the management of Ronnie Allen, a former centre-forward of arch-rivals West Bromwich Albion – Wolves have never regained the status of Cullis's era. In the 1980s they slipped into Division Four, with regular gates below 3,000. They were nearly wound up twice.

Some suspect that the roots of Cullis's dismissal went back to an incident when he had angrily ordered his players onto the team bus after a 5–1 defeat at Luton. He instructed the driver to leave for the railway station without a player, Peter Broadbent, and John Ireland, who was a junior director at the time. Ireland got a taxi to the station, where he gave Cullis a public dressing down. Many believe his days were numbered thereafter.

When he was sacked by Wolves, Stan Cullis was just 48 years old. For all his achievements, experience and expertise, he was largely ignored by the wider football world. After a short period out of the game selling squash courts for Coventry City chairman, Derek Robbins, he managed Second Division Birmingham City for five years. He couldn't rework the old magic and retired from football management in 1970. He wrote passionately about the game and was a Player of the Month adjudicator but despite his mighty contribution to football, he was never knighted or decorated. 'Being sacked affected him deeply,' says Andrew Cullis, who is a vicar in Nottingham. 'He internalised a lot of it. He didn't express it to me or my sister but it did hurt him. In a funny way it was never talked about.'

John Ireland went on to become a president of Wolves and have a stand built in his name 20 years before others were dedicated to Cullis and Wolves' legendary captain Billy Wright. Cullis was persona non grata at Molineux, although when Billy Wright became a director he did at least try to heal the wounds. To add to the folly, while Wolves were winding their way downwards, and might have benefited from the wisdom of an elder statesman, Cullis was managing a photographic shop in the town centre. 'After Birmingham, he should have stayed in the game in one capacity or another,' says Andrew Cullis. 'He had two shops – the other was a chemists – but the photographer's was a hoot to us, because he could never take a photo to save his life.'

It's worth pausing to think about that. A man whose only life's trade had been football running a photography shop during a period when the club whose only sustained success had been under his management and then went through 12 managers in 25 years after his dismissal, refused to call on his help or to even encourage him to come along and watch games at the ground he knew so well. There was little family sympathy for Wolves' decline in fortunes. 'Within my own heart I wasn't sorry,' recalls Andrew Cullis. 'Even for me, it was Wolves have done that to Dad, we don't want to know.'

Thankfully, when Jack Hayward took control in 1990, he insisted that Cullis was welcomed back. The family are now keen Wolves supporters. Unfortunately, Cullis was not in a good state of health, nor a wealthy man by then. His wife, Winifred, needed day care towards the end of her life and Stan, worried about their financial plight, sold his mementoes for £100 to an opportunistic memorabilia collector. 'As a family, certainly the boys (Stan's grandchildren) feel we would like to have the England caps somewhere. We have lots of photos and letters, but all the caps have gone,' said Andrew.

In 1992, Wolves held a testimonial match to coincide with the opening of the Stan Cullis Stand, symbolically against Honved, the Hungarian club side Cullis's team beat to restore English pride in the wake of the defeats inflicted by the 'Magnificent Magyars'. It raised £70,000. It is worth noting, though, that this was the supporters' money, contributed through gate receipts. 'The testimonial match was a great healer. He hadn't been to a match at Molineux since John Ireland was around,' recalls Andrew. 'It was a big healing moment. He really looked forward to going to games in the later years, though not during his final few years when he was too ill.'

The sacking of Stan Cullis in 1964 was a sign of things to come. The untouchable gaffers who ran their clubs without question from top to bottom were on their way out. The game was spinning in a different direction. Cullis's dogmatic style of management became obsolete. Like other aspects of society, football changed dramatically in the 1960s. What happened to Cullis has been repeated time and time again since. Doubtless there were many chairmen and directors at the time, even if they were shrewd enough not to admit it publicly, who probably nodded along with John Ireland's actions.

In the 1960s football managers took on a different role. They were shorn of their overall power in running the clubs and directly aligned to the success or failure of the team. 'A new phrase came about, "the tracksuit manager",' recalls Tommy Docherty, who would become one of the new breed of football managers to emerge in the 1960s. 'He stepped out of the office, put his coat and watch and chain away, put on a tracksuit and became a totally different man. Suddenly everybody realised he was the whipping boy if things didn't go too well, and the chairman would not have to carry the can.'

The control freak in most managers, and the fact that clubs did not always seek to bring in other people to replace the traditional side of their job (the overall management of the club), meant managers were saddled with a hopelessly large brief. They simply could not be a full-time head coach and carry on with their former duties. Yet many, to this very day, try. That is why so many work ludicrously long hours regardless of the dangers to their health. They are just guys who can't say no.

The changes sweeping football weren't just inspired by Walter Winterbottom's call for the game to improve tactically and technically, but by the new freedom footballers would enjoy after decades of being chained to their clubs on restricted wages.

Wage negotiation and transfers had been fairly straightforward up until the early 1960s. With a maximum wage in place for players, their demands were limited. The retain and transfer system effectively meant clubs could sell the players they didn't want but it was difficult, sometimes impossible, for a player to leave a club he no longer wished to play for. Under Jimmy Hill's charismatic leadership the PFA forced the maximum wage issue. In 1960, the PFA threatened strike action. The threat was repeated again in 1961, and this time the clubs gave way. Two years later George Eastham, a Newcastle United player, challenged his club's right to retain him against his will. The case went to the High Court. Eastham won. The shackles were off professional footballers.

'The game had been so unfair,' recalls Tommy Docherty, who played for Preston North End in the 1950s. 'In our day, the players were slaves. You were getting £10–£12 a week. The club had you for life. You couldn't leave the club but the club could get rid of you. When freedom of contract was introduced in February 1962 the whole game changed. It soon went from £100 a week to £150, £200, £250. Moneywise it just took off. Now it's unfair the other way. The demands of the players today are crazy.'

Pitched at a level slightly above the average wage, the maximum wage had been introduced with good intentions – to prevent a few very rich clubs buying all the best players and winning all the trophies. To an extent it had achieved its aims. There had, naturally, been periods of domination, like Arsenal in the 1930s, and Wolves and

Manchester United in the 1950s, but the trophies were generally spread around a lot more than today. However, it was a hopeless, unjustifiable, hark back to Victorian times. All the power was in the hands of the club owners, there were appalling industrial relations, and footballers (usually called solely by their surnames) were treated as little more than pawns.

Management under these circumstances had been fairly straightforward. It was easy to stand up to disgruntled players because they couldn't leave without the club's consent. John Barnwell, now chief executive of the LMA, started his professional career with Arsenal. 'There were 65 players on the team photo. We were all on a one-year contract on a maximum wage. When they lifted the maximum wage they said the game would be ruined. It wasn't. Then the freedom of contract came in. We've had the Bosman affair since. The game will always survive its traumas.'

The end of the maximum wage was a blessed relief to professional footballers, but it posed problems for managers. Some clubs had been so entrenched in the patrician era that they even held some of their players' wages for them. 'When I left Arsenal after nine years I had a sum of money which I invested in my first business,' recalls John Barnwell, who used the money to open the first coin-operated launderette in the Midlands and later ran a financial services business, which he cheerfully admits he knew nothing about. It didn't last long, but it did give John an eye for business and an interest outside the game. His route into football management came later via coaching. 'I didn't set out to manage. Your personality pushes you that way. I set out to coach because I enjoyed that.'

Although they had to deal with the wage negotiations and transfers (which escalated rapidly from a British record of £50,000 in 1960 to £1 million in 1979), most managers were ex-players who did not have any control of the purse strings. They were caught in no man's land between the directors and the players. They couldn't hide behind their desks, or for that matter on the training ground.

Some did not handle the transition particularly well. John Barnwell moved from Arsenal to Nottingham Forest in 1964. 'The manager was John Carey, a great player and one of the few people to have been picked in every position for Manchester United, including in goal. We rarely saw him without his trilby and never in a tracksuit. He employed Tommy Cavanagh as coach. Coaches were coming to the fore at the time. Carey bought and sold the players, and did the contracts. Having been there a couple of weeks I remember asking him how he wanted me to play. He said "Jesus Christ, I've paid all this money for you, and you're asking *me* how to play!" He bought me for what he'd seen and that was how he wanted me to play. He picked players for what he required. He saw what he wanted and that was what he expected, and if you didn't deliver you were out. When the tracksuit managers came in, they spent more time on the training ground and they tried to do everything which we're now realising is physically impossible.'

The manager's role was changing dramatically. Not only did he spot and sign the players, and usually sort out the transfer fee and decide how much they should be paid, but he also had to coach them, and select them for his team. Tommy Docherty went into football management at Chelsea in 1961. An irrepressible character who would manage a dozen clubs (despite his name being synonymous with the sack, he was actually only dismissed from two of them for football reasons), Docherty was at the forefront of the new wheeler-dealer world of the football manager.

'I went into managing because I didn't know anything else other than football,' admits Docherty. 'I went on a coaching course with people like Jimmy Hill, Bobby Robson, Malcolm Allison and Don Howe. I went to Lilleshall and got my full badge and then went to Chelsea as coach during my playing days. It was a natural progression from playing and coaching to managing.'

He would soon find himself handling players who were earning far more than he ever had as a player. 'Bob Lord at Burnley said "We'll pay Jimmy McIlroy £100 a week," and Tommy Trinder at Fulham said "We'll pay Johnny Haynes £100 a week." Then the game went crazy until the Bosman ruling. It was a lot to deal with.'

Frank O'Farrell had been one of the celebrated members of the so-called West Ham Academy, but had also been a colleague of Docherty's at Preston. He, too, started his management career in 1961, at non-league Weymouth. 'In those days lots of top players ended their careers in non-league football because it didn't cost the clubs as much as now.' O'Farrell took his West Ham team mates John Bond and Ken Brown with him. The timing couldn't have been better. 'I started managing when the maximum wage ended. Preston had wanted me to take a drop in wages to £18 from the maximum which was £20. I refused and left. I went to Weymouth as player/manager and was better off. I was on £25 a week, with a car and a club house,' recalls O'Farrell. 'A result of the maximum wage being abolished was that clubs released lots of players. I would travel up to the PFA offices in Manchester and get the lists of the latest players released and their addresses so I could get to them first. I would travel from Yorkshire down to East Anglia and work my way home signing players.'

Snapping up players this way had huge financial implications. The directors had to be seen to be doing something if results weren't going well – and it was easy to blame the manager. 'We all went into it with our eyes open. It was part of the system. A lot of talent was lost on those decisions and results. People forget that successful managers like Joe Mercer, who won the championship at Manchester City (with Malcolm Allison in 1968), had failed at Sheffield United and Aston Villa. Some were not lucky enough to bounce back.'

Rather than take the strain off their overburdened managers, most club boards let the managers take the blame for results. Since the 1960s, they have hired and fired at will. Loyalty and continuity has been rare. For every West Ham Academy (the Hammers have had the fewest managers of any Premier/Football League club) or Liverpool Boot Room (the Reds employed from within during Shankly's reign, which began in 1959, through to Kenny Dalglish, who left in 1991), there have been clubs who have replaced their managers with alarming regularity – and not, one has to say, with much conspicuous success.

The statistics are telling but, unfortunately, they probably aren't that shocking to people who know the way the football industry works. Twenty clubs have had twenty or more managers in the past forty years. Forty-one clubs have had ten or more managers in the past twenty years. Fifty-three clubs have had five managers or more in the past ten years. If you look at the statistics prior to the 1960s, there was much more managerial stability. Only eight Premier/Football League clubs had more managers in their 60–80-year histories prior to the last

40 years than since. In most of these cases it is because one, or maybe two, managers have had remarkably long periods in office.

There has also been a spiralling effect. There is a belief among many people in the game, Tommy Docherty and Jimmy Armfield, for instance, who have suggested that there were more sackings in the 1960s and '70s than now, but the statistics do not support that view. Writ large, more managers were sacked in the 1970s than 1960s, more managers were sacked in the 1980s than the '70s, ditto the 1990s than the '80s. It *is* getting worse. Clubs will always lose managers, through better offers and retirement, and there will always be a ripple effect when one manager moves on and someone else fills his shoes that can run along a few clubs. But there is no ignoring the fact that British football management became more precarious in the 1960s.

The 1960s were changing times. Respect in society dwindled and deference to authority waned due to factors such as the Profumo affair, plays and television shows depicting the realities of working-class life, the upturn in trade unionism, the rise in conspicuous consumption and youth culture. Young people were breaking down social barriers and defying authority everywhere. Football was inevitably part of this change. The new well-paid footballers (though modestly paid compared to today) had expendable cash with lots of ways to spend it. They were role models. Their lifestyle, their outlooks, their acquisitions were an anathema to their managers, whose own youth had been spent in austere times.

Stan Cullis was a classic case. He managed Birmingham City in the late 1960s, but he couldn't relate to the players or crack the whip as he once had at Wolves. 'Towards the end of his time at Birmingham he found it difficult to be with the players because of money and these were changing times,' recalls his son Andrew. 'He couldn't understand the players or how to motivate them. And neither did he understand the things going on in a footballer's life. I would go to matches with him and I remember saying to him that one of the player's wives had had a baby recently, and maybe that was why he wasn't playing well. This was obviously a total revelation to him, that if you had a baby you might lose some sleep because he probably didn't do with us.'

Tommy Docherty became manager of Chelsea in 1961, when he was 33 years old. He built a team of talented young stars, but there was a wayward tendency among them. In April 1965, Chelsea were challenging for the First Division and with consecutive games at Blackpool and Burnley they stayed in a Blackpool hotel to prepare for both fixtures. On the eve of the first game, eight players slipped out via the hotel fire escape for a night on the town. Docherty decided to lay down the law. He sent them home, played a side made up of reserves and lost both games. The players included future managers George Graham, Terry Venables and John Hollins. Docherty's authoritarian stance, though understandable, seemed harsh at the time.

'I had warned them five times before on previous occasions about their behaviour,' recalls Docherty. 'It was a case of them or me. So when they did it for the sixth time I sent them home and fined them all I could fine them: two weeks' wages. I was criticised for that at the time but today the press are calling for stricter management. Today, they're treated with velvet gloves. I had a great squad of kids, but they were led by one or two players who got too big for their boots. Terry Venables and George Graham were the ringleaders. I had the full support of the board.'

Matt Busby, for all his legendary status and the huge swathe of public sympathy that enveloped him and his team, had similar problems. In football, very little seemed to illustrate the difference between generations in the socially liberated 1960s than Busby and the outrageously talented George Best. Few young people summed up the 1960s better than Georgie, the 'fifth Beatle', boutique owner and flared trouser-wearer. Best would later go off the rails and it has been said many times that Busby simply could not relate to him. But there was dissent within the Old Trafford ranks long before Best went on boozy binges. Busby paid his players relatively small sums compared to the sort of cash they could get elsewhere, despite United's huge crowd-pulling appeal. While top stars were earning more than £100 a week, Johnny Giles, a young forward in those days, was transfer listed for asking for a rise from his modest £25 a week.

Noel Cantwell had signed for United and brought some of the continental influence that had seeped through the walls at West Ham. Players were demanding coaching, Busby was an old-style gaffer. He ran a tight ship and left the coaching of players to others, like Jimmy

Murphy. It is even conceivable that Busby could have suffered the same fate as Stan Cullis during the occasional lean season in the early 1960s – he was looking like a man out of time – but United stuck with their popular manager and he delivered the Holy Grail, the European Cup, in 1968. Unlike Cullis, he would become an influential director who could never quite let go of team affairs. He made management particularly difficult for his successors, Wilf McGuinness and Frank O'Farrell.

Coaches had come of age and tactics were changing. England had undergone such a transformation at international level that they lifted the World Cup in 1966. Alf Ramsey was a shrewd tactician. Never afraid to ignore his critics, he produced a winning, rather than merely crowd-pleasing, side. His switch from an old-style formation to a modern 4–3–3 served England well. Jimmy Adamson at Burnley had done the same, and Bertie Mee, a former physiotherapist, was bringing in new types of training at Arsenal including meditation and aerobics. Management was moving into a new age.

Howard Wilkinson caught the coaching bug in the 1960s. His career began at Sheffield Wednesday, where he had been an England Youth player. He was released and went to Brighton and Hove Albion for four years. Fed up with hanging around his digs, he went on a coaching course organised by club coach Steve Burtenshaw.

'He was running a preliminary coaching course. From the very first session I was hooked. I thought I would like to do this. It was absorbing. I took my full badge a year later [now called the A licence]. My preparation was always watching people. I was interested in systems. You just pick up things and apply them to your own coaching.' Wilkinson quit playing to go part time with Boston and study for a PE degree. He was hedging his bets with one foot in teaching and another in football as player/manager of Boston United. He used education to bring fresh techniques to football from other sports and would become the ultimate tracksuit tactician.

Managers were now actually expected to coach – for the first time most were seen wearing tracksuits. But they were also media men. Television changed football in lots of ways. Firstly gates dropped as fans preferred to stay at home and watch games on TV at a time when the cost of admission was rising because the clubs needed more revenue to pay the players. In those days, at least, there were not huge sums to be earned from lucrative television rights deals. This only increased the pressure on the manager to succeed. Failure hit clubs in the pocket. If you can't afford the best players you inevitably lose your chance to compete in the transfer market, which affects results. More pressure. But managers, at top clubs in particular, were also expected to do TV interviews. Their image affected their club. Some of the older managers weren't equipped – a rising generation were more at ease. Managers became iconic figures. They were wary of how they looked and performed on screen. It was an essential part of their job. The same went for radio. Were they given training to prepare for this new aspect of the job? Of course not. The demands have steadily increased, but actual media training for managers is fairly new and certainly not widespread.

The sack, or the threat of the sack, has defined football management since the 1960s. It has led to instability, to short-term thinking, to some managers looking to line their pockets while they've got the chance, to widespread mistrust. 'Don't ever trust anyone in this business,' one manager I interviewed for this book told me. What a sad opinion for anyone to have about their business. Managers are relatively easy to sack. You can force them to resign, but you can't do that to players or directors. Fans speculate, feverishly, about their fate. It has to be a real disaster for them to shout 'sack the board'. Sacking the manager is far easier.

Narrow-minded Tory right-wingers like to locate the 1960s as the decade when just about everything in society started to go wrong. It is often their blithe justification for dismantling everything from the education system to council housing, and 'reform' (by which, they usually mean privatisation) of the NHS and town planning. They reject the liberal consensus of the '60s, preferring an imagined Golden Age, which never really existed, but which is conveniently used to parody the present. But British football management did change irrevocably in the 1960s. It was the start of the sack race.

– CHAPTER SIX –

A Change at the Top: Do Sackings Work?

There's one thing for certain in football management and that is that one day you are going to get the sack.

Tommy Docherty

'TWO HUNDRED AND SEVENTY-FIVE MANAGERS HAVE BEEN sacked in five years. Only 34 are still managers, 63 have been recycled back into football in another role. That means 178 have left the game.' John Barnwell wearily reels off a deeply depressing though telling statistic. These are the grim results of football's failure to offer any semblance of security to the majority of managers and stability to football clubs of this country. John knows them so well because it is the major concern of his industry. It is *the* major question surrounding football management. He is asked it all the time: why are so many managers sacked?

The LMA was formed ten years ago when England boss at the time, Graham Taylor, believed managers needed their own organisation, having previously been part of the wider Football League Executive Staffs Association, which had diverse interests, including chief executives and directors – the people the managers worked for. Barnwell has been chief executive for six years. The LMA's offices, on a nondescript industrial estate in Warwick, are far removed from the game's power base in the industrial heartlands. Nonetheless, Barnwell is a busy man. Our conversation is punctuated by phone calls from concerned managers. Should they sign this, how should they deal with that. Signing and settling contracts seems to be a big bugbear.

'He's a nice man but has to dot all the i's and cross the t's, then do it all over again,' smiles John, referring to one of his calls. He is a model of calm and efficiency, adept at calming his agitated members. He has been through the trials and tribulations of management, success and the sack. While managing Wolves, he was involved in a near-fatal car crash (briefly touched upon in the preface to this book, and described in greater detail in Chapter Ten) and finally gave up management following a hip-replacement operation six years ago. He badly misses the training ground.

That Barnwell spared almost two hours for our interview says more about his concern for the subject matter of this book than his availability. I am extremely grateful to John, a wise old managerial owl with an erudite knowledge of the football business. He is remarkably candid about the sack race. 'The reasons so many managers lose their jobs and never get back into it is because they are ill-prepared and the appointments, in many cases, shouldn't have been made. Because it is a winning and losing profession it is inevitable there will be a high turnover but when they are dismissed they should be better protected by their contract and should be better skilled to be recycled back into the game. We've got to improve the standard of managers. If they manage better they will keep their jobs.'

John is keen to gear up the gaffers so they can cope with the high-pressure demands of the job, but he also believes it is too easy for clubs to sack managers. In the face of flak from fans and the media it is all too often a first, rather than a last, resort. 'The Premiership isn't too bad. We've had one season where only two managers were sacked, another where eight lost their jobs, but that isn't too bad. The majority are in the Football League.' The Football League has different rules to the Premiership clubs who have to settle the contracts of their outgoing manager before they can appoint a new one. Attempts to introduce this system into the Football League ran to ground.

'Three years ago we had an appeal panel process in the Football League for the first time and the dismissals were reduced by 50 per cent,' says Barnwell. 'If you were dismissed the manager and club had to settle his contract within 28 days or the manager had the right to ask an appeal panel to sit. It focused people's minds. The manager is asking for a loaf and the club are offering a slice of bread. As you get nearer to 28 days reality sets in and both parties negotiate.'

David Sheepshanks, the Ipswich Town and former Football League chairman, was influential in persuading his fellow chairmen to accept this system, but when Ipswich were promoted to the Premier League, (which meant Sheepshanks had to resign from the Football League committee) it was scrapped. 'It only sat twice. We've been fighting for it to be reintroduced for the past two seasons,' explains Barnwell. 'We've had meetings with the Sports Minister Richard Caborn so a regulation can be put into the rules which will slow down these dismissals. In reality they can sack a manager and drag you through a long legal process which can be very expensive, and if you take another job that is seen as mitigating circumstances. They can appoint somebody on the same money or less, and it still hasn't cost them anything. They've got rid of you but they haven't honoured the contract. If you were headhunted and were successful they wouldn't just want your contract quashed, they would also want compensation. So they can't have it all their way. A contract should reflect both parties' intentions. New managers coming in are so keen to get a job they sign what is put in front of them.'

The statistics that effortlessly trip off Barnwell's tongue have worsened this season. Divide the 275 managers by season and it's an average of 55 per season or 2.98 managers per club in that period of time. The average managerial tenure is currently 18 months. By the time you read this is it will probably have lowered. I make no apologies for being out of date. It is impossible to keep up. Indeed, many of the interviewees for this book have changed jobs since I spoke to them. It is a rapidly changing environment. In any other form of business such a high turnover of key personnel would be viewed with dismay. It would be a sign of failure. So it is understandable to ask why so many? And do sackings actually work? There must some logic suggesting that the replacement of the manager leads to improved fortunes – otherwise why do it?

This is a more complex question than it first appears. Despite the obvious conclusion from media speculation, more managers resign than are sacked. But are their resignations, in reality, due to the same thing as sackings – results? Do they jump or are they pushed? The clear answer in two-thirds of managerial changes is 'yes' to the latter. These are known as involuntary dismissals.

Academics have struggled to find convincing answers to the results of sackings. It isn't just a question of comparing the performance of the club either side of replacing a manager. How long before and after do you take into account? Weeks? Months? Years? Most academics prefer to condense their studies into a very limited period, often as little as ten games, because circumstances can change so quickly. An outgoing manager may have had a particularly difficult run of matches, for example, played against the top teams in the division. A new manager is unlikely to be appointed in the face of this sort of fixture onslaught. If he has a string of winnable games he is hailed as a hero. The change is deemed to have worked. Then there are changes in the resources available. Players change too: some look to leave, new ones arrive. A new manager might also bring in his own coaches. For academics, these are all contributory factors.

A manager might also take over a relegated club, or one preparing for the consequences of relegation. That was certainly the case when Dave Bassett took over from Peter Taylor at Leicester City in September 2001. Although Leicester were obviously committed to keeping themselves in the Premiership, especially so early in the season, they quickly became cautious, even fatalistic. Bringing in Micky Adams – an experienced manager in his own right – as 58-year-old Bassett's number two gave the impression that Leicester were looking to rebuild longer term with younger managers taking over. With a new stadium being built, were they anticipating they might have to accept a step back in order to go forward? In these sorts of circumstances it would be harsh to compare Bassett's performance with Taylor's. Leicester did not invest heavily in their playing squad under Bassett. Equally, to compare the results of a new manager at a relegated club with those of his predecessor can be misleading, given the likely decrease in commercial income, in particular TV revenue. An incoming manager in this situation often has to operate on a totally different budget. Obviously the last manager failed (the club were relegated), but what is his successor expected to achieve?

Academics are also keen to acknowledge the so-called 'shock effect' of firing a manager. Players may have become disillusioned under the previous boss. They might have had bad luck with injuries or the wider availability of players. When a new manager arrives players respond by trying to impress him. After all, they may want a new contract. Poor form can lead to reserve team football and/or the transfer list. Footballers, like most of us, are an essentially selfish breed. They seek to look after their own career. Nothing wrong with that – but it does muddy the waters if you are trying to make direct comparisons in the performance of incoming and outgoing managers. There is also an element of professional pride. The dismissal of a manager will inevitably follow a period of expectation in the media. Fans will have blamed the players for poor results. Professional pride means they will try to prove their detractors wrong after the manager has been sacked. Quite often a temporary or caretaker manager will have been appointed (an odd phrase – does he wear a brown coat and carry out routine maintenance?). Results often improve dramatically. It's all part of the shock effect.

So what do academic studies tell us? John Goddard and Stephen Dobson, authors of *The Economics of Football*, published in September 2001, found that the shock effect led to an immediate improvement in results. Their research was limited to six games prior to a manager being dismissed and the six games afterwards. 'It is difficult to assess the financial consequences,' says John Goddard. 'It is a very complicated picture.' Their research found a dip in results is followed by a longer-term improvement.

'Statistically it is often inevitable that there will be an uplift because a string of poor results doesn't normally last too long. It is inevitable they will turn things around at some stage. Also very few clubs sack their managers when a set of tough games is coming along. A team at the foot of the Premiership won't appoint a new manager if his first three fixtures are likely to be Manchester United, Liverpool and Arsenal in quick succession. It wouldn't be fair.' Goddard's observations, to a degree, do answer the question of whether the dismissal was worth making. 'Overall the teams who replace their managers do better than those who stick with their managers.'

A study reproduced in *Insight* magazine, the FA coaching department journal, written by Daniel Abraham, a management and business administration student at Reading University, came to a slightly different conclusion. 'In the short term, changing the manager does not affect results, and although in the longer term other factors do influence results, there is no evidence to suggest that managers do not make a difference. But managers are only one of a number of variables influencing team results.'

Ruud H. Koning, of the Department of Econometrics at the University of Groningen in Holland, has evaluated the effects of firing coaches of teams in the Dutch Premier League between 1993–94 and 1997–98. Koning acknowledges many of the points above, and even throws in variables like the number of home and away games played and the quality of the opposition. He uses complicated mathematical formulae in order to reach his conclusion that teams earn more points and score more goals per game than under the previous coach. But when you include all the other factors, 'the performance of a team does not always improve when a coach is fired'.

Koning believes new coaches tend to concentrate on defence rather than attack, staving off defeat rather than winning matches. There is a key conclusion which many other academics pull short of. He says: 'Firing a coach occurs too often since it is not clear that the results on the field improve after a change of coach. It is likely that the board of a team intervenes for other reasons. It is likely that fan and media pressure are also determinants of the tenure of a coach.'

Which brings us back to square one. The inconclusive results of this number crunching tell us very little. Or maybe that in itself is significant – there is very little change.

Tommy Docherty, a man who has learnt much at the University of Life, says: 'Directors don't sack managers. Players get managers the sack. The manager selects the players, picks them and produces them through the youth policy. If he doesn't get the results he gets the sack. The supporters sack the manager with their response to the team's performance and the players by not performing and getting the results. Chairmen don't sack the managers. They have to say, "I'm sorry, the results aren't to the standard required so we're making a change."'

My own unscientific research has been longer term, among what academics call 'involuntary' dismissals, those managers sacked or forced to resign – roughly two-thirds of managerial dismissals in the

Premier/Football League in season 2001–02. I have taken an anecdotal look at the results and what I would call realistic expectations. Few people, not even, I suspect, the most die-hard of Leicester City supporters, will have expected them to win the Premiership or even finish in the top three last season, for instance. It is probably safe to say that a reasonable expectation would be for Leicester to finish mid to lower table. Above that would be overachieving, finishing bottom (as they did) is obviously below par – but not, I would suggest given the resources available to them, by much.

Peter Taylor, Leicester's former manager, was dismissed in September and feels he was prematurely rejected. 'It was frustrating because we did have a bad start to the season but so did three other clubs and they all kept their managers. I felt I was the man to turn things around. But they thought the results weren't acceptable and that is their decision. They felt a change was needed. You hope you're going to get the backing of the board during those sorts of times, but I didn't. That is disappointing but you move on older and a bit wiser. No one who's had success hasn't had a lean spell or a period when they could have been sacked. It's inevitable.'

In my research into the frequency of managerial changes, I have found it is fair to say that in ballpark terms the clubs that change their manager the most have had the least stability. Could they have benefited from a more stable regime? And what about those clubs who have found their Mr Right (manager)? Have they achieved better than reasonably expected? If we look at the managerial changes in the Premier and Football League clubs in season 2001–02, among the 'involuntary' changes just under half of the managers were sacked (15). Five went by mutual consent – which is the sack, but with a gagging order attached in exchange for an immediate settlement of your contract. The rest were resignations and in one case demotion to another job within the club. When we take a closer look at what happened to those clubs that changed their manager in the involuntary category, 23 out of the 33 clubs saw no particular change in their fate or fortunes. There may be longer-term policy implementations that will take time to mature but for the vast majority of clubs there was little discernible difference in their performances. For a further seven clubs, I would say there was a slight improvement in form, and a genuine improvement in four clubs. A couple of changes were made too late in the season to make any difference (one of these, David Moyes at Everton, did manage three vital wins in his first five games – a better ratio that his predecessor).

It was hard to say that any of the clubs actually performed worse, but that isn't surprising as most clubs sack their manager because results are poor. With so many clubs sacking their managers, within the opening two or three months of the season they were at or near the foot of the table and stayed thereabouts. Again, classic examples were Leicester City in the Premiership, Stockport in Division One and Cambridge United in Division Two. You can't do worse than end up at the bottom.

It is notoriously difficult to assess those clubs that had been relegated. Coventry City, for example, parted company with Gordon Strachan after a month of the season – and there was an immediate upturn in form – but this was City's first season out of the top flight for 35 years and they were spiralling into debt, estimated at around £40–£50 million depending on the figures you read. In these circumstances it is difficult to say what would have been a realistic aim and to assess performance before and after. The club clearly felt they had underachieved and sacked Strachan's replacement Roland Nilsson and his assistant, the much-travelled Jim Smith, at the end of the season.

They were one of the clubs to see a marked upturn in form. Ditto Kevin Keegan at Manchester City. But did he do better than Joe Royle, his predecessor, might have? Keegan certainly won promotion handsomely, but City had far bigger resources then any club in their league. They were expected to win it. Keegan's true test comes in the 2002–03 Premiership season.

This brings up an often-contentious factor. Were the clubs right to sack their manager because he was underachieving? This again is difficult to assess, but judging the size and support of clubs, their past, their pulling power and financial backing, it is fair to make some basic assertions. Manchester United, the biggest club in the world, would be failing if they were outside the top five of the Premiership. Torquay would probably be overachieving if they finished in the top half of Division Three.

On this basis, looking at those clubs who changed their managers it would be fair to say that most were underachieving clubs – slightly less underachieving than those in absolute freefall. A couple were, frankly, overachieving. I would include Grimsby and Walsall in this category (small clubs at the lower end of the First Division who both survived the drop) and about a third were clubs who were performing at an expected level.

If the changes were minimal and, on the whole, if changing the manager doesn't necessarily bring worse results, what does that say about the long-term future of the club? The logical conclusion would be that constantly changing the gaffer restricts your chances of going down, or at least maintains the status quo. It suggests other factors, like a new cash-rich owner taking over the club, the development of young players, selling players for lots of money or some other circumstance leading to a change in fortunes. It isn't all down to changing the manager – which makes you wonder why there is a gargantuan effort by the industry to replace so many managers every season.

'The number of sackings is a direct derivative of the inability of chairmen and directors of football clubs to appoint properly,' says Steve Coppell, the former Crystal Palace and Manchester City manager, who left Brentford in June 2002. 'Every management appointment is an emotional, not an analytical one. Decisions are made on the basis of what will please the public rather than who is best for the job.'

Bringing in a new manager causes inherent instability within the club. After all it isn't just a manager that is changed. Quite often he will bring his own backroom staff to the club. That means those belonging to the previous regime are sacked, not necessarily unfairly but without having done anything wrong. In other industries you would need a damn good reason to do this, or face an industrial tribunal. Not football.

One of last season's sacked managers was Ray Graydon. We met a few weeks after his dismissal from Walsall, a time when many managers are understandably down. Not Graydon. He is one of life's optimists. He had served a 20-year apprenticeship as a coach and enjoyed every minute at Walsall. He wasn't bitter towards his former

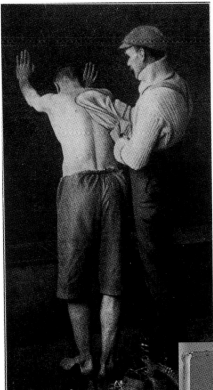

Recuperation 1906 style – West Brom players enjoy a post-training rub down.
The National Football Museum

SOCCER COACHING

Walter Winterbottom

AN OFFICIAL PUBLICATION OF
THE FOOTBALL ASSOCIATION

Walter Winterbottom's seminal text on football coaching.
The National Football Museum

The 1950s manager at work – a trio of championships
didn't save Stan Cullis from being mercilessly sacked.
Supplied by Andrew Cullis

Sir Matt Busby's message of support to Stan Cullis after his sacking in 1964.
Supplied by Andrew Cullis

The Doc calling – Tommy Docherty was one
of football's first tracksuit managers.
Birmingham Post & Mail

John Barnwell (left)
celebrates Wolves'
1980 League Cup
final win, with Geoff
Palmer (centre) and
Andy Gray (right).
Less than a year
earlier, Barnwell was
nearly killed in a late-
night car crash.
*Birmingham Post &
Mail*

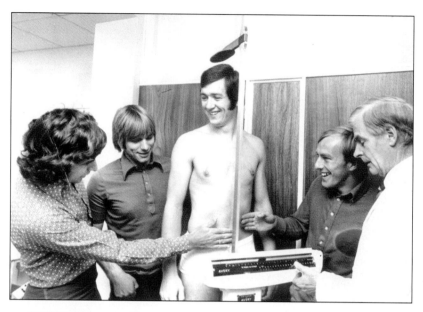

ABOVE: Bruce Rioch: a rare breed of manager who weighs the same now as during his playing days (here with Aston Villa).
Birmingham Post & Mail

BELOW: George Graham: banned from football management for a year following the Bungs Inquiry.

ABOVE: David Platt: Former England captain and current England Under-21 coach – but do ex-players deserve to be fast-tracked to the top?
Stuart Clarke

BELOW: Ex-England boss and League Managers Association founder, Graham Taylor, in his 'turnip' era – here being interviewed by David Davies.
Stuart Clarke

Fit to Manage? The League Managers
Association are funding research into
the health of their members.
The Adidas/Wellness Centre

Howard's Way: The FA's Technical Director,
Howard Wilkinson, has revamped the
training of coaches in England.
Mooneys photo agency

Bhoys our hero: Martin O'Neill has worked his
way up from non-league football with Wycombe
Wanderers to the Celtic hot seat.
Stuart Clarke

ABOVE: Jim Smith: dugout doyen in a praying pose.
Smith is the ultimate journeyman manager.
Stuart Clarke

BELOW: Brian Clough: the people's manager.
Stuart Clarke

Joe Royle (preferring not to get his shoes wet). One of seven managers Manchester City have had in the past ten years.
Stuart Clarke

Sir Alex Ferguson (with Brian Moore), Man Utd's most successful manager, could easily have been sacked in his early days at Old Trafford.
Stuart Clarke

employers but was surprised when he worked for them to go on a scouting mission and discover he was the fifth longest-lasting First Division manager at the time and twelfth in the Premier/Football League. He had been with Walsall for just three and a half seasons.

'There are too many sackings. Clubs should have the faith to stick with the people they've appointed,' insists Graydon. 'If you're the man for the job you should be given time to do it. They wouldn't give you the job in the first place if they didn't think you could do it.

'Matt Busby said "to get continuity we first of all need unity" and that's true – everyone has to be pulling in the right direction whether you are managing a football club or writing a book – people have to be behind you and back you all the way.'

Graydon admits he has been in a strange position, trying to get back into the game, which inevitably has to be at someone else's expense. 'I'm waiting for people to get the sack unfortunately – which is unusual – but I think it's great that I'm having a rest and I don't have to dive back in. But you don't want to be away too long.' At the end of the 2001–02 season Graydon was back in management – at his hometown club, Bristol Rovers. The myth of a managerial merry-go-round isn't true. As John Barnwell of the LMA says, where do all those managers who lose their jobs go?

The sack race doesn't just include managers, but also their assistants. It happened to Ray Graydon when he was a coach at Southampton. When Graeme Souness replaced Dave Merrington, Ray was shown the door.

Chris Evans is the academy director at Wolverhampton Wanderers. He is the longest-standing member of their coaching staff. An articulate and sincere man, he sits proudly in front of photographs pinned to the wall of the players he has passed on to the first team, seven of last season's first team squad including England Under-21s players Joleon Lescott and Lee Naylor. Pride of place goes to Robbie Keane, the Irish striker Wolves sold for £6 million at the age of 18. You can do an awful lot of youth development for that sort of money. Evans' own playing career ended at the age of 27. An ex-Arsenal apprentice, who played for Stoke City, York City and Darlington, he took college and university courses while playing and set up the country's first council-run youth football development programme in

Anglesey before joining Wolves in 1990. He manages a team of 10 full-time coaches, 20 part-time coaches, 10 physiotherapists, 25 landladies and 50 scouts across the UK and works with 140 academy players aged between 9 and 19. 'I like to find raw material and help those players realise their potential. Footballers predominately come from working-class backgrounds, as I have myself. Robbie Keane came here on £40 a week – now he's one of the top earners in the Premier League. He contacts me for advice.'

His academy is autonomous. Evans reports to the chief executive rather than the manager. 'The manager is results oriented. We are not, we are development oriented.' Evans insists he's had a 'great' working relationship with all the Wolves managers during his time at the club including Graham Taylor, Mark McGhee and Dave Jones, but football's wider climate of 'all change' when a new manager turns up can be a time of trepidation for all coaches.

'When managers come into the football club quite often they come and clear the decks because they feel what has gone before has to some extent failed. I don't accept that. They are worrying times. I have a wife, three children and a mortgage. I have relocated to this part of the country. My children's education is based locally. I haven't been in a position to affect first team results, so why should I be subject to them? This is an autonomous programme. I think there are too many things that happen in football because they've been happening for 100 years. I don't agree. I have been loyal to this football club and it has been loyal to me. I don't believe I should be forced onto the dole queue because of results.'

Continuity is seen as a key to success, which is why Howard Wilkinson, the FA's technical director, insisted academies stay clear of football management when he drew up 'A Charter for Quality', which brought them in. But the same does not happen in the professional game. If we look at the clubs that have changed their managers the most times there is little conspicuous sign of success. Three clubs – Cardiff City, Crystal Palace and Wigan – have had ten managers in as many seasons. This cannot be good for continuity. None of these clubs have experienced a significant upturn in results. Palace, indeed, have had a turbulent time which threatened their existence. Their rapid turnover of managers reflects that problem. They have yo-yoed between the Premier League and Division One. Steve Coppell (who was manager until 1993) has been back a further three times, Alan Smith twice. Cardiff have prospered recently only because of Sam Hammam's investment.

If we look at the clubs which have had eight or more managers in the past ten years it is easy to identify instability. Notts County have had nine managers in ten seasons, including three last season, and have slipped from the old First Division to Division Two. Lincoln City have also had nine managers. Halifax (who have had eight managers) have been in and out of the Football League twice, Carlisle have flitted between Divisions Two and Three and flirted with demotion from the League a few times. Southend, Stoke, Swindon and Norwich have all had eight managers in ten seasons.

Take a longer view and it is even more telling. Halifax have had 18 managers in 20 seasons, Cardiff City 17 in 20 years, Hull City and Bristol Rovers 16 each. It is a truly depressing picture and this lack of stable leadership cannot be good for any club. Obviously there are financial restrictions and some managers resign or are sacked simply to get the debts down or because they no longer want to work on a shoestring budget. Others progress, but constantly changing the manager does not and cannot work.

Let's take a closer look at how it affects the operation of a club. Manchester City have had 13 managers in the past 20 seasons, 18 in the past 30 years. Frank Clark was one of the managers who fancied his chances at turning round the fortunes of this legendarily underachieving club with its huge support. The last time City won a trophy was the League Cup in 1976. Clark's track record before going to Maine Road had been as a general manager at Leyton Orient for more than ten years. Money had been extremely tight at Orient and his task of taking over from Brian Clough at Nottingham Forest was notoriously difficult, but neither of these hurdles compared to the difficulties he encountered at Maine Road. 'It was impossible. Because they'd had so many managers, they had a huge playing staff – 50-odd pros, most of who knew they weren't going to get a game, and had been brought in by different managers on good money so they didn't want to leave and you couldn't get them out on loan because their wages were too high.

'It was a very difficult boardroom situation where on the surface it was all sweetness and light but underneath when things went wrong all the divisions surfaced. It was a club surrounded and infiltrated by ex-players, ex-vice-presidents and ex-directors all with their own agendas, all with a spoon to stir and all with access to the club.'

When he was appointed, Clark recalls how he had to sit in a car at the far end of the training ground with the vice-chairman, now chairman, David Bernstein because his temporary predecessor Phil Neal was clearing his desk: 'Talk about embarrassing.' Clark would remember this incident when he left two years later. He found out he had been sacked by listening to the radio. 'I had 30 minutes to clear my desk and to say "cheerio" to everybody before Joe Royle walked in. The nature of the job is what is your misfortune is somebody's else opportunity.'

They might be literally queuing to get the manager's job at Manchester City, but Clark believes the economics of continual change are wrong. 'We need an education programme. We have to show the chairmen why it is wrong. If they can't see the turnover is wrong then they should look at the cost. It is so expensive to keep paying someone off and bringing a new guy in.'

Lincoln City have not had managerial stability for a long time: they've had eight managers in the past ten years. Small wonder their supporters inevitably hark back to Graham Taylor's five-year reign in the mid-'70s, when he would march his players around factories on meet-the-fans tours in order to build a closer bond between the club and the community and to boost gates. More recently, the Imps have accrued accumulating debts. In 2001, they became the first club to be taken over by a supporters' trust – a new, democratic and somewhat obvious form of ownership, given soccer's 'people's game' status – where fans club together to buy shares in a trust and the trust buys a block share of the club. It is democratic because the trust members (fans) elect people on to the trust board. If they have control of the club like they do at Lincoln, sold to them by former chairman John Reames, then the fans are on the board.

I met Lincoln's chairman, Rob Bradley, near Cheltenham Town's ground. Despite having the obligatory Crombie draped across his arm and being suited and booted, Rob is still a fan. He carries out his statutory duties of glad-handing it with the opposition directors and watches the match from the directors' box, but he travels on the supporters' coach and still has a lunchtime session in the pub with his mates – hence the Taylor talk. His heart is on the terraces.

One of the first things Rob, an architect by trade, wanted to establish at Sincil Bank was managerial stability. It had become a managers' graveyard in recent years. Conversely, the first thing he did was sack the manager, Phil Stant. 'Obviously Phil was upset because it was his first management job and it hadn't been an easy time for him. It wasn't a pleasant thing to do but it was right for the club,' recalls Bradley. The board appointed former Grimsby and WBA boss, Alan Buckley. 'We met him at a hotel in Market Rasen. I don't think he'd met an entire board before. We wanted to let him know where we were coming from.

'We wanted a manager who we felt would take a long-term view. The club had suffered too much because each manager wanted his own backroom staff and players. There had been too many changes. And the youth system hadn't produced any players. We wanted Alan and Keith Alexander, his assistant, to get that going.' Unfortunately for Bradley and Buckley, the debts mounted and amid the uncertainty of future income following the collapse of ITV Digital (and the inevitable knock-on effect for Football League club finances), Lincoln went into administration in April 2002. Buckley was released from his contract as a cost-cutting measure. He was replaced by Alexander. It was continuity of sorts.

There is ample evidence to show that those clubs who keep faith with their managers tend to prosper. No one would advocate sticking with someone who is out of his depth or doing a poor job and there is a question of how far you go in letting a manager stay in charge but the relatively rare cases of loyalty do show that stability works.

There are only eleven managers who have been in charge of their current clubs for five or more years, only three of those for more than ten and one of those, Alan Curbishley at Charlton Athletic, shared the job with Steve Gritt for the first five years. But these tend to be the more stable and successful clubs. Charlton have established themselves as a mid-table Premiership club. The clubs managed by the two longest-lasting managers have been even more successful: Dario Gradi at Crewe (appointed in 1983) and Sir Alex Ferguson at Manchester United (1986). Notably, neither manager had any conspicuous success in their formative years. They were given time. It took Ferguson four years to put a trophy in the cabinet at Old Trafford, and although he has enjoyed unprecedented success since with the Champions League, several Premiership titles, FA Cups, a League Cup and European Cup-Winners' Cup, he could have been sacked early doors. But he wasn't and the rest, as they say, is history.

A few train stops along from Manchester is Crewe. If it wasn't for the fact Crewe has a large railway junction, most people would barely have heard of this small Cheshire town at all. Oh, and the local football team have a funny second name. That was until Dario Gardi hit town. 'Where's Crewe?' an old joke used to go. 'Near the foot of Division Four.' It wasn't particularly funny but it was pretty accurate. For 20 years between 1969–89 Crewe Alexandra had been locked in the Football League's basement division. In the decade before Dario Gradi arrived, Alex had seven managers in ten years. No stability. Gradi, a former pre-Crazy Gang Wimbledon and Crystal Palace manager, is not your average football boss. He never played League football, was a former FA regional coach and an assistant at Chelsea and Derby County. Employing him was a gamble and he was barracked in his early days in charge.

It took Crewe six seasons to make any progress. But Gradi got the youth policy working. After a two-year spell in the Third Division, Crewe were relegated, but bounced back in 1994 and were promoted to the First Division three years later. Despite small average gates of 6,000, Gradi kept them in the division for five seasons. They were relegated in 2002. Gresty Road has been rebuilt and the club is now on a sound financial footing, thanks to Gradi's youth policy. Gradi either developed his own players or picked them up cheaply from other clubs, improved them and sold them on for significant sums of money. David Platt, Geoff Thomas, Rob Jones, Craig Hignett, Robbie Savage, Neil Lennon, Danny Murphy – the list is endless. If Gradi hadn't been given time none of this would have worked.

The clubs who have appointed the least number of managers have generally been more successful. West Ham have had just six in the past forty years, only nine in their entire history, Liverpool just seven, including several successive promotions from their infamous Boot Room, and Arsenal seven also. Nottingham Forest and Southampton have had nine managers in forty years and Ipswich just ten in their entire existence.

In all these cases stability has worked. Managers have left but the clubs have been kept on an even keel. Success for clubs like Ipswich, West Ham and Southampton – who all won the FA Cup in the 1970s – is being in the Premiership. Go back to the 1950s and none of these clubs were in the top flight. If you don't agree, ask the fans of former big clubs like Blackpool, Stoke, Preston North End or Burnley who have spent decades in the wilderness.

Ipswich are proud of their family club status. Their current manager, George Burley, is a popular former player from Bobby Robson's era and has been in charge at Portman Road since 1994. Ipswich chairman David Sheepshanks says the club have made a conscious effort to stick with their manager, even though they were relegated in his first season in charge and missed out in the First Division play-offs for three consecutive years.

'It was a long-term appointment,' says Sheepshanks. 'When we chose George we set out on a course to give him both time to develop the playing side of the club and to develop his own skills. He was clearly a young manager who had never managed above the Scottish First Division. We saw it as our role to support him.'

Ipswich believe in staff training – everyone at the club, from the chairman and the manager down, is encouraged to go on training courses every year. Burley, who eventually achieved promotion via the play-offs in 2000, acknowledges he is a lucky man. 'Some of the things happening at Ipswich don't happen elsewhere in football. It is partly because it is a family club but it's also because the management of the club is right. The supporters see that, they understand it, and so they get behind you.' Even though Ipswich were relegated from the Premier League at the end of the 2001–02 season, there was neither speculation nor expectation that Burley would be dismissed.

David Sheepshanks is critical of the approach adopted by his fellow chairmen. 'A lot of the criticism is subjective rather than objective. Appointing a manager is the most important decision a chairman has to make so it shouldn't be taken lightly,' says Sheepshanks, who is also an FA councillor. 'Too many appointments are made with a short-term view and a lot of management candidates are players with good playing records that say nothing about their coaching record.'

It is, indeed, all too often a case of jobs for the boys.

– CHAPTER SEVEN –

Jobs for the Boys: The Case for Qualified Football Managers

> It's just jobs for the boys these days, just jobs for the boys.
>
> Tommy Docherty

SO HERE'S THE DEAL. YOU'RE A CLUB CHAIRMAN AND YOU'VE fired the manager. Who are you going to hire to replace him? You may have come in for some stick yourself, your own stock is low with the fans. You'd better appease them. So who do you choose? The easiest option is someone well known, a face the fans can trust, like an ex-player, a big name – a good motivator.

The huge number of dismissals indicates that all too often the wrong choices are made. Yes, football is a results-based business, and yes, there are unreasonable expectations and, of course, there is enormous pressure. But the facts remain that the average league manager lasts just 18 months. Something is going wrong – the clubs must be appointing the wrong people at least some of the time.

One of the problems is populist appointments: a returning prodigal son, a big-name former player, a much-travelled 'gift of the gab' manager. Chairmen love to bask in the reflected glory of famous names; they hope some of the magic will rub off on them. Few chairmen or directors ask for more detailed credentials. Is the manager qualified? Is he a good coach? Can he handle a team of players and coaching staff? Is he a good communicator? Is he the right manager for this club?

Sadly, English football has a long legacy of dismissing qualifications as a load of old hogwash. It was slow to embrace any kind of coaching culture, and although steps have been made to catch up, we are still a long way behind the other top European football countries, who refuse to let managers coach unless they have taken the highest available qualifications. Over here, at present, anyone can manage a football team. You, me, the bloke next door: if you were to win the lottery, buy your favourite club and install yourself as manager, no one could stop you. You wouldn't need to sit a single exam. You could bawl and shout at a group of professional players to your heart's content.

Small wonder sports coaching in this country has a low standing. 'On the continent a coach carries a great deal of respect,' says Howard Wilkinson, the FA's technical director. 'A coach in Italy, France or Germany will be given a certain amount of room when they walk down the street, whereas here, if you get a shout from across the road, being called "dickhead" would be nice. The position doesn't command any respect.' Character is perceived as more important than qualifications. Coaching isn't seen as a worthy profession.

On a sports field on the edge of a prosperous town, a First Division squad are about to start their day's work. It's midday, late summer, sunny with a slight breeze. Perfect for strenuous activity. I have a pre-arranged interview with one of the club's goalkeepers and his manager, and also hope to record a few training-ground sounds: the ball thudding into the goalkeeper's gloves, shouts, coaching – essential 'colour' for a radio feature. To be honest, I'm hoping to get the interviews done first, then record a few minutes of the training session and head off.

I arrive early and spot the manager, head down, walking towards a far-off pitch. Great. As a stranger it's always difficult to break into the conversation if people are together, so to spot the boss on his own is a bonus. I race up to him with a cheery introduction. 'How are you?' 'Nothing a few wins wouldn't put right.' No smile. No other response. Oh well. He doesn't stop walking, listens to my request but says nothing. To break the silence (we're well ahead of the players), I mention I had seen a recent game his team had played (and lost – they were anchored to the foot of the table). The early-season signs did not bode well. 'We bloody battered them for an hour, then they nicked it.' Hardly. It is a warped version of the game. True, they had been in front, fleetingly and against the run of play, and had only lost 2–1. But they had been run ragged. I can't recall any hint of the battering the opposition were supposed to have survived. It hadn't helped that a player had been dismissed for dissent, and I'm about to find out why.

'Fuck off, bollocks, you cunt.' In a seven-a-side 'gaffer's word goes' end-of-session game, the manager had the temerity to award a throw-in against one of the club's defenders. It was an instantaneous reaction from the player. He would have said it to anyone. I knew him years ago when he was a quietly spoken youngster at a previous club. He has changed. Several years of hard-bitten 'professionalism' has turned him into a snarling, bad-tempered ball of frustration. He had been booked for a similar outburst aimed at the referee in the game I had seen a fortnight earlier. His response: 'What? You must be joking, ref?' This is no way to speak to anyone, let alone your boss – especially someone you call 'gaffer'. Not with the radio man recording. He wasn't admonished.

The rest of the session isn't any cheerier. The 'warm-up' consists of a gentle jog. The players spend the first hour whacking a ball from the centre spot to the right wing, then running into the penalty area to meet the cross and hopefully lash the ball past a literally defenceless goalkeeper. This is performed solo, then with a colleague, then with a single defender at the near post (can't imagine where the cross is going this time), then with three forwards, then four. The alternating goalkeepers don't stand a chance. There is no coaching for them (they told me so between shots and headers). It looks like an exercise in pointlessness and is performed without purpose.

When the players run back to the centre circle the gaffer isn't happy. 'Don't you ever do that again, you cunt.' He rounds on the goalkeeper I have come to interview for throwing the ball back from whence it came – the centre circle. The gaffer had wanted it thrown out to the wing. 'Are you trying to trip my players up, you wanker?'

Why, if he is so incensed, didn't he tell the goalkeeper about this much earlier, I wonder? Maybe it is a not-too-subtle attempt to gee him up? It may, of course, have been a bit of reverse flattery for my benefit (people are often showy when a microphone is around) – the goalkeeper was to be pulled down a peg or two. He looks genuinely embarrassed. I want to shout out 'Hang on a minute!' He simply sits there, demoralised.

The club are struggling. It isn't easy for them to bring new players in and they need to extract the maximum out of each and every player, to pull together – to 'gel' in football parlance. It is hard to see how they could improve with this type of coaching, with this manager, with his attitude. The club were duly relegated at the end of the season. Having seen them train it was hard to sympathise.

At the end of the session, despite my obvious presence (I was the one without shorts on and holding a microphone) and patience (I had been there for two and a half hours), the manager literally sprinted for his car. No apologies, no hesitation, no explanation, no shower, no warm down, no tracksuit. Amazingly, he was followed by his players – well-paid professional sportsmen. They merely slapped on tracksuits and baseball caps and fled to their sports cars. All, ironically, except for the supposed 'unprofessional' goalkeeper who trudged off disconsolately. 'I can't do a thing right here anymore,' he complained as he ripped off his gloves. He was one of three players to shower, was effusively polite and after our interview phoned the club to find out why the manager had stormed off and arranged an interview with his assistant instead. I drove to the ground and an hour and a half later he grudgingly performed this simple task. 'He had someone to meet at the station,' was the rather lame excuse I was offered for the manager's disappearance.

On the way home, I wondered what the supporters who pay £15–£20 a ticket to watch this team play would think if they had witnessed the session? Or the chairman and his board of directors? How much of this undisciplined, random bullying and obsessive swearing is accepted in our football coaching culture? Not much, I hope.

In 1999, Kevin Keegan was appointed England manager. It was a time of crisis: Glenn Hoddle had resigned in the wake of comments made in a national newspaper interview and England looked unlikely to reach the European Championships. Could charismatic Kev turn the tide? He is a redoubtable advocate of devil-may-care attacking football and a household name. His enterprising Newcastle United team had charmed the nation and almost won the Premiership twice in the mid-'90s. His new club Fulham were working their way through the leagues with Mohamed Al Fayed's substantial backing.

Keegan's permed presence as a player in the 1970s belied the grit of an Armthorpe lad who strained every sinew to inch his way above more naturally gifted performers of the day like Rodney Marsh, Stan Bowles, Frank Worthington and Laurie Cunningham. He had pop-star status and retired in the early 1980s after a two-year spell with Newcastle United. He showed little inclination to go into coaching or management, preferring the golf courses of Marbella to the mud, sweat and tears of Football League management. He was lured back to Newcastle in 1992 when Sir John Hall took charge of what was then a Second Division club. With a huge pile of cash at his disposal, Keegan got the Magpies promoted and the momentum took them to the top of the newly formed Premiership. King Kev could do no wrong on Tyneside but he quit in 1997, the season after Newcastle had let a 12-point Christmas lead slip and his infamous 'I'd luv it if we beat Manchester United now' quotes near the end of the season. He resurfaced at Fulham a year later, in the curiously titled role of chief operating officer, and was in the process of leading them to the Second Division title when England came a-calling.

It did not work out. Having initially taken the job on a temporary basis, attempting the near-impossible task of doing both jobs, he quit Fulham. Although England just about edged into Euro 2000 after a two-legged play-off victory over Scotland, their performances in Holland and Belgium were disappointing. England lost their final group game to a late penalty and Keegan was lambasted in the press for his lack of tactical nous, which was seemingly embodied by his puffed-out chest and 'be big' instructions to his players towards the end of the Romanian game when they desperately needed a goal.

Keegan quit, literally in the loos, after England lost the first game of their World Cup campaign at home to Germany in October 2000 – the last game to be played at Wembley Stadium. Seven months later Keegan popped up at Manchester City as a replacement for Joe Royle. It was a familiar task: a big club with huge resources at his mercy, far more than their opponents. Not surprisingly, Keegan guided City to the First Division title. City scored more than 100 goals and were ten points clear of their nearest rivals. They went up in style.

For all his King Kev majesty and amiable charm, he remains a controversial figure among football's coaching community. He doesn't have any formal coaching qualifications but is constantly able to jump into high-profile posts. 'Why was he appointed England manager?' asks Dennis Mortimer, the former Aston Villa captain who is now a regional coach with the PFA. 'Because of his personality more than anything else. That sort of person is always fortunate because they get picked for the clubs who have got money.'

Mortimer is concerned that the professional players he coaches on courses don't stand a chance when they apply for jobs against big names. 'I get angry when guys are put into place without people actually having the opportunity to apply for the job and send in their CV.

'The top managers are on huge wages, and some might say that is right because they're in the firing line, so you get a manager on maybe £1 million a year and his first team coach on £70,000 or £80,000 a year. Now that is still very good money, but I say why is that the case? Why is the manager on ten times the money when he isn't coaching the team and may not be qualified? I think the whole structure is wrong.'

English football has a tiny percentage of qualified coaches in comparison to other European countries. But that doesn't prevent coaches who don't have the highest available qualifications from being fast-tracked to the top.

The FA's new Soho Square HQ is a far cry from the dreary corridors of Lancaster Gate. It is emblematic of the new FA, honed by chief executive Adam Crozier. Light, bright and airy, it effuses modernity and energy – words that would never have been applied to either his predecessors or their dowdy old home. Lancaster Gate might have been in central London, but it was dark and sleepy. Okay, so you have to dance around the drunks who occasionally inhabit the dark streets of Soho, but you're only 100 yards from the bustle of Oxford Street.

There are new departments and new personnel. An FA regional officer (who will have to remain nameless) likens the new FA to New Labour: lots of spin, not quite so much substance. The effort is getting the message across. Bright young things with mobile phones seemingly grafted onto their arms breeze through the corridors; the older staff members are wary.

David Platt, England's Under-21 coach, races into the reception area and greets me with a warm handshake. All smiles and casual dress, with a white T-shirt deliberately showing beneath a formal shirt, Platt has an air of continental flair. 'Good to see you,' he smiles. His diary is over-running, he has more appointments to race through and a couple of camera crews are anxiously hovering to make sure they don't miss their interview as we slip into a side room.

Platt, a former England captain with 62 appearances to his name, is the country's first full-time Under-21 coach. Although he had worked with the Under-18s with Howard Wilkinson briefly, his was a surprise appointment, and a dramatic promotion. His only managerial experience had been an uneventful two-year stint with First Division Nottingham Forest. He had famously been manager for a few weeks at Italian club Sampdoria, a great first move into management, but didn't have the required qualifications and was barred by the Italian FA from sitting on the bench during matches. He left within weeks.

Platt expressed surprise that I wanted to ask him about his Italian experience. A cursory glance at the e-mail I had sent to his office before the interview would have confirmed it was one of a range of issues I wanted to talk about. Did he want me to run through them prior to our interview? 'No, shoot.'

Minutes into our interview, I was accused of being 'obsessed' when I asked three questions about his Sampdoria experience. Given the lack of depth to his coaching/management career and his rapid rise to the England Under-21 job, and as an apparent heir to Sven-Goran Eriksson's throne, it didn't seem unreasonable to ask for his version of events.

With all sectors of the game calling for the introduction of mandatory qualifications, Platt at the time had a UEFA B licence (there are three advanced levels: UEFA B, then A, and the Pro licence) and it seemed appropriate to ask how he felt about continental-style qualifications coming in over here. It is his Achilles' heel. Having been rejected in Italy, he headed home and found a willing English employer in Nottingham Forest. While the first inaugural batch of managers were taking the new UEFA Pro licence in the summer of 2001 (new to England not the rest of Europe who have had it for ages), Platt was starting on his UEFA A badge, the next one down. England's bright new coach couldn't take the new top course for bright young coaches because he didn't have the right qualifications.

Platt's strength is his vast playing experience: an apprenticeship at Manchester United, released and turned around by Dario Gradi at Crewe, sold to Aston Villa where he was managed by Graham Taylor;

he then went on to Bari, Juventus, Sampdoria and finally Arsenal. He has played under some of the game's finest coaches from Eriksson, Van Gaal, Wenger, Robson and Taylor, to Gradi. 'I've picked things up from all of them,' he observed. In Italy he discovered the benefits of biometrics, a technically specific form of exercise designed to build strength through powerful movements like leaping or hurdling rather than the gritty endurance of six-mile runs. The fitness technique is 'just coming to the fore over here', he noted.

We talked about his first managerial job at Sampdoria. Platt accuses the Italian authorities of 'picking holes in things and making his position untenable'. He needed a UEFA A licence to coach, but didn't have one. With hindsight, he acknowledges he should have waited until he had taken the course. 'Theoretically, I had the right qualification, as long as my assistant had the one that was above me to work.' His assistant, note, not him. The Italian authorities didn't recognise that. 'They didn't want a young English manager coming into the game,' is the England Under-21s manager's conclusion.

Platt found few such problems getting a job back in England. He took over from Ron Atkinson at Nottingham Forest following their relegation from the Premiership in 1999. Platt views his elimination from coaching in Italy as 'a restriction of trade' because if the president wants to employ a coach, 'it has nothing to do with the badges you've got or haven't got'.

He is an advocate of the qualification system, but Platt did not immediately brush up on his qualifications when he was back in Blighty in 1999. He took the first part of his UEFA A licence in the summer of 2001, prior to getting the England Under-21 job, and completed it in summer 2002. He has now started working towards the Pro licence. There are those who question whether someone who only had the UEFA B licence at that time should have been promoted to such high office after just two unspectacular seasons at Nottingham Forest.

Our interview covered further ground. It became clear Platt is a diligent coach with many fresh ideas and a passion for coaching. He was a different, less cautious, man when talking through the sort of problem-solving issues all young coaches encounter, and his observations of player motivation were genuinely interesting. But, like Keegan, there are people who are concerned about why he was promoted at such speed.

The Café Royal in Regent Street is a short walk away from Soho Square. It is the salubrious venue for the Sports Coach UK annual coaching awards for 2001. Sports Coach UK, formerly the National Coaching Foundation, is an organisation dedicated to developing the profession of coaching in the UK. It is a registered charity and this annual dinner is held to celebrate the achievements of sports coaches. They are, so often, the unsung heroes of sport.

At the 2001 ceremony the awards were presented by the Patron of SCUK, HRH The Princess Royal. Sports Minister Richard Caborn also attended and there was an address by the paralympian, Tanni Grey-Thompson. BBC Sport's Steve Rider was compère. This was more than a bit of opportunistic glad-handing over a glass of bubbly; each year SCUK inducts a list of notable coaches into its Hall of Fame. There is the Dyson award, in memory of the influential track and field coach, Geoffrey Dyson, and the Mussabini Medal, in memory of Sam Mussabini, who coached Harold Abrahams to success in the 1924 Paris Olympics (featured in the film *Chariots of Fire*). Normally it is an event which passes without too much media interest. Not in 2001. Coach of the Year was Sven-Goran Eriksson, and a large bank of photographers were poised to take snaps of Sven with the Princess Royal. Then they noisily departed, eagerly pursuing Eriksson. Richard Caborn struggled manfully with his speech as the pandemonium moved outside.

It was a significant appearance. Football-wise, former Scotland manager Craig Brown and Howard Wilkinson, the FA's technical director, were also honoured (joining Sir Alf Ramsey and Sir Alex Ferguson, who won the Mussabini Medal, and former FA coaching directors, Allen Wade and Sir Walter Winterbottom, members of the Hall of Fame). Football coaches are a small part of the SCUK picture. Eriksson, England's first foreign national team coach, lifted the award within a year of taking charge of the England team.

Sports Coach UK's home is a less glamorous Victorian house in suburban Leeds. Their chief executive, John Stevens, is the sort of 'been there, done it' coach and sports administrator who reels off virtually every local authority in the country when you enquire about his background. Suffice to say, John knows what he's talking about, coaching-wise.

The number of unqualified coaches teaching sport at all levels is a major concern for Stevens. The figure may be as high as 500,000 nationally. Football, he believes, doesn't set a good example. If people are perceived to have made it to the top without having attained the highest qualifications, why should those at grassroots level bother? 'It's a dire, disastrous message to send out,' says Stevens. 'They are slowly addressing the issue but they aren't making the progress they would like.'

Stevens is prepared to name names. 'It is a matter of great regret that people like Kevin Keegan can become national team manager when he doesn't have a coaching qualification. I think David Platt's experience is very interesting. He is very keen to become a very high-quality coach and he has demonstrated his ability with the England Under-21s. He went to Italy in Serie A and was appointed coach of Sampdoria. After a few weeks they said "Sorry, you cannot do it." Why? Because they have a rule that says unless you have this qualification you cannot coach a Serie A team. Basically, he couldn't progress. He comes back to the UK and gets a coaching job with Nottingham Forest without improving on his qualifications.'

While some say a qualification is only a piece of paper, Stevens would argue there are bigger issues at stake. 'You have dangers associated with health and safety. You have dangers associated with inappropriate practice, so you might ask players to do things they are not physically capable of. You have physical risk to players through using the wrong physical training techniques, the wrong volume or frequency of exercise. You have potential problems with the social or mental side. If you don't know how to work with players, if you have a player who isn't working very well or is going through a difficult patch, you might cause him psychological damage if you pick the wrong technique.'

There are many people in football who refute suggestions that the football industry pays scant regard to qualifications. Even some of those who have the former full badge (now the UEFA A licence) don't favour mandatory qualifications. Tommy Docherty is one of them: 'I think it is ridiculous. If you can't coach, you can't coach. A certificate isn't going to give you the ability to coach. You're going to have a situation where a schoolteacher has got a better chance of getting a job than a football man because he can lay it down in black and white more professionally than an ordinary football man. The FA have got more coaches than Wallace Arnold – but they're mainly schoolteachers.'

Steve Coppell, who only had a Preliminary badge when he accepted his first managerial post at Crystal Palace, is also against mandatory qualifications. 'It really irritates me. All the qualifications are about are coaching. Management is something totally different. I think it is totally wrong for coaching qualifications to be the criteria for running football clubs. Who can say that someone who's done a couple of courses at Lilleshall is better equipped to run a football club than somebody who has been a manager for 700–800 games?'

Some say the number of games you've played should count, too. 'A coach is something that takes 42 people to London for the day,' quips Kenny Hibbitt, the former Wolves player, who has managed Walsall and Cardiff City, and last season, non-league Hednesford Town. 'It doesn't matter what qualifications you have got, you have to have been in situations to know what its about. With due respect to schoolteachers and the like, there is a place for them in the academies and centres of excellence because they are fantastic organisers . . . but at the professional level there's only the experience of being involved in it that will give the experience of handling it. Players respect ex-players and they find out if you've never played. I think people teaching football should be able to express what it is like, physically, to be able to do it. I would go as far as to say that if my son went to a centre of excellence or academy I would want him to be taught by an ex-professional. Otherwise he doesn't go.'

John Stevens believes this attitude is simply wrong. 'I think that is a disgraceful view. I feel a lot of football managers do a disservice to the term manager. Because if you look at what they do, they don't manage. They aren't given responsibility for the club's strategy, for the financial management of the club, I suspect very few are given responsibility for handling budgets and transfer negotiations and legal issues – all the sorts of things a manager has to do. Most of them are called managers but are actually coaches. The only aspect they should be managing, in my view, is the environment in which players, assistant coaches, support coaches, support staff, and medical people can actually focus on the athlete/coach interaction.' Stevens also believes it is difficult to tell grassroots coaches to take qualifications if they see top football managers working without them. 'It is an almost indefensible position and it does the concept of coaching, the quality of coaching, the status of coaching, the profile of coaching as a profession a huge disservice.'

On a typical Saturday morning in south Birmingham the junior players of Callowbrook Swifts FC are practising their skills. Two hundred children aged between six and sixteen, proudly bedecked in the club's green and black colours, are put through their paces by a team of qualified coaches.

Callowbrook are an FA Charter Standard club — a new kite mark awarded by the FA to grassroots clubs who meet a range of quality criteria, including employing qualified coaches. 'We check out everyone to make sure only the right people are involved with the club,' says secretary Nigel Brindley. Every manager or coach of Callowbrook's 12 teams must have a coaching certificate. 'It is a prerequisite and a credit to people who have given their own personal time and expense to get their qualifications.'

'If Kevin Keegan came here, I couldn't let him coach our kids,' says Tony Allison, who holds a UEFA B badge (the second highest soccer coaching standard). 'It has taken me four years to get to this level. The children are the ones who benefit.'

This is where so many young footballers begin their soccer education. Callowbrook, who started six years ago and whose single team in that formative year were mercilessly hammered, would love to fund the building of toilets and changing-rooms and a car park — but there is neither the money nor space available. Yet they have to jump through hoops in order to coach these children. 'It seems strange and unfair that people in the professional game don't want to, or can't be bothered, to set an example for the rest of the game,' says Nigel Brindley.

In 1997, Howard Wilkinson, who had been appointed as the FA's technical director a year earlier, released a document called 'A Charter for Quality'. Among its aims was the introduction of academies and centres of excellence at Premier/Football League clubs. One of the mandatory rules for coaches is that they must have a minimum of the UEFA B licence and undergo continuous personal assessment in order to work in an academy. Although these rules apply to academies, which train players between the ages of 9 and 18, there are no mandatory qualifications for those people working in professional clubs: in other words, working with players who might be worth millions of pounds.

Chris Evans, academy director at Wolverhampton Wanderers, believes this is wrong. 'What profession with such phenomenal resources allows its core decision-makers to have no qualifications?' asks Chris. 'My opinion is that we should protect the people who are in position now because they were in post when there were no mandatory requirements, but the way forward is that you should not become a senior coach unless you have a minimum award of UEFA A.'

Some managers would seek to side-step these rules by saying they don't actually coach, so don't need the coaching qualification. Evans agrees: 'Many managers don't directly coach their players. They are overseers and recruiters. I don't have a problem with that, but I believe people who are educating others shouldn't educate unless they are educated themselves. There is no hereditary transfer of information from football player to mentor. The problem has been no formal training, no education, the old pals act, and that doesn't work. Knowledge and expertise does in my opinion.'

The 'old pals act' runs deep in British football. Managers, coaches, directors and chairmen are often recruited through friendship rather than proven expertise or ability. Ian Atkins, director of football at Third Division Oxford United, believes this approach stifles the development of managers and coaches at his level. 'Some of these people have mates they want to bring in who aren't really managers. They ruin football clubs or leave them in a hell of a state and someone has to come in and pick it up again. That's why there is a rapid turnover of managers. It is frustrating when you've achieved but you see other people who have a year or two here and there and they get First Division jobs.'

Frank Clark, who now works as an adviser to the LMA, believes mandatory qualifications will drive up standards of football management. 'It's madness that somebody can finish playing one day and manage the club the next. It's crazy. Passing a coaching course doesn't make you a good manager – but preparation and training for a profession must give you a better chance of success. It will eliminate the timeservers who go into management because they can't think of anything else to do. We need a smaller pool of well-trained, well-motivated people who are going to be top managers and coaches.'

There are also concerns among football managers that without any qualification criteria the job, unlike other forms of management, has no professional standing. John Duncan, the former Ipswich and Chesterfield manager, says, 'If somebody came to fix my telly I would need to know he could do it before I would let him start. I think the logic of that extends to football management.' Aston Villa manager Graham Taylor goes further. 'To give the position some status I think you've got to be in a position where we give the manager some mandatory qualifications. Everyone feels they could do the manager's job but I never feel I could a doctor's job or a solicitor's job or anyone else's job. But any profession – and we're called professional football managers – should have a professional ethos.'

David Moyes, the manager of Everton, believes the old pals act is holding a lot of good managers back. 'That's not to say qualifications are going to make you a good coach or manager but I feel players are looking for a little bit more than a name and because there's a lot of money being put in they've a right to ask a prospective manager "What have you got, and what can you offer to prove you can do the job?"'

Allen Wade, a former FA director of coaching between 1963–82, says professional footballers have always believed they know best – and that a solid playing career is enough to earn them a top managerial position. 'If you're being asked to study for something you see it as a threat,' explains Wade. 'The logic was that if you had been a good player you would automatically know how to coach. It isn't true. How many top managers today were top players? Alex Ferguson wasn't, Graham Taylor wasn't, Howard Wilkinson wasn't. By that logic Billy Wright, Bryan Robson, Peter Shilton, Bobby Moore and Bobby Charlton should have been great managers – they weren't. Club directors have little knowledge of football and almost certainly no knowledge of physical education or coaching which means they will appoint people they perceive will make them popular.'

It isn't such a problem north of the border. Scotland has a more developed coaching structure. Craig Brown, the former Scotland national coach, ran their coach education programme before becoming Preston North End manager in May 2002. He says the Scots have few of the cultural problems with coaching courses that have held back English coaching. 'It was common to go on coaching courses when you were playing. I had an A licence when I was 26,' says Brown. 'The contrast in England was that top players wouldn't go on courses. International players in Scotland did. Big-name players like Bryan Robson, Kevin Keegan and Glenn Hoddle, I think, felt their playing reputation was enough and that they wouldn't learn enough from the courses.'

Scotland developed the UEFA Pro licence well before England. Forty-two Scottish coaches hold this qualification, the special course for top coaches – a managerial degree, in effect. Many of these coaches now work in England, like Archie Knox, Walter Smith (until recently), Paul Sturrock, Mark McGhee, Gordon Strachan, David Moyes and George Burley. In Scotland, Craig Levine, Alex McLeish, Bobby Williamson and Jimmy Nichol also have Pro licences. Several English managers have sneaked across the border to take their coaching qualifications.

'Because of the high quality of staff on the courses in Scotland everyone respects them,' says Brown. 'We try to make it as inexpensive as possible and they enjoy the courses and get a lot from them. We're proud of our coaching heritage.'

John Barnwell of the LMA says the key is getting mandatory qualifications accepted by the professional clubs rather than enforcing them. Clubs entering the Champions League will need to have at least one UEFA Pro licence coach on their staff in order to enter the competition from 2003. 'We can't tell PLC companies who to appoint, but we can say while you continue to make mistakes, here are a list of names who have these qualifications and are highly prepared coaches.' Barnwell says 17 Premiership managers have got at least the A licence and the rest (other than Keegan, who has no qualifications) have a B licence. Sixty of the seventy-two Football League managers have an advanced coaching licence. 'You're giving the chairmen a kite mark to look at, a standard to reach. It is only a guide, because you cannot replace experience, but the days of managers starting lower down and working their way up are going. They don't want to make that long trip, and the people who appoint them want personalities, so what we have to do is replace the philosophy and thinking.'

But then a lot of things need to change in Britain's football boardrooms.

– CHAPTER EIGHT –

Money Matters: The Wheeling, Dealing World of Football's Bosses

Mr Macari told the court: 'If you don't break the Football League rules . . . you don't have a side.'

Report on the Swindon Town Inland Revenue
fraud trial in 1992

OKAY, LET'S TALK DIRTY. THERE IS A CYNICAL, TIRED-EYED VIEW that all football managers are on the take and on the make. That a major part of the boss's job is sealing deals, especially transfers, by any means available – and if it involves late-night liaisons in motorway service station car parks, brown paper envelopes and the lining of pockets, then so be it.

There have certainly been enough allegations, investigations and actual charges brought against people employed in the football industry – not least in the so-called Bungs Inquiry which ran between 1993–97 – to suggest that some managers have engaged in unscrupulous activity (and for that matter directors, chairmen, agents, players and administrators). It would, however, be harsh to say that *most* managers routinely hop either side of illicit lines.

The Bungs Inquiry, set up by the FA Premier League to investigate the increased role of agents or intermediaries in transfers in the 1990s, discovered there was a 'cult of dishonesty' running through football. Although it effectively called for the registration and regulation of agents, there are many in the game who believe a further tweaking is needed to define the precise part they should be allowed to play, especially in transfers. For example, there have been concerns expressed over the potential conflict of interests for those managers who hold shares in players' agencies (who then do business with that particular agent), and agents who have managers' family members working for them.

Impropriety of one form or another – be it bungs, bribes or backhanders, whether it is payment to and from agents to outright match fixing – has tainted football virtually since it began. Other chapters of this book have sought to explain how the football manager's job in the UK developed, not primarily as a coaching role, but as a club administration function. Managers are usually at the heart of soccer scandals.

Football has had to amend its rules to keep up with changes, starting way back when it was supposed to be an amateur sport but players were in fact being paid. In 1884, Preston North End's manager Major D. Sudell openly admitted it. He threatened to form a breakaway organisation, the British Football Association League, unless the FA backed down. A year later they legalised professionalism. Then transfers. Then wages. Then contracts. Then the accepted role of players' agents can be seen in a similar light.

From its inception the grim reality is that football's prime mover has usually been money. It is a cash-driven business. Yet, unlike conventional forms of commercial activity – because it is seen as sport and therefore, in the minds of many people, somehow exempt from the rigours of normal business practice – the same standards of professionalism have largely been ignored. It's a hackneyed old phrase, but nonetheless true, that many directors do not run football clubs in the same way as they run their other businesses. If they did they would never have made the money to buy a substantial stake of a football club in the first place.

As Robert Reid, one of the Bungs Inquiry team said: 'A lot of the problems with agents developed because football managers cut corners to get the job done. The history of club administration . . . is that, quite often, the club secretaries (and secretary-managers) inherited the job without sufficient expertise. They grew with the job, so to speak. We found that some were clearly unsuited to handling contracts and negotiations worth millions of pounds. It was sometimes a question of the blind leading the blind. So it is no wonder that a culture developed where managers took over and started to offer what you might call incentives to sweeten a negotiation or to help things along because they were so "hands on". I think this is particularly true of the "old school" managers.'

Undoubtedly, the recent developments of PLCs, who prefer to bring in their own experienced industry professionals, have redefined this element of the manager's role. He is now largely restricted to coaching and kept at arm's length from the detailed negotiations. But this does not happen everywhere – and there are still many grey areas. But the question remains: why are we only talking about these standards coming in some 120 years after the game was professionalised? The fault does not just lie at the manager's doorstep.

Actually proving illegal activity has always been difficult in football. So many of the people I have interviewed for this book have their suspicions about uncomfortably close connections between different parties, and fears about colleagues in the football industry, but they will not, understandably, permit themselves to be quoted. The phrase '. . . and this is strictly off the record, Chris', has been endlessly repeated.

Managerial impropriety is nothing new. Even the great Herbert Chapman, who managed Huddersfield and Arsenal to five First Division titles in the 1920s and '30s, was suspended in 1919 following an FA investigation into illegal payments to players at Leeds City. The club refused to show their books to the Football League and were subsequently thrown out by the League and wound up by the FA. They soon re-formed as Leeds United. When Chapman managed Arsenal, his chairman Sir Henry Norris was banned from football when an FA Commission of Enquiry found that a £125 bill supposedly to pay for the team bus had in fact been used as an inducement to attract Charlie Buchan to Arsenal. Subsequent managers at two of Chapman's clubs, Leeds United and Arsenal, would take centre stage in later financial scandals.

Don Revie was undoubtedly a great manager. In 13 seasons in charge at Leeds United between 1961 and 1974, he transformed them from a nondescript struggling Second Division side into one of the most powerful football clubs in Europe. They won two First Division championships, a Second Division championship, two European Fairs Cups, an FA Cup and a Football League cup under his stewardship. His methods were undeniably thorough and ruthlessly efficient. He handed dossiers to his players about their opponents, he was ultra competitive in the transfer market and in snapping up youth players. Revie even changed the Leeds strip from yellow and blue in favour of the pristine all white of Real Madrid, in the hope that some of the magic would rub off on Leeds. In an attempt to make Leeds a family club, he sent flowers and presents to players' wives on their birthdays. He assembled a wonderful team of star players: Giles, Bremner, Clarke, Lorimer, Gray and co. What a team.

But Revie's career would always be tainted by allegations and insinuations of match fixing. Years of enmity over supposed underhand dealings finally exploded when Revie walked out on England in 1977.

Former Bury and Sunderland boss Bob Stokoe claimed that, in 1962, Revie had offered him a £500 bribe to throw a relegation battle. 'After that I lost all respect for Revie,' insisted Stokoe, who famously got his own back when Sunderland (then in Division Two) pulled off a remarkable FA Cup victory over Revie's mighty Leeds in the 1973 final. There were also allegations, though never substantiated, that Revie tried to get the final game of the 1972 season thrown, when Leeds, having already lifted the FA Cup, went to Wolverhampton Wanderers in search of the First Division title and, therefore, the Double. Mike O'Grady, a former Leeds player who was at Wolves (but was on loan to Birmingham City at the time), claimed he had been approached by Revie. Leeds lost 2–1 but months later the *Sunday People* reported allegations that three players claimed they had been approached to take bribes of up to £1,000 each. FA and CID investigations were inconclusive.

It was often suggested that Revie was obsessed by money. He was the first England manager to introduce win bonuses for England players. On 12 July 1977 he shocked the football world by announcing that he had signed a four-year deal worth £340,000 to manage the United Arab Emirates. He told the *Daily Mail* first, rather than the FA. He was subsequently banned from English football management for ten years, which effectively quashed his career. Revie took the FA to the High Court in 1979 to get a number of breach of contract fines overturned – but he did not receive any damages, didn't get his ban overturned and was only partially awarded the cost of the case. He died of motor neurone disease in May 1989.

When Brian Clough replaced Don Revie at Leeds United in 1974, he told the players they could throw their medals away because they had won them by cheating. As the Bungs Inquiry found some 20 years later, Cloughie's own dealings in the game were not exactly squeaky clean.

Match-fixing has always shocked the British football community's essential sense of decency. We all want to believe that the results of games we see and play in are the result of honest endeavour and not because they have been rigged. There have been several cases around the world that suggest this is not always the case. When it happens abroad to Johnny Foreigner we are not surprised – when it happens in Britain we are stunned.

In England, three Sheffield Wednesday players were banned for betting against their own side in a match against Ipswich in 1962. One of them, Tony Kay, was a promising young player who had just joined Everton when the allegations surfaced. He was widely tipped to be a future England international. Instead he was banned for life. The other players, Peter Swan and David Layne, were given ten-year bans.

The most recent charges brought against footballers for match fixing at English clubs came in the 1990s when Bruce Grobbelaar, Hans Segers and John Fashanu were alleged to have thrown three matches in the early 1990s in exchange for payments from a Malaysian betting syndicate. All three were cleared of conspiracy in 1997 although Grobbelaar's claim for damages (given and subsequently taken away) against *The Sun* newspaper continues.

In 1989 Lou Macari was fined £1,000 by the FA for betting against the club he managed, Swindon Town, in an FA Cup tie at Newcastle, which the Wiltshire side lost 5–0 in 1988. Swindon chairman Brian Hillier was also fined, having made £4,000 out of the same bet. That case instigated an Inland Revenue investigation into under-the-counter tax-free payments to players by Swindon in the late 1980s. In 1992, Hillier and club accountant Vivian Farrar were jailed for tax fiddles and banned from the game. Swindon Town, who won the 1989–90 Second Division play-offs, were denied promotion by the League as punishment for their financial irregularities. Macari was acquitted of conspiracy to defraud the Inland Revenue and was allowed to carry on in management. He had told the court: 'If you don't break the Football League rules . . . you don't have a side.' It was, he argued, the way of the world.

Macari's former Manchester United manager, Tommy Docherty, went into management as a short-haired, sharp-suited, quick-witted manager whose gift of the gab was matched only by his ability to create flair teams. His Chelsea side of the 1960s was full of talented young players including Peter Osgood, Charlie Cooke and, later, Alan Hudson. His success at Chelsea was the backbone of a classic nomadic gaffer's career: spells at Rotherham, Aston Villa, QPR, Porto and as Scotland national team manager followed. Then came the big one. Manchester United, in the wake of Sir Matt Busby. It was a job too big for both Wilf McGuinness and Frank O'Farrell (whose tortuous time at Old Trafford with constant interference from Busby is told in the following chapter). Docherty suffered the ignominy of taking Manchester United down to Division Two. He then bounced them straight back up and on to an FA Cup win in 1977. Just when things were going swimmingly for The Doc, he was sacked – not because of results, not because of bribes or bungs scandals, not because he fell out with the chairman, but because he fell in love . . . with the physio's wife. Bye bye.

Docherty was soon back in management at Derby County. But Manchester United weren't behind him. Docherty made 'the worst decision of his life' by bringing a libel case against one of his former United players, Willie Morgan, who had described Docherty as the 'worst manager he had ever known', in a Granada TV programme. 'I took offence and I shouldn't have done,' recalls Docherty. 'It was a person's opinion of me and during my life I had always encouraged people to speak freely and say, "Well, it's only his opinion, it doesn't matter."'

It led to a spate of court cases, of accusations and counter-claims between Docherty and former United players. Docherty was accused of selling over-the-odds cup-final tickets to touts – charges that were never proved – and receiving a £1,000 inducement to let George Best play for Dunstable (managed by Barry Fry).

Although Docherty's libel case was dismissed, it cost him £30,000 in legal bills. A year later he was interviewed by police concerning allegations of backhanders paid in the transfers of three Derby County players, Colin Todd, David Nish and Gerry Daly. He was also charged with perjury following the Morgan case. Docherty was never found guilty of any charges, but the biter of the 1960s who had clamped down on Chelsea's young boozers had his reputation tarnished.

Ironically, it would be the two ringleaders of the eight players Docherty had sent home and fined after their drinking spree in Blackpool the night before a game in 1965 (see Chapter Five), Terry Venables and George Graham, who would be key managers named in the Bungs Inquiry, long after Docherty had stood in his final dugout at Altrincham. Oh, and Brian Clough.

They were three of the giant gaffers of English football management in the 1980s. Clough may not have repeated his startling successes of the 1970s (championship wins with Derby and Nottingham Forest, where he also won two European Cups) but he kept Forest consistently in the top flight challenging for the game's major honours. Graham would be Arsenal's most successful manager since Herbert Chapman and adopt some of the same defensive nous. Venables would manage Barcelona and Spurs.

When Tel and Clough walked out hand in hand onto the Wembley turf (for what was effectively Cloughie's swansong and the only time, incredibly, one of his teams had ever reached an FA Cup final) in 1991, Graham must have looked on in envy. He and Venables were good buddies – more than just drinking mates who defied Docherty in their young playing days. Venables, a Spurs player, was Graham's best man at his wedding on the morning of a Spurs v. Arsenal derby in 1967. Tel Boy and Stroller, the streetwise Essex lad and the dapper Glaswegian. The astute coach who built the '80s Crystal Palace team and the staid damage limitation expert who revelled in the '1–0 to the Arsenal' aura.

Venables always had a business brain. He turned himself into a limited company, 'to exploit the talent of Terence Venables', when he became a professional footballer at the age of 18. He is the only player to have represented his country at six different levels (schoolboy, youth, amateur, Under-21, Under-23 and full international). He co-wrote the detective series *Hazell* and could croon with the best (or worst, depending on your view) of them. He managed his own West End club, Scribes. It was small wonder he was one of the first football managers to fancy his chances of owning a big PLC club.

Graham, from Bargeddie near Glasgow, played for Villa, Chelsea, Arsenal, Manchester United, Portsmouth and Crystal Palace and won 12 Scotland caps. He was part of Arsenal's 1971 Double-winning side. When it came to coaching, Stroller lagged behind Tel Boy, whose grasp of tactics was spotted by Crystal Palace boss Malcolm Allison. When Allison left, Tel took over, but when the team of the '80s dream died, he hopped over to Shepherd's Bush to manage QPR. Graham was his youth team coach. They soon parted. Venables became El Tel, the surprise choice as head coach of Barcelona at the awe-inspiring Nou Camp in 1984, Graham tried his luck in management at downmarket Millwall in their hooligan heyday. Nou Camp, old Den. Catalonia and the catastrophic.

While El Tel was charming the socks off the Spaniards, Graham was enjoying life with the Lions. Arsenal's stock was so low in 1986 that Stroller's minor achievement at Millwall, winning promotion from Division Three to Division Two, was deemed success enough to deserve a crack at the sought-after Highbury hot seat. But they chose right – in Graham's nine years at the club they won two Football League championships, an FA Cup and League Cup in the same season, and the European Cup-Winners' Cup. Stroll on.

Venables returned to English football in 1987 to take over as Spurs boss. Unlike his friend Graham's North London 'oppo', he had to be content with a single FA Cup win – over Cloughie's Forest in 1991. By then, Venables, who always had his sights set further than mere football management, was in the advanced stages of buying Spurs. In 1983, they became the first English football club to float on the Stock Exchange, but chairman Irving Scholar's ship soon ran into stormy waters. He had to get Robert Maxwell to underwrite building work at White Hart Lane, which cost £10 million, and with the massive magnate shaping to buy Spurs, Venables launched his own counter bid. He needed a partner. He found Alan Sugar, owner of the Amstrad empire.

Between them Venables and Sugar bought a controlling interest in Tottenham but Sugar had by far the bigger stake. They soon fell out – big time. Sugar sacked Venables from his job as chief executive in May 1993 and four years of bitter legal wrangling in the High Court followed, with Sugar winning again and again.

It was during one of these cases in 1993 that Sugar, when being quizzed about the details of the purchase of Teddy Sheringham by Tottenham from Nottingham Forest, claimed Venables had uttered the infamous words 'Mr Clough likes a bung'. It kick-started an explosive chain of events.

Had he been a football man, Sugar would have realised he had broken the *omerta* surrounding the game's wheeling and dealing. Bung? What bung? The public hadn't heard of this word in football before. Why do you need to 'bung' managers money? It soon became clear.

Agents had been creeping in to football throughout the 1980s. All the governing bodies from UEFA to FIFA, from the FA to the Football League and the newly formed Premier League had slightly different rules, but basically agents or intermediaries weren't legally allowed to be paid to represent players or anyone else for that matter in transfers. The Sheringham deal exemplified the complexity involved.

At the time of the transfer, FA rules stated that 'no payment in respect of the registration or transfer of registration shall be made to an agent'. On 27 August 1992, Sheringham (still a Forest player) went to the Spurs training ground and, after negotiation with Venables, Frank McLintock, a representative of agents First Wave management, and Ronnie Fenton, Forest's assistant manager, an agreement was reached on the player's personal terms. The transfer fee of £2.1 million was agreed. Tottenham also paid £58,750 to McLintock in cash. It was alleged, but never proven, that £50,000 was paid by McLintock to Fenton, although both Fenton and Clough deny receiving any money. The remaining £8,750 was returned by McLintock to Spurs.

This incident, described by the inquiry as 'common practice among clubs', and allegations of many more like it, sparked the FA Premier League's Bungs Inquiry, which was set up in October 1993 and ran for four years, submitting an interim report in 1995 and a final report in September 1997.

The three-man panel, consisting of Rick Parry, the chief executive of the FA Premier League at the time, Robert Reid QC, and Steve Coppell, who was chief executive of the LMA when the inquiry began, scoured 12 specific transfers in minute detail, interviewed 66 witnesses and sifted through 629 items of evidence and 10,200 pages of documents and transcripts. It revealed that rivers of readies were flowing into the pockets of intermediaries or agents, often in bizarre clandestine circumstances. It delivered a damning indictment on the probity of football and several of the men involved: 'We are satisfied that several witnesses have attempted deliberately to mislead the inquiry in their evidence.' The inquiry also concluded that the regulations at the time the inquiry began had 'in effect, created a cult of dishonesty under which many transfers took place with the assistance of agents/intermediaries'.

The interim report, published in 1995, recommended the licensing of players' agents and a code of conduct to be drawn up. It also discovered that George Graham had accepted £425,000 in 'unsolicited gifts' from Norwegian agent Rune Hauge after signing John Jensen and Pal Lydersen. Graham, who admitted the charges, was sacked by Arsenal and banned from football for a year.

When the final report came out in 1997, several other cases were added. Some were serious, others seemed farcical. The deal taking Paul Gascoigne from Spurs to Lazio was brokered by an Italian waiter. A witness told the Inquiry team that Ronnie Fenton, the assistant manager of Nottingham Forest, received £45,000, left for him in a fishing box off a trawler at Hull, as his share of a deal that took Thorvaldor Orlygsson to the City Ground. It was suggested he collected another parcel at a motorway service station.

Football was indeed fishy. It stank. The Inquiry claimed Fenton 'probably' used his cut of the £2.1 million Sheringham transfer in 1992 to pay for his daughter's wedding reception. But there were bigger names than Fenton, or, indeed, Steve Burtenshaw, Arsenal's chief scout who the inquiry said had set up the deals with Hauge for George Graham.

Submissions made to the inquiry were slammed by the panel. In the

Sheringham transfer they found parts of the evidence given by Terry Venables (who was England manager during part of the period of the Inquiry) to be 'self-contradictory', yet the report exonerated him. 'Whilst the conduct of Mr Venables cannot be justified, it should be borne in mind that, in our view, he regarded the obtaining of Mr Sheringham's services as being essential for the good of the Tottenham team. He did not make or intend to make any personal benefit from the payment of the £50,000. In our view he regarded that payment as being an essential prerequisite of obtaining Mr Sheringham's transfer and therefore something which could properly be done on behalf of the club.'

The handover took place at a meeting attended by Fenton, McLintock and Sheringham. All three initially omitted telling the panel about the rendezvous 'with the intention of misleading the inquiry', the report claims. And even when the witnesses did admit they had met, they 'gave accounts which did not accord with what actually occurred'.

Other Tottenham transfers involving Vinny Samways and Andy Gray involved 'disguised invoices' to agents who claimed payment for non-existent promotional work. This created a 'cult of dishonesty' in transfers involving agents/intermediaries who produced 'invoices which falsely recorded the work undertaken'. The report on Nottingham Forest's part in the Sheringham transfer was less conclusive: 'We have heard evidence that payments were made in cash to members of the Forest staff arising out of the transfer but we do not have evidence on which we can determine at whose instance those payments were made.'

The report concludes: 'The various accounts of events relating to the [Sheringham] transfer differ to an extent beyond that which can be attributed to the results of fading memories . . .'

In the middle of the inquiry, on 30 January 1995, Kate Hoey, at the time an opposition MP, spoke in the House of Commons of 'the many allegations which have yet to be proved or disproved'. She inferred that she had seen evidence of transfer deals to the UK and from Spain and other deals involving Venables. However, Ms Hoey would not submit evidence to the inquiry.

Clough and Fenton were the subject of other transfer

investigations. The inquiry accused them of profiting from the transfer of Tony Loughlan and Neil Lyne from non-league Leicester United to Forest when Clough was manager and Fenton his assistant. 'There is direct evidence of a fraudulent arrangement by which Mr Clough and/or Mr Fenton acquired a substantial sum of money from the two transfers,' the report alleges. 'A deal that should have cost the club £15,000 eventually saw £61,000 leaving their funds.'

It concludes: 'Forest appear, in effect, to have paid Leicester United on three separate occasions. The total amount spent by Forest . . . was £61,000, notwithstanding evidence that the price initially discussed for both players was £15,000.' Fenton allegedly received money in a brown envelope at Leicester Forest East service station on the M1, and £45,000 from Hauge after Forest signed defender Alf Inge Haaland from Norwegian club Bryne in January 1994.

The role of Fenton and the chief scout at Arsenal, Steve Burtenshaw, who received £70,000 from the agent Rune Hauge as part of a massive hand-out paid by the agent for introductions to men who were involved in the trading of players, like managers and coaches, came under scrutiny. Burtenshaw, whose involvement with Hauge began in the late 1980s, paid his cash into bank accounts in the South of France and Dublin.

The FA was left relatively powerless to impose fines on those named and shamed. Clough and Fenton were charged with misconduct in 1998, but it was largely meaningless because Clough had retired from the game and was suffering from ill health so did not face disciplinary action, and Fenton had left football and was living in Malta. Only Steve Burtenshaw, who worked for QPR after being sacked by Arsenal following the 'bungs' revelations in 1995, was fined by the FA. They hit him with a £30,000 fine for what he described in his own words as a 'careless error of judgement'. Forest were also charged with 'wholly inadequate' supervision of transfers under Clough, but with a new regime in charge at the City ground, there was no point trying to impose any penalties on the club.

The wider authorities, particularly UEFA and FIFA, have not managed to curb the power of agents, like Rune Hauge, who still trades players across countries and continents often via other agents. Hauge was banned in 1995 by FIFA but still has a powerful hold over

Scandinavian footballers looking for clubs abroad. The inquiry said Hauge did not 'provide any meaningful evidence to the inquiry'.

In the wake of the inquiry, the FA asked Sir John Smith, the former Metropolitan Police deputy commissioner, to expand his investigation into football's betting rules to include a report on the way the game regulates its financial affairs. The FA also established an independent compliance unit (later changed to an 'advisory unit') with powers to examine all aspects of the game's complex finances.

One of the more disturbing results of the Bungs Inquiry, though largely ignored by the press, came when the transfer of Andrei Kanchelskis from Shakter Donetsk to Manchester United was being investigated. The inquiry team couldn't interview members of Shakter's board because 'the persons who were directors of Shakter at the time have been murdered'. They were blown up by a car bomb believed to have been planted by the Russian Mafia. Then there were revelations, apparently held back from the inquiry team, of Manchester United being given a £40,000 bung by Kanchelskis's Russian agent Grigory Essauolenko when they sold him to Everton in 1996 – slap-bang in the middle of the inquiry. This only came to light with the release of Alex Ferguson's autobiography *Managing My Life*, published in 1999. It was handed to United in a silver pot – and was retained for a year when it was returned to Mr Essauolenko.

Judge Robert Reid says he was 'disappointed' that the inquiry had not been told. 'I don't know whether that would have been relevant, but I'd have liked to have known.' No one from Manchester United gave oral evidence to the Inquiry, but they almost certainly would have been called had this piece of information been supplied. The FA asked their new compliance officer, Graham Bean, to look into this matter. He compiled a report but it was left to gather dust at Lancaster Gate. No action has ever taken against Manchester United for failing to report the bung to the inquiry.

The Bungs Inquiry highlighted just how reliant football clubs have become on players' agents. There is no shortage of managers or directors who are keen to publicly decry the involvement of agents, yet they often rely on their advice for talent spotting and to check the availability of players. Kenny Hibbitt, former Cardiff City and Walsall manager, believes there is too much negativity about the work they do. 'A lot of managers use agents now, so whenever I hear them criticising I don't listen because most of them couldn't operate without them. They use them to identify talent and to get advice. The agents are there to earn a living – so you can't get free advice and then complain when they ask for a cut of a fee.'

But why were managers ever entrusted with contract negotiations or the buying and selling of players? Many managers will share Howard Wilkinson's view that it was a necessity he hated doing rather than an aspect of management he openly enjoyed. 'You had to do the non-coaching parts of management because you had no expert support. Now increasingly you can call on expert help.

'You do it because you've got a wife and a baby on the way, and no house. Something predisposes you to football management. You're not easily put off so there is a blissful disregard of some of the pitfalls. When it came to negotiating I just did it and learned as I went along. I was the best one there because I was the only one there. I never wanted that – I never enjoyed it. I wouldn't have left Notts County if it weren't for the wheeling and dealing. It was the modus operandi of managers that had evolved over time because that's what they were: managers and trainers. A trainer told 'em to run round a track and took care of the kit and the manager signed, sold and picked them and decided the rudiments of the tactics.

'I don't know a manager in his right mind who wouldn't want to get rid of that responsibility. You've got no skills to cope. You do a deal, you save £10,000 or £100,000 or you spend too much. What does it matter to you? And then you negotiate a salary. Much better to get someone who has got a picture of the budget to do that. You've got enough problems winning matches or not without being criticised at a board meeting because you've paid somebody £10 a week too much or something.'

For Bruce Rioch, it was only when he joined Arsenal, replacing George Graham, that contract negotiations were taken out of his hands. 'After what had happened, Arsenal said "You will not be involved in the transfer of players. You can select the players but we will deal with the negotiations," and that was the case with Dennis Bergkamp and David Platt coming in.' But it didn't always last, especially when it came to players who were already at the club. 'In the run-up to my first season, Dixon, Bould and Winterburn were offered terms they wouldn't accept. They came to me and I went to the directors and said, "Look, you have to get these boys tied on contracts." I still had an input. I signed Stephen Hughes and David Hillier, who were young boys, on contract so although it said in my job description "you don't get involved in contract negotiations" there were some cases where, if you didn't, they may not have had deals at all and players would have left or gone elsewhere.'

Newspaper reports around the time this book was written suggest that the naming and shaming of more managers who are involved in the deep-rooted 'bung culture' in English football may be imminent. But the climate creates the weather. Club directors and many of their fans prefer to have a winning manager to a principled manager. It is part of the sack race. Is any one really surprised to see managers offering inducements to players, bungs to agents, or seeking to line their own pockets in this notoriously precarious profession? Are impeccable beacons of honesty and integrity to be found in the boardrooms of British football clubs? Not always.

– CHAPTER NINE –

Blame it on the Boardroom

THERE WOULD BE NO SACK RACE – NO BREED OF FOOTBALL manager whose job is constantly on the line – if they weren't hired and fired with astonishing regularity. So who do we blame for this situation? Ultimately the buck has to stop with the employers, those club chairmen and directors with itchy fingers on triggers who constantly make the wrong managerial appointments, pander to pressure from fans and frequently apply standards that would be unacceptable in other forms of business.

The football industry has a sad legacy of clubs failing to define an exact role for the football manager, to keep adequate tabs on the sort of things he is doing or is expected to do. To give him support when he needs it or to curb his powers when he is exceeding his role. In short, many managers have been allowed to do what the hell they like because no one else at the club has been capable of stopping them or helping them. There are exceptions – many notable exceptions – but the high turnover of managers has to be a reflection of the boardroom incompetence at football clubs. And if we're calling for managers and coaches to be qualified, how about some best practice in the boardrooms of football clubs, too? Heaven knows, the game needs it.

When Danny Bergara arrived in England at Luton Town in 1973 he couldn't believe the type of training he was asked to do. 'Your organisation, teamwork and preparation is right but you don't consider the technique, skill or fitness side of it enough,' he told a group of coaches at Lilleshall. 'You're only working on one side of the game . . . on the tactical situation.'

It was a big disappointment for Bergara, who used to watch newsreels of English games in the 1950s at cinemas in his homeland. At the time, his small South American country (population: two million people) of Uruguay were world champions, having beaten Brazil (population: 200 million and rising) in the 1950 World Cup final. It was the second time they had hoisted the Jules Rimet Trophy. England, who couldn't even beat the USA in the 1950 finals, had been wondering whether to grace the tournament with their presence.

The Bergaras were a football-mad family. Danny and his four brothers all played for their local team, Racing Club in Montevideo. In one game they fielded all five Bergaras. The eldest, Mario, was a Uruguayan international who played in World Cup finals in Chile in 1962. Danny, who played in the Uruguayan First Division at the age of 15, was an Under-18 international. He moved to Spain with his older brother, Nacho, at the age of 20. European clubs were snapping up the top South American talent. Danny followed fellow Uruguayans like Juan Schaffino (transferred for a world record of £72,000 to AC Milan in 1954) and Jose Santamaria (who moved from Nacional to Real Madrid in 1957).

'It was every kid's dream to play in Europe,' recalls Danny, who signed for Spanish First Division club Real Mallorca in 1962. He got off to a fantastic start. In his second match, the mighty Real Madrid flew in with their host of stars – Puskas, Santamaria, Pachin, Muller, Gento and co. – and were routed 5–2. Danny scored the fifth goal, but was dropped for the next game. He later moved to Seville (for a club record fee of 2.5 million pesetas) and Tenerife.

Danny ended up in England for a non-football reason: love. In the 1960s Majorca became the British package holidaymakers' favourite destination. Danny met 'a gorgeous English girl' there, a blonde air stewardess called Janet, who worked for Sunflight Holidays, owned by one Herbert Douglas Ellis. Jan and Dan. It was a romance reminiscent of the era: Dan the flair Latino footballer, she the Hertfordshire girl looking to broaden her horizons beyond the exotica of St Albans. They met, they fell in love, they married – in June 1966, the month England won the World Cup.

In 1973, they moved to England with Danny joining Luton Town, because it was near Jan's parents. Danny, signed on the recommendation of much-travelled English football manager Vic Buckingham, was struggling to recover from a calf injury sustained in Spain, but had to attempt to play in order to justify his visa. The injury hadn't been treated properly in Tenerife. A doctor (not the normal club medic) drained several syringes of fluid, about a third of Danny's calf, into a bowl. He has never walked freely since.

Bergara might not have been able to play but quickly became a coach at Luton. In the kingdom of the blind (and coaching-wise British football was myopic in 1973) the one-eyed man is king. Danny's continental expertise matched by his infectious effervescence made him a sought-after coach.

He got his full coaching badge within a year, and spent five years at Luton before following manager Harry Haslam, to Sheffield United. Danny worked with the England Under-18s in Ron Greenwood's era, and after a brief sojourn in Brunei was coach under Bruce Rioch at Middlesbrough. In 1988, after a 15-year 'managerial apprenticeship', Bergara became British football's first foreign manager when he took charge of Rochdale. It was short-lived, but he soon had another chance, this time at the struggling Stockport, perennial Fourth Division re-election applicants. They were going nowhere (well, certainly not upwards), had never really been anywhere, anchored to the bottom division for 21, mainly desperate, seasons. Until Danny Bergara rolled into town.

In his six years in charge, Bergara won promotion to Division Three (then renamed Division Two) and they went to Wembley four times (twice in the Autoglass Trophy, twice in play-off finals). He made the club millions of pounds in the transfer market by what Danny calls 'polishing diamonds', developing his own young players, or spotting underachievers, improving them and selling them on. His side would form the backbone of the Stockport team that would, two years after Bergara was sacked in March 1995, go on to play in the First Division – dizzy, unimaginable heights. Stockport in the First Division; it beggared belief. They made the quarter-finals of the FA Cup too.

'I would say we made two-and-a-half to three million pounds profit,' says Bergara. His role call of players includes: Andy Preece, signed for £15,000, sold for £350,000; Paul Williams, who cost nothing, sold for £250,000; and Kevin Francis, bought for £55,000, transferred for

£800,000. Others moved after Bergara left: Alun Armstrong (for £1.6 million), goalkeeper Paul Jones and forward Tony Dinning. 'It was a magnificent period,' recalls Bergara. 'If someone would have told me that would happen when I arrived in England I wouldn't have believed it. The way I had to go, it was the saddest day of my life.'

So what caused Bergara to be sacked? A row over a £64 expense claim.

Bergara, who lived in Sheffield, had a cheap and cheerful arrangement to lodge at a terraced house opposite Stockport's ground, Edgeley Park, a few nights a week. He had an expenses allowance of £50 a week, which Bergara claims he never reached. He even bought, and cooked, his own food to keep the costs down. Even though Bergara was making millions of pounds for the club, this small allowance was taken away.

A subsequent employment tribunal recalls the events. In March 1995, Stockport County's chairman Brendan Elwood sought to take Bergara's meagre allowance off him. Bergara disagreed, but Elwood told a subsequent board meeting, in Bergara's absence, that the manager had agreed to this new arrangement. When Bergara submitted his expense claim for £64 on 29 March he was refused payment. Bergara, in language hardly unfamiliar to the football industry, was verbally abusive to the club's chief executive David Coxon, and called the club's finance director David Jolley and chairman Brendan Elwood 'bastards' for withholding his expenses. He repeated these abusive remarks at a subsequent meeting with his deputies Dave Jones and John Sainty.

The tribunal heard that Bergara went to a dinner at a local hotel that evening, attended by Jolley and Elwood and other Stockport County board members. He met the club's vice chairman, Grahame White, and described Jolley and Elwood as a pair of 'fucking gangsters'. At the conclusion of the dinner, in the hotel foyer, Elwood swore at Bergara and sought to strike him twice across the face and told him 'not to bother coming to work tomorrow as he no longer had a job'. Jolley, who had intervened, later became an aggressor, poking Bergara in the chest and giving him what was described to the tribunal as a 'Sheffield volley', a tirade of swearing. He told Bergara to come to a meeting at his office the next day, where he would 'tear up his contract and shove it up his arse'.

Not surprisingly, Bergara did not accept this invitation and at a board meeting later that day, where their interpretation of the previous night's events had been presented by Elwood and Jolley to the rest of the board members, Bergara was dismissed. They said he had attacked them, not vice versa. The tribunal noted that the Stockport chairman, Brendan Elwood, had lied to his own board members by saying that Bergara had agreed to having his expenses withdrawn and by presenting a false version of events at the hotel. The tribunal found that Bergara had been unfairly dismissed and 'was not satisfied that the respondents [the club] had a genuine belief that the applicant [Bergara] was guilty of misconduct warranting dismissal based upon reasonable grounds. The evidence . . . showed the allegations which were ranged against the applicant . . . to be misconceived and inaccurate.

'This was an employer who had treated this manager with a complete lack of frankness and in a disingenuous way . . . For whatever reason, Mr Elwood and Mr Jolley wished to terminate Mr Bergara's contract.'

Bergara was found to have contributed 25 per cent to his dismissal (and had his compensation claim reduced accordingly) as a result of the bad language he had used. The tribunal panel also noted that Bergara's successor, Dave Jones, who along with a fellow coach, John Sainty, gave evidence on behalf of the club against Bergara (conversations usually held secure inside the confines of the manager's office), was employed at a third of Bergara's salary.

This opportunity allowed Jones, who had been given his break in full-time coaching by Bergara, having previously worked in a care home, the chance to build a notable career in management. He took Stockport into the First Division, then joined Southampton, and is now manager of First Division Wolverhampton Wanderers. John Sainty is now chief scout at Southampton.

For Danny Bergara, things have turned out differently. Since he was unfairly dismissed by Stockport he has not found a job in football equal to his expertise. He has coached at Sheffield Wednesday, and managed Rotherham, Doncaster Rovers and Dr Martens League club Grantham, but there have been few job offers. He now scouts for Spurs and supplies statistics for the Press Association.

Bergara believes he has been shunned by the game because word has spread around the boardrooms that he attacked his chairman. 'I'm a waste,' says Bergara. 'I've got all this knowledge to impart but I'm playing golf and doing jobs around the house. I send off applications. As far as I am concerned the fracas caused by the chairman and his fellow directors in a public place has ruined my career.

'It is a matter of record who attacked who but the reputation is out there – and it took four years before I got a penny and then I had to give half to the solicitors. But Stockport County will live with me forever. Nobody can ever take away what I have done at the club.'

Bergara's story is all too typical: a qualified coach with a solid track record in development and motivation, who even now in his early 60s talks with fervour and passion about the game, is left on the sidelines while clubs employ coaches with limited tactical outlook.

Managers take pot luck with the chairman they work for. As Tommy Docherty says, and let's face it, 'the Doc' should know – he has worked with the odd chairman or 12: 'The relationship between the chairman and the manager is the most important one at the club. You've got to get the players playing for you and you've got to have the respect of the chairman. You need to know that he supports you 100 per cent in what you're doing.' Docherty says the most difficult chairmen to work with are those 'who promise you the moon but give you nothing. No money to buy players or to let you make decisions. Some try to pick your team for you. That's why I left QPR the first time after 28 days.'

Most managers are not so willing to join the dole queue. Danny Bergara has shown the difficulties of getting back into management after you've been sacked, and trying to overcome a reputation for being a 'quitter'. That is why some managers are prepared to put up with all sorts of circumstances.

Frank Clark's first managerial role was that of assistant to Ken Knighton at Sunderland in 1979. They won promotion to the First Division in their first season, but then the chairman changed. Tom Cowie, a car dealer, took over. Cowie sacked both of them in April 1981. 'I learned it's better not to fight battles you can't win. We didn't have the experience to handle Tom Cowie. You've got to fight from a position of strength.' Clark's biggest challenge came at Manchester City. He joined a club full of directors with diverse aims and intentions and a hopelessly large 50-odd-strong playing staff, amassed by a succession of managers. Clark didn't realise how ludicrous the situation was at Maine Road until he got the sack. He found out by listening to the radio.

'I was driving up to Sunderland on a scouting trip and the secretary rang to ask could I pop in to see the chairman. I said, "Well, I haven't gone very far, so I can turn back if it's urgent." He said: "No, it can wait until tomorrow." So I went to the game, got back to my car and there was a message on my answerphone from a journalist friend of mine saying, "My paper is running a story tomorrow saying you're going to be sacked." Still no official word from anybody. People were leaking stuff to the press all the time so I wasn't unduly worried. I was getting ready to go to work and I heard on the radio that I had been sacked. Twenty minutes later I got a phone call from the chairman, Francis Lee, asking me to pop round to his house. He was very apologetic, he said it wasn't his decision, he was being undermined by others on the board, and said he was sorry.'

The nature of football management is that one person's misfortune is someone else's opportunity. Clark discovered that the phone stops ringing when you're perceived to have failed. At the time of writing, he hasn't worked since leaving Maine Road in 1998. 'I thought people would remember what I did at Forest and Orient and that I had been working under difficult circumstances, but the phone didn't ring.'

It's a fact of managerial life that before a manager is sacked the club look to manoeuvre someone else into position. They need to know if the potential new manager wants the job and what his conditions might be. The chances are he is already working. It is an illegal approach and against the rules, but, in reality, it happens all the time.

Frank O'Farrell had done rather well for himself since joining Weymouth. He had moved on to Torquay (and got them promoted), and to Leicester, which he had taken to the FA Cup final, relegation, but straight back into Division One. Then came a call that would change his life – from Manchester United. Wilf McGuinness, a former United player, had not fared well as Matt Busby's successor. He was out, Frank was wanted – but he was still at Leicester, which made it an illegal approach.

One man could swing the deal: the legendary Sir Matt Busby, now supposedly a 'junior director' (as he told the press), but as O'Farrell was to find out still a major influence at Old Trafford. Busby was a man who couldn't quite let go of his management reins. 'I wasn't daunted about going there. It didn't bother me,' insists O'Farrell. 'But I couldn't shake off the influence of Matt Busby.'

At their first surreptitious meeting Busby told O'Farrell: 'It's all yours, Frank.' He laid out the terms – a five-year contract at £12,000 a year plus bonuses. At a later meeting, in a lay-by on a B road in Derbyshire in United chairman Louis Edwards' jag, Busby repeated the terms. 'Edwards turned to him and said, "I thought we agreed it was £15,000?" Immediately, I was concerned,' recalls O'Farrell. 'He'd tried to screw me for £3,000 a year. I later heard that Busby told Jimmy Murphy [his long-time assistant] that "the old man" had let him down. So before I started there was this question-mark over Matt.'

This level of interference wouldn't have been tolerated from any other director, but Matt Busby was special. To many people he *was* Manchester United. Moreover, he was a stable influence, a wise old head the younger manager could call upon when he needed advice. When O'Farrell arrived at Old Trafford, he discovered that Busby intended to keep the manager's office, while a smaller one was built down the corridor for the mere manager. 'I thought, I must make a stand here,' says O'Farrell. 'I said to Matt, "This isn't going to look right. I should be in the manager's office." He agreed, and moved out to the office intended for me, but it showed he was going to stay around.'

O'Farrell made a good start – United won their first five matches. George Best was back and Denis Law was scoring goals. Busby told the press: 'Frank is possibly the best signing *I* have made.' But this rather special 'junior director' played golf with his former charges, and they took their moans to him. 'I left George Best out of the game against Wolves because he had missed training and had gone on a drinking spree in Ireland. When he returned his landlady phoned to say he's back and will be able to train. I told her to tell George he wasn't playing. I had to take a stand, but the truth was we were lost without him. The rest of the team wasn't good enough. We lost 3–0.' United finished eighth in the League, not bad in a rebuilding season. 'Then I dropped Bobby Charlton in my second season and we lost the game to Spurs. He wasn't up to it anymore.'

If Matt Busby was the grandfather of Manchester United's family,

Charlton was a kindly uncle. A one-club man from the Babes era, he had been on the Munich plane. He had been a member of England's 1966 World Cup-winning team, and had won 105 caps for his country. Busby's loyalty was understandable, but it made life difficult for O'Farrell. 'He said he wouldn't have dropped Bobby Charlton, but he was undermining the team and the manager.'

Busby began to openly criticise O'Farrell's signings. Martin Buchan, who turned out to be a fine servant and club captain for many years, was mistakenly singled out by Busby for an error he was supposed to have made in a game against Spurs. 'Busby said he didn't mark his player for the flick on from Alan Gilzean, but he was wrong. It was David Sadler who should have marked tighter.' Sadler was one of Busby's former players. 'He believed what the players told him because they were trying to put the blame elsewhere. I corrected Matt and he didn't like that. He had lied to me in the past and I knew he was talking to the players behind my back.'

O'Farrell was sacked after a humiliating 5–0 defeat at Crystal Palace, which left United third from bottom in Division One. Younger readers might find it hard to believe that could actually happen – some United fans called for Alex Ferguson's head in 2001 when United plumbed the relative depths to eighth in the Premiership. Prior to Ferguson's era, it wasn't always uncommon for them to slip out of the top half of the table.

'I was asked to go to the boardroom. They said they would be relieving me of my post. I asked why and they wouldn't give me an answer. I insisted because I wanted it recording in the minutes. So they said it was the results. But it was a clash of personalities. I was independent of Matt Busby and he didn't like that. He still wanted to be in charge.'

The immediate years after Busby's reign as manager ended are seen as a period of decline. United would slip further after O'Farrell left in 1972. Tommy Docherty would take them down to Division Two, before turning their fortunes around. O'Farrell believes Matt Busby failed to accept his part in their downfall during these barren years for the club. 'Busby had allowed the side to get too old, but wasn't held accountable. Wilf McGuinness, myself and Tommy Docherty didn't get the backing from Busby we might have expected. He was talking to players behind our backs.'

It was nine months before O'Farrell's contract was settled. He was obliged to sign on at Salford labour exchange. 'They were being vindictive; they did it to humiliate me,' says O'Farrell. 'In the end they settled out of court at the last moment. I'm not bitter because I've had a good life but until I went to Manchester United my career had been on an upward curve. Afterwards it went downhill because the impression was that I failed but the club went down some distance after I left before it was turned around.'

Meddling is one thing, working for dishonest directors is a totally different question. One of the problems in football is that there is little monitoring of the people who are allowed to buy clubs. The football authorities have few checks and balances. The FA's sole rule on ownership is that a person should not have a substantial stake in two clubs. The Football League rules go slightly further – they actually demand to know more about the owners. But there is no proper test. As long as you aren't barred from being a company director, as long as you have the collateral, a football club is all yours. There are few hoops to jump through. If the game is going to demand that coaches and managers are qualified, what about directors? Shouldn't they have to prove their suitability to purchase major stakes in football clubs, which after all, are cherished community institutions. What do managers think?

'How do you stop people from selling their property to who they like?' asks John Duncan, the former Chesterfield manager. John Barnwell believes the owners of clubs should be licensed. 'The Football League should have financial criteria and grant licences which are periodically checked for anyone owning or seeking to own a major stake in a football club. If necessary clubs should be prevented from trading until they comply.'

Steve Coppell, a former PFA chairman and a Bungs Inquiry panellist, says football has to prevent people buying clubs simply to get their hands on the real estate. 'The game should be more responsible to its member clubs. There is an asset-stripping mentality where at some clubs the football ground is separated from the football club and the football bodies are happy to let this go on until a crisis occurs. It must not be allowed. The people who are running football clubs must not be people who have a dodgy financial background.'

Ray Graydon believes that it can be difficult to assess in advance. 'At Oxford, I worked for Robert Maxwell. We know now he wasn't a good guy and he ruined a lot of people's lives. But he was remarkably successful at Oxford. You couldn't have stopped him coming into the industry.'

The antidote to individual owners snapping up clubs to do whatever they like is for fans to group together to buy their clubs. Until recently, this seemed a fanciful notion, but supporters' trusts are being set up at many clubs. Supporters Direct is a government-backed organisation providing help and support for fans looking to set up a trust. The aim is to buy blocks of shares within a club and if they are big enough, they can influence decision-making and get their own directors appointed. Because the representatives are voted into office the trusts are a democratic form of ownership. At many clubs who have hit financial hard times, this might be the only way forward.

The first club in the country to be run by a trust was Lincoln City, whose chairman is Rob Bradley, an architect and long-standing Imps fan. He took the chair in 2001 when previous owner John Reames sold his stake in the club for a nominal value. Unfortunately, the trust was not able to reduce Lincoln's debts and the club were plunged into administration in April 2002. Bradley and his colleagues wanted to change how the club had been managed.

'When we took over I thought the powers of a manager seemed wide and vague,' says Bradley. 'It wasn't just the manager, it was the whole staff. People were working without job descriptions and it became a real problem. When we had to sack some of them because of financial problems we were hit by legal actions from the bar staff to the chief executive. In one dispute we had to refer to a newspaper because there was no proper documentation around.

'Because it was a football club rather than a ball-bearing factory it was like it didn't matter. We have tried to introduce proper contracts and job descriptions so everyone knows where they stand, including the right paperwork.'

Unfortunately, the trust could not cope with Lincoln's spiralling debts and had no option but to place the club in the hands of administrators. On a wider scale Bradley supports calls for tighter controls on the ownership of clubs. 'This has to come in. The Football

League's stance is that clubs only have to comply with company law, but football clubs aren't ordinary businesses. They are a special case and should be treated as such by the governing body. They need to be safeguarded from asset strippers and property developers. The way some clubs have been run leaves a lot to be desired. It must be impossible for managers to work under those circumstances.'

On a warm Friday evening in late April 2002, West Bromwich Albion chairman Paul Thompson and club manager Gary Megson stood arms aloft and hand in hand on the balcony of Sandwell Borough Council's offices in Oldbury. Below, thousands of Albion supporters waved their blue and white flags and scarves at the clubs' players and officials. This was a special moment. The Baggies, as they are known, had won promotion to the Premier League (a return to the top flight for the first time in 16 years) and edged out their neighbours, Wolverhampton Wanderers. After months of public and private rowing, manager and chairman, arguably the two people who had done most to turn around the club's fortunes, appeared united at last; their joining of hands seemed hugely symbolic. Sharper-eyed supporters may have noticed it was the chairman who had grasped his manager's hand, not vice versa.

The harmony wasn't to last. Four days later Thompson resigned after a brief but bitter meeting with Megson. Thompson claims he was left with three unenviable choices: to sack Megson and risk the condemnation of fans who see the club's manager as God after he steered them to an unlikely promotion; to try to muddle along in the hope they could reach enough common ground for a working relationship; or to quit. He decided on the latter.

'I couldn't win either way,' claimed Thompson, who didn't go quietly. He issued an immediate broadside against Megson and criticised 'Victorian attitudes' among the wider football industry. He wrote to both supporters and Premier League chairmen to explain his decision and give his version of the arguments which had run all season and were shrouded in claims, counter-claims and innuendo. While, on one hand, this looked little more than a spot of local difficulty – albeit a major headache for West Brom and the sort of problem which led to 63 of Gary Megson's colleagues losing their jobs in 2001–02 – on the other hand, the differences between Megson and Thompson are symbolic of the relations between managers and chairmen, with repercussions far beyond the confines of the Black Country.

Here are two men who did a remarkably successful job together. Thompson is a Barnsley-born businessman, and accountant by trade who built up the information technology services group Sanderson into a £100 million a year turnover business. He joined the Albion board in 1996 and took over as chairman on Christmas Eve 1999, at a time when the club was losing £30,000 a week, which meant they had to sell star asset Kevin Kilbane to Sunderland for £2.5 million in order to balance the books, with young Italian starlet Enzo Meresca following close behind, this time to Juventus for £4 million.

In March 2000, Thompson appointed Megson as manager. West Brom were sinking and heading for relegation. A fully committed midfielder who had played most of his football in the top flight, Megson's managerial career had not caught the eye. He had managed four clubs in five seasons prior to joining West Brom, and although he had steered Stockport to eighth in the First Division in 1998 (carrying on the good foundations laid by Danny Bergara and Dave Jones, mentioned earlier in this chapter) he had not enjoyed conspicuous success elsewhere.

Together, Megson and Thompson forged a formidable partnership, Thompson keeping a close eye on the finances and Megson using his coaching nous to bring committed players to the club – and improve those who remained from previous regimes. Off the pitch, losses were turned to profit with 17 players bought for a relatively modest £8.5 million. A new £6 million stand has been built and a £1.8 million training centre is due to open in 2002. On the pitch, relegation was staved off in 2000, a year later West Brom made the First Division play-offs, and in season 2001–02 they were promoted, despite selling star striker and local hero Lee Hughes in the week leading up to the start of the season for £5 million. Three million of it remained unspent.

So why the row? Most of it has centred upon the role of the manager in a modern football club. Megson is a traditionalist, whereas Thompson has sought to introduce a more modern business approach. 'There is a fundamental conflict within football which is to do with who is running the club as opposed to who is running the team,' says Thompson. 'At most successful clubs the chairman and the board run the club and the manager runs the team and that's the way it should be.'

Thompson believes that football managers have enough on their plates. 'Dealing with team affairs is a full-time job,' he explains. 'The footballers are finer-tuned athletes than they used to be, they train professionally and for longer than they used to. There are diet and fitness trainers and proper preparation. The problem is that there isn't an agreed job description for a football manager so there is a misunderstanding of where the scope of the manager's job ends and other people pick up. The manager is a senior employee at the club and the most important person at the club other than the chairman. I think a better title would be "coach". It would distinguish the fact that the manager is running the first team and not running the club.'

The key to the 'professional business principles' Thompson sought to introduce is joint decision-making. 'The basic rule in industry and commerce is that you have segregation of duties and checks and balances. I believe there should be more than one person involved in every major decision. With the first team the buck stops with the manager – but when it comes to spending money then the buck has to stop with the chairman and the board so it is only right that they are involved with those dealings.'

But there are problems with this approach. Firstly, football professionals are sceptical when perceived outsiders encroach on their area of expertise. They believe, rightly or wrongly, that they know best. They will not readily accept advice from non-football people. Secondly, managers have to carry the can when the flak flies from fans and the media and if they are going to take the blame, the way they see it, it is only fair they make the decisions. And thirdly, football managers as a breed tend to be control freaks. This book is littered with endless examples of such behaviour. They will not, or sometimes cannot, let go regardless of the implications for their health or wider ability to do the job.

The most obvious advantage of Thompson's shared decision-making approach for the manager should be job stability. 'If the manager gets the sack because of the performances of the team then that's fair enough but if it is because of the players he has brought in then you've got to ask what were the chairman and the board doing because they should have appropriate input into that,' says Thompson.

In theory, taking all the complicated financial aspects of handling transfers and negotiating player contracts, deciding who to offer contracts to and how much they should be paid, away from the manager should make his job easier, freeing up time to do what most managers do best – coaching. It would also clear some of the suspicion about bungs and backhanders that has surrounded football and was the backdrop to the Bungs Inquiry of the 1990s.

If only things were so simple. Unfortunately, Paul Thompson's seemingly sensible business approach does not easily cover the awkward shades of grey. Gary Megson found he could only 'recommend' players he wanted to retain or release. The final decision rested with the board, and he was sometimes overruled. It is surely too much to expect a football manager to meekly accept this. Then there are those areas of the clubs which are outside his immediate control but which he will obviously have a huge say in developing and running, like youth programmes and scouting networks.

In a letter to supporters Thompson claimed his disagreements with Megson came down to two elements: the public nature of the comments and criticism by the chairman and board, which Thompson says is 'never acceptable', and the club's scouting system. Thompson favours an integrated scouting system, where various parties including the chairman, chief executive, first-team manager, assistant manager and chief scout sit down to discuss the players they may be interested in.

Megson, who has long insisted that scouting at West Brom was inadequate and consisted of 'his dad (a former player and manager) and a couple of mates', wants greater input into the scouting operation. This, linked to Megson's understandable concern about not having the final say on the players who are signed, released or pursued, made for an uneasy relationship. With the club going into the Premier League, Megson clearly decided this approach could no longer work and told his chairman so.

Thompson insists all he tried to do was operate the same way as top continental clubs and the more enlightened British clubs. He argues that not only did this approach work, but that the image of managers and chairmen, and the relations between the two, should be raised by such an arrangement. 'I think supporters are starting to realise that not only has a club got to have a good manager but it's also got to have a good chairman. At the moment a lot of high-calibre company chairmen won't come into the game because of the flak and criticism that they get.'

Whether football has lost Paul Thompson remains to be seen. He resigned as chairman and a board member of West Bromwich Albion in May 2002, but at the time of writing (July 2002) has retained his 23.21 per cent shareholding in the club. In June, a former boardroom colleague of Thompson's, Jeremy Peace, took over as chairman and forced Thompson's favoured successor, Clive Stapleton, and another director, Barry Hurst, off the West Brom board. The club's chief executive, John Wile, also left. Stapleton issued a Thompson-esque broadside claiming that the good work of the past two years could soon come undone if the principles applied during that period are ignored. Peace has brought in new directors, most notably Wile's former playing colleague and former PFA vice-chairman, Brendon Batson.

Within a week of Peace becoming chairman, Gary Megson expressed his optimism for the future and indicated he would be willing to sign a new contract. The irony is that if Megson does progress to a higher-profile club it will undoubtedly have been down to his success at West Brom, an opportunity given to him by a board led by Paul Megson.

Either way you look at this argument, one thing is certain – the current relations between managers and boards of football club directors by and large are not working, a fact reflected in the high turnover of managers. Something has to change. Football needs stability, not only in the dugout but also in the directors' box. At the moment too much of the pressure rests on the managers' shoulders, and it is taking a toll on their health. The question is – are they fit to manage?

– CHAPTER TEN –

Fit to Manage? Health, Wealth and Heart Attacks Among Britain's Football Bosses

When you're in football management you sometimes think 'Why the devil am I doing this job?' and when you're out of it you want to get back in.

John Barnwell, Chief Executive of the LMA

It's with you from the moment you wake up to the moment you go to bed. And you wake up in the middle of the night thinking about football. It's part of your make-up.

Bruce Rioch

Perhaps the saddest aspect of British football management is not the number of sackings or resignations, but the effect the stress of the job has on the men who choose to become seasoned soccer bosses. It is the grimmest part of the sack race.

Everyone knows that managers are under pressure, but how does that pressure actually manifest itself? Of course managers must endure the highs and lows of their job, in particular the tension of matchdays – it is, after all, a results-based business. But what about the cumulative toll the role takes on people who are, as we have seen, often ill-equipped to be football managers in the first place? Long working hours and anxiety even in leisure time, media scrutiny, poor diet and lack of sleep, drinking too much (the link between long working hours and drink problems in many industries has been long established); all of these factors have a detrimental effect on managers' family lives and health. Living in a pressure-cooker environment is a recipe for disaster.

There are startling admissions in this chapter from managers who feel they have missed their children growing up. They complain of feeling constantly tired and not being able to concentrate on anything other than football, of not being able to delegate. Small wonder many managers seek solace in drink or end up with serious health problems. I have put some late nights into writing this book – 16-hour days. But I know it won't last forever, and I'm not doing it every day for ten months of the year, under intense public scrutiny.

Not that, on the whole, employers are unduly concerned. The industry has a sad record of ladling the pressure on with the largest available spoon. Rather than help, many directors hinder the manager by passing the blame for other problems at the club directly onto his shoulders, cranking up the pressure on the gaffer. Fans don't, or won't, consider the wider implications of their criticisms. The media are, well, the media. It's always the manager's fault. The clubs don't care. They rarely ask managers to take medical examinations before being given a job or offer health insurance packages (standard practice for most senior managers in other industries), and they often make a manager fight for compensation when he leaves, often through ill health, at best because results haven't gone his way. Regardless of how well they are paid, the ill-treatment of managers is heartless. Football's motto is use 'em up and wear 'em out – there are plenty more fish in the sea.

The high number of resignations in the game is significant. Why are managers quitting in such numbers? Is it because they find themselves looking over the edge of an emotional abyss? If so, this is truly shocking.

'I was left in a field in Derbyshire. I don't remember anything about it. I can't remember anything for three months.' In April 1979, John Barnwell, then manager of First Division Wolverhampton Wanderers, had a near-fatal car crash. 'The police think somebody may have cut me up at 12.30 at night. I had been speaking at a Cancer Research dinner so I hadn't been drinking.'

John was driving back from the East Midlands to Wolverhampton to be back on the training ground early the next morning. He never made it; instead he nearly lost his life. He had a fractured skull and a car wing mirror had stuck in his head. A millimetre either way and he could have died.

'I suspect the cause was sheer tiredness. The long hours of rushing up and down motorways, and not eating properly. When you're in football management you sometimes think "Why the devil am I doing this job?" and when you're out of it you want to get back in. I used to look in the mirror after my operation and I didn't recognise who was there. I thought someone was stood behind me.'

John had been worried about Wolves' dip in form. They needed a win or two to steer clear of relegation. He had joined them earlier in the season, after they had lost 10 of their opening 12 matches. It was his second managerial position; he was previously boss of Peterborough United. 'We had three matches left and needed one point for survival. The team took what happened to me on board and won all three matches.'

Clearly the players could cope without him, but that didn't stop the club's directors from rushing him back to work, ahead of his doctor's advice. 'I remember the surgeon who saved my life saying it would be two years before they could allow me to do any physical work. I came back far too early. The season was starting. My hair was shaved. I wore a gold and black woolly cap. I looked a right fool. A couple of the directors encouraged me to come back because it was pre-season and the great strides we had made were in danger of slipping backwards. I shouldn't have gone.'

A director persuaded John to leave his home in Peterborough, where he was recuperating, to watch a pre-season friendly match in Cardiff. 'We were losing 1–0 at half-time. I went into the dressing-room, had a word with a few players and we went on and won 3–1. That convinced me that just my presence there would help the situation.'

Soon after Barnwell had been ushered back into his chair it became apparent that all was not well. 'Whenever I took a phone call of some intensity, which was most of them, I would suddenly feel as if two screws on the side of my head were being turned and my scalp was getting tighter and tighter. I would say "Excuse me, I've got to go," and put the phone down. That stayed with me for several months. It's called scalp tension – which isn't unusual after the injury I had. The doctors weren't keen on me going back so soon, but I did.'

Not that he was eased back into the post, or had any major duties taken away from him to ease the pressure. 'I bought and sold the most expensive players in British football history during that period. I remember sitting in the office one Monday morning and my head was exploding. I had no hair. I had sold Steve Daley to Manchester City and bought Andy Gray, and that deal had been going on for several months, so I was capable of handling that. But I remember thinking "I'm going to pay for this at some stage in my life". You make decisions at the time because they seem the right things to do.'

Barnwell's choice to return prematurely appeared to be vindicated when Wolves won the League Cup in 1980, the season he returned after his accident. He could do no wrong. He was the toast of the town. But football club directors have short memories. The same club that had treated Stan Cullis so shabbily less than 20 years earlier was about to make a similar mistake. Ironically, a new stand built and named after John Ireland (the chairman who sacked Cullis) was at the root of it.

In January 1982, club chairman Harry Marshall gave Barnwell an ultimatum – either sign a new contract or leave. 'I terminated my contract,' says Barnwell, who insists Wolves were attempting to sell Andy Gray behind his back. 'The building of the new stand was eating into our budget. The club had to find half a million pounds a year. There was only one place they were going to find that sort of money and that was from me.'

The new stand, into which Wolves ploughed their cash instead of investing money in new players, was a slap in the face for Stan Cullis. It put the current incumbent in an impossible position. 'We had a few young players coming through and a lot of older ones. We won a League Cup, we had reached two FA Cup semi-finals, we were back in Europe from being bottom of the league. But suddenly, with no youngsters coming through, we needed to buy and we had no selling value apart from Gray.' Gray was one of the best strikers in British football at the time. A tall, fearless (and highlighted) forward, he was good in the air and quick on the ground. Barnwell had pulled off a real coup by bringing him to Molineux from Aston Villa. To see him sold so soon was demoralising.

Barnwell's own willingness to return to his job almost immediately after his crash was not being rewarded. 'I had a three-year contract waiting to be signed. When the chairman came back from holiday (in the summer of 1981) he wanted to change the terms and the length of the contract. We had a confrontation and from that day on I was always going.'

Even leaving Molineux was messy. 'I was advised by my lawyers to terminate my contract, which I did. Looking back, it was the wrong thing to do. It took nine months to get them into an arbitration tribunal. I was advised to attempt to get a job but didn't really do so. I went to the USA. I was advised to take Wolves to a tribunal in Birmingham. I ended up with a massive legal bill and I didn't get a penny.'

Barnwell's story is worth telling in all its inglorious detail, because it demonstrates the pressure managers are under: an accident probably caused through tiredness and worry over how the team will cope and the threat of relegation; an employer urging a manager back to work against medical advice and then making him fight for a settlement. He was expected to put his health on the line for the club, yet they showed little loyalty in return.

The health of football managers has remained a passion of John Barnwell's. As chief executive of the LMA, which was formed in 1992, ten years after his exit from Wolves, he has been the driving force behind a project called Fit to Manage, launched in May 2001, to monitor the cardiovascular health of football managers.

'After I left Wolves I left the country and went to AEK Athens. From a physical point of view it was the best move I could have made. I was in a warm climate; there was less pressure although it was a massive club. I could get on the beach during the day in warm sunshine, have a swim, get enough rest and train during the afternoon. I didn't have to worry about buying or selling players or any of those other stressful things that managers have to do. I totally recovered physically and came back to England.'

Barnwell argues that health problems often start early in a manager's career. 'Most of us have been professional players – we've lived a healthy life and everything is done for you. Suddenly, we're in a stressful job, under high public circumstances. It is a very pressurised job. You work long hours, you're in a car, you eat at the wrong times, grabbing food that you shouldn't be. You're probably stopping to have a drink after a game with the press and then you go in the boardroom and have another drink. It's probably 8 or 9 p.m. before you get home and you haven't eaten. It doesn't take long for the body to get out of shape and for your aerobic fitness and muscle quality to depreciate.'

Barnwell believes managers need to learn to look after themselves because the clubs won't help. It all goes back to the high turnover of dismissals. 'The philosophy of the people running the clubs goes way back. The fallout of managers is so phenomenal clubs say "What is the point of us spending time and money on health care when he won't be here that long?". I would say if they prepare better coming into the job, and if they stay fit and healthy while they're in the job, perhaps they'll still be in the job. But they don't always see it like that.'

Football has a long legacy of managers suffering from ill health, especially heart trouble. Scotland boss Jock Stein died of a pitchside heart attack. In 1997, Joe Kinnear had a heart attack when managing Wimbledon at Sheffield Wednesday but survived. Barry Fry and Graeme Souness have had heart surgery, and Liverpool manager Gérard Houllier had life-saving treatment after complaining of feeling unwell at half-time during a Premiership match between Liverpool and Leeds United in October 2001.

This produced great waves of sympathy and concern. Newspapers and magazines questioned the amount of stress in the game and the high number of sackings already happening in the 2001–02 season. But it didn't last. Thankfully, Houllier was back in charge of Liverpool before the end of the season. Unlike Barnwell at Wolves 22 years earlier, he wasn't rushed back to work.

A Carlton TV programme, *Tonight With Trevor McDonald*, recorded and screened in January 2002, revealed the matchday pressure football managers are under. Heart and blood pressure monitors were attached to the bosses of two competing Premiership clubs: Sam Allardyce of Bolton Wanderers and Dave Bassett of Leicester City. The producers could hardly have chosen a better game to indicate the rocketing stress levels of the managers of two relegation-threatened clubs. Bolton had two players sent off and were two goals down in the first half. They sneaked a goal back before half-time, then Leicester had a player dismissed after the break. Bolton scored a last-gasp equaliser in injury time and Allardyce went from despair and agony to the ecstasy of earning a precious point. For Bassett, it was all too typical of Leicester's season. They weren't holding on to the lifelines being thrown their way.

Allardyce, who called the referee a 'fucking disgrace' six times on the trot after the first sending-off, saw his heart rate rise from a resting rate of 46 beats per minute to 162 – almost quadruple. His blood pressure went up to 192. Bassett's heart rate leapt from 56 beats per minute to 120 beats with a similar blood pressure rise as Allardyce, but Bassett's heart showed an irregular beat.

Bassett concluded: 'Although I love football, I'm not putting my life at risk for it.' Allardyce was amazed to find that his heart rate peaked to dangerous levels when Bolton grabbed their late equaliser, a moment of joy, rather than during his outburst when he had reeled off a string of expletives.

Cardiologists from the Wellness Centre, based in Stockport, carried out the research. They are also working with the LMA on Fit to Manage. The project will run for four years. 'The game is littered with managers who have had cardiovascular problems,' says Dr Dorian Dugmore, the centre's director. 'Medicine is so often practised downstream, where we wait for something to happen and then try to treat the person. With Fit to Manage we're saying, "Can we assess the risk and look at some likely outcomes and can we intervene before heart problems develop?" We are hoping to give football managers an overview of their lifestyles and particularly to minimise the risks to their cardiovascular health and the impact on the major diseases like cancer and degenerative disease caused by not looking after yourself.'

The LMA are ploughing £100,000 into this long-term project, which began with an initial batch of 11 league managers in 2001. The first results will not be produced for two years. 'We're rolling it out over four years,' says John Barnwell. 'I think the clubs should be doing this anyhow but the managers are never at the club long enough so the clubs don't see it as their responsibility.'

Dorian Dugmore likens this attitude to an old analogy he uses in treatment. 'A cardiologist is standing beside a riverbank and unbeknown to him there is a bystander standing on the other side. Suddenly the cardiologist sees someone drowning and he dives in and saves their life. He then sees someone else in the same predicament and repeats the process. And again. He is lying on the riverbank exhausted and the bystander says, "I've just seen what you've done, you've saved three lives in succession – that's amazing, well done! Do you mind if I give you a tip?" The cardiologist says, "Of course not." The bystander replies, "Have you ever thought of running along the river to see which bugger is pushing them in?"'

Dugmore is the sort of down-to-earth doctor the managers respond to. He works mainly with busy, stressed-out executives from all walks of life, and recalls an American businessman urging him to 'get on with the test'. He didn't have a moment to spare – not even to be told whether his life was at risk. He was the sort of person who likes to book their heart attack in at 2 p.m. when they 'have an open window'.

It is sad to think that a steady stream of overworked football managers will be heading for this corner of Cheshire without the support of the fat wallets running major football clubs. 'An ounce of prevention is better than a ton of cure,' says Barnwell. His members are in dire need.

So where does the pressure come from? 'There's pressure from the media and supporters but also the pressure you put on yourself,' says Steve Cotterill, the former manager of Cheltenham Town, now at First Division Stoke City. 'If you want to be successful you put unwarranted and unmerited pressure on yourself. I think you have to learn to enjoy the ups and try not to let the downs affect you quite as much.'

'If it is your first job, it is your career that is at stake,' says Steve Coppell. 'It means everything and it is understandable how it can invade every aspect of your life.'

'The stress affects everybody,' says Peter Taylor, former England Under-21 coach, who was sacked early in season 2001–02 by Leicester City and resigned from Brighton and Hove Albion at the end of the season. 'Sometimes it is disappointment, other times it is desperation.'

Millwall manager Mark McGhee says learning to live with stress doesn't make it any easier to cope with failure. 'It's like being struck by lightning. Just because it might have happened to you before, it doesn't mean you're hardened to it. It still hurts. You need to look after yourself and to take advice, whether it's from colleagues or friends. Even Alex Ferguson does. It does affect your family and home life. There's no way it can't, when you're out all hours.'

Former Scotland manager Craig Brown, now manager of First Division Preston North End, feels guilty that he spent so much time away from the family home, he missed his children growing up. 'I didn't give as my attention to my family as I should have. That's quite normal for football managers. I've got two boys and a girl – all married now – and I've got to say I didn't have the input into their growing up I should have. I don't think they are the worse for it, but they could have been. I'm the one who lost out because I neglected their formative years. And you can't get them back.'

But even when they are physically at home, some managers are mentally elsewhere. Like Steve Coppell, for instance. 'You might be watching a film in the cinema and halfway through you start to worry about who you're going to play in midfield on Saturday. And what about their centre-forward, how are we going to cope with him? So it dominates every aspect of your life, no matter how much you try to prevent it.'

Everton manager David Moyes reckons he works somewhere between 80 to 100 hours a week. 'The only hours you aren't working are the hours you're sleeping. Even on Sunday when you might be at home with the family there won't be a manager who isn't running things over in his head. If we don't win I don't enjoy my weekends and we don't go out. I hope I'll get better when I'm older!'

'I can fully understand that some managers come under so much pressure it makes them ill,' says Jan Molby, of Hull City. 'You're putting your neck on the line 50 to 70 times a year in front of a lot of people, who all have an opinion on what you are doing. That brings pressure.' Ray Graydon, manager of Bristol Rovers, agrees. At Walsall, his first managerial job, he says he felt the pressure of not wanting to let down the fans who had been so loyal to him. 'They didn't expect us to be successful and I had a great rapport with them. I didn't want to let them down. I felt it when we got relegated and when we won promotion.'

A frequent complaint of managers is tiredness caused by the long working hours of football management, and in particular never being able to sleep or switch off. 'I worked at least 90 hours a week,' says Bruce Rioch, who, at the time of writing, has been out of football since being dismissed by Wigan Athletic in February 2001. 'It's with you from the moment you wake up to the moment you go to bed. And you wake up in the middle of the night thinking about football. It's part of your make-up.'

Late-night driving is a particular concern for managers, justifiably so when you look what happened to John Barnwell. 'People say, yes, well, you're well paid, but money doesn't keep your eyes open at 12.30 a.m. at night when you're driving home from a game,' argues Steve Cotterill. 'You can have all the money in the world but if you fall asleep at the wheel because you've had an early start, you've done training, you've done this, that and the other, that is not going to stop you from driving your car off the road.'

Managers often feel guilty for taking time off. 'Brian Clough got it right – he'd go to Spain for a week's break and come back refreshed,' says Bruce Rioch. 'Alex Ferguson has his interest in horseracing. Anything to temporarily take your mind off things.' Sadly, Rioch never took the sensible measures he advises for others. 'Managers need rest at certain times to recharge themselves. I've never done that. There's always another match to watch, another player to see, something else to do. You can do that when your team is winning but if the team loses and you go to Spain for a week people say "Why's he doing that? He should be on the training ground working with the players."'

When Ray Graydon was coach at Southampton, the manager Ian Branfoot wanted all his staff to take a week off during the season. Graydon didn't. 'I never took my Saturdays off. I wanted to be with the reserve team, or whatever. But you do need a break occasionally. It should be written in stone.' This is part of the problem; managers cannot relax. John Duncan, the former Chesterfield manager, says the job is constant. 'It's almost 24 hours. There wasn't a moment when I wasn't thinking about the job. It's never out of your mind. There's always something to do or someone to deal with.'

The stress and worry turns managers into control freaks. While they should leave talent-spotting to scouts and training sessions to their fellow coaches, many don't. They feel a need to do everything, to burn the candle at both ends. They are poor delegators. Steve Cotterill reckons he's got it pretty bad. 'It's something I've had to address,' he admits. 'I find it hard because I always think "I can do that better than him, so I'll just do it". And if you do delegate things they don't necessarily do them wrong, but they do them differently to you.' He gives an example: 'Anything on coaching, especially things being set up properly. I like all the cones to be in a straight line, I like the pitch to be the right size, the goals netted up nicely, the balls spread around the pitch, the bibs laid out for the players, not just chucked in a heap with everyone scrapping over them. The players notice clean balls. I don't like balls that are dirty from yesterday, so that type of thing you want done properly. Attention to detail.'

Cotterill has even tarmaced the club car park and painted the players' bar. Steve Coppell, a former LMA chief executive, says the demands are different but just as intense in the lower leagues as at the top clubs. 'At lower league clubs, it's hard work in a different way to a higher-profile club. There is no delegation. At a higher club the demands aren't so much physical, whereas here you have to be involved in everything. Higher up the pressure is the buck stops with you, lower down there is more understanding of the limitations. Everything is driven by cost. Things aren't done because it's right, they are done because it is the cheapest option.'

Startlingly, most managers breeze into their posts without undergoing a medical to assess whether they are physically fit enough to do the job. In 20 years of management Bruce Rioch was never asked to take a medical. 'The only medical test I ever had was one for myself when I took out some personal insurance when I joined Arsenal. But it was for me, not for the club. No club has ever asked me to undergo a medical. You're not even offered things like private medical cover – PPP or BUPA, that sort of thing – it has to be negotiated. We would never sign a player without him undergoing a very thorough medical, but managers are key men in the organisation of the football club and they should also be examined.'

Given this apparent lack of care, and the frequent demoralisation when they get stick from fans and the media, how do managers keep going? 'I've spoken to chairmen who have admitted "I wouldn't have your job for any amount of money,"' laughs Bruce Rioch. 'Who motivates the player? The manager. But who motivates the manager? Players? Maybe. Chairman and the board? Can be. Mainly it comes from within. We're in management because we have leadership qualities that others have recognised. No one ever needs to put pressure on me to get results, I have my own standards. You're a masochist really. You keep coming back for more only because you really believe you can be a success, and when you see that success and the happiness it brings to people, it's worth it.' Rioch was one of the first managers to sign up for Fit to Manage. He was manager at Wigan when selected, but soon lost his job. The stress of the sack is another consideration.

Dr Dorian Dugmore rates football managers among the highest risk group of employees for potential cardiovascular problems. 'The key concerns are the pressures and stresses of the game. It's a precarious job involving long working hours, stress, pressure and high demands. These guys are in a cauldron. A lot of football managers have been players. While they were players they kept themselves very fit, they were looked after and assisted to look after their own health because everything was geared to their performance.

'Suddenly – and it can happen within weeks – they may move into a whole new way of living. They may be working 18 hours a day, travelling all around the country and overseas for major competitions and the transition from sports performance related fitness to lifestyle fitness is hard to make.' This new lifestyle has no consistency. 'The football season ebbs and flows. There are critical periods where the pressure is going to be very high. That is why it is no good monitoring managers during average times. It's something you have to track over a long period of time and that is what the programme tries to do. All the research worldwide on all successful programmes points to one thing: you influence the person at the top, because if they do a great job then the effect of that will percolate down to the workforce.'

When you see managers waving their arms around bellowing out instructions, it isn't hard to spot the tell-tale signs of those seemingly at risk. But are the ones who express themselves so graphically really those in danger of suffering a heart attack? Dr Dugmore says that isn't always the case. 'It's not always the ones you'd think that have the problems. Appearances can be deceptive. You get some people who blow a fuse and have steam coming out of their ears and you say "He's destined for a heart attack". Yet he can be the guy who doesn't have the heart attack, whereas Mr Cool, who puts on a good front, who always seems in control, might be a seething cauldron of stress and pressure inside. He's just doing a great job of masking it.'

The tension of matchdays, exemplified in the *Tonight With Trevor McDonald* programme, is another crisis point, according to Dr Dugmore. 'If people become persistently angry and hostile because of the stresses and pressures of the job, we know from all the latest research that the likelihood of a cardiovascular problem can increase quite dramatically. In the USA they talk about the "corporate athlete"; they say that managers train 80 or 90 per cent of the time but "perform" 10 or 20 per cent of the time, when their leadership and decision-making is important. Football managers do that for maybe 20 or 30 years. But how much do they do in their own lifestyles to avoid the risks of heart disease and cancer?'

So how does Fit to Manage work? Dorian Dugmore says they start by assessing the managers' health and what condition they are in. 'They give us a background on their lifestyle, from how much and when they eat to how many hours they work, to how much exercise they take, to their family history and risk associated with that through to their own risk and own history to the sorts of stresses they are undertaking and being subjected to. Everything down to how much driving they do – the whole scenario that makes up the lifestyle of a football manager.

'At the Wellness Centre, we physically measure as many of those things as we can. So we measure their blood lipids and blood fats and we can see the sort of profile they have. We measure their blood glucose, look at their diabetic potential and lung function.

'They go from these resting assessments to detailed investigation in our exercise stress-testing laboratory. In essence, they are put onto a treadmill and monitored with electric cardiograms to see how their heart is working through ECG tracings. We measure how much oxygen they are using by looking at their oxygen costs during exercise. We look at their blood pressure. We take them from rest in a graded way towards what we call Maximum Volition Exhaustion, where they have reached the peak of their energy effort. They are then monitored as they recover. The last bit is so important because you have to exercise slowly to make sure you do it properly.'

Dr Dugmore goes on: 'When we've done all of those things we sit down with the manager one-to-one and go through their complete lifestyle. We set them short, medium and long-term goals to get them to either continue their great state of health or to improve their health and fitness parameters so we can minimise risk for the future. Lifestyle coaches design a tailor-made programme for each manager and track them on a regular monthly basis. Then we ask the managers to supply a detailed synopsis of what they have done over that month and we get back to them within 24 to 48 hours to give them all the latest findings and advice on how they can maximise their health and lifestyle. It's an important ongoing process.'

Dugmore admits it can be difficult to persuade some managers to spare the time to carry out their Fit to Manage programme, even though it is in their best interests. 'Football managers are the chief executives of the football world and chief executives are busy people. So there'll always be reasons why they won't do things. A couple of them have been hard to get in but as soon as they've got here they've been fantastic.'

The results of Fit to Manage will be revealing. What sort of overall shape are our football managers in? Obviously, much of the exact detail is confidential. During my visit I wasn't allowed to speak to one manager who had been tested because there were complications. The question of whether the game itself, or the clubs, should directly fund projects looking into the health of their employees remains.

'The open and honest answer to that is "yes",' says Dorian Dugmore.

– CHAPTER ELEVEN –

Tough at the Top,
Harder at the Bottom

> There are people who say, 'You couldn't manage at the top level because you never played any higher than the old Second Division.' Well, let them come down to our level and see if they could manage here.
>
> Jake King, Telford United Manager

THE COMMON CONCEPTION IS THAT ALL OF THE PRESSURES OF football management are at the top end of the game. This is only partly true. The big-time bosses of the Premiership may be under intense media scrutiny. They are certainly under pressure to deliver. Their performances can cost their clubs millions, if not multi-millions of pounds. But when all is said and done, they are also very well paid and have plenty of professional support staff.

Managers in the lower leagues, or at non-league level, don't have any of that security. The budgets are small, money is tight. There is no margin for error. Football's skewed finances have pushed the power towards the rich and mighty, making it tougher for the small clubs to survive. It is harder than ever for them to sell their way out of trouble. Since the Bosman ruling, players can leave a club for nothing when their contract runs out. The wider influx of foreign players into British football means that clubs look overseas. The traditional filtering through of players from bottom to top is thinner. Even the youth development rules have changed to benefit the big clubs. Since the introduction of FA licensed academies and centres of excellence for Premier/Football League clubs, talented Under-18s in non-league club youth development programmes can join a league club without a penny in compensation being paid. This does not happen between league clubs. It gives freedom of choice, yes, for the players, but acts as a disincentive for smaller clubs to engage in youth development. It also blocks an escape route from poverty. Most managers and players at non-league level are part-time with these changing circumstances and work immense hours for a part-time employment. You wonder why they do it.

For many, it is the first rung on the ladder to a career in full-time football management. John McGinlay, the former Scottish international forward, falls into this category. Since our interview, when he was managing Gresley Rovers in the Dr Martens Western Division, he has already made the step up to Ilkeston Town, a division higher. Progress.

Nigel Clough, son of his legendary managerial father Brian, is the boss of Burton Albion, promoted to the Nationwide Conference last season. His name has been linked with several managerial posts. Kenny Hibbitt has managed in the Football League but spent a short period out of the game and, after clawing his way back at Hednesford Town in the Dr. Martens Premier Division, was surprisingly sacked by them at the end of the 2001–02 season after less than a year in charge. Others, like Worcester City manager John Barton, are now putting something back into the game. Telford United boss Jake King hopes the hard work he has put in will pay dividends.

All these men work long, torturous hours. Without them, and many other willing workers, our grassroots football would wither away. They are an essential part of the football management scene. That is why they are included in this book. Their stories deserve to be told. It might be tough at the top – but it is certainly harder at the bottom.

It's 10 p.m. on a freezing Thursday night and John Barton has his head in his hands. He furiously rubs his eyes. It's not an injury crisis (well, not a new one anyway) or selection headache that is troubling him, or even a particularly awkward question I've posed. It's just that John is mentally exhausted. He can't quite summon up the words he wants. It's frustrating. He's tired. Very tired.

We're sitting in a small, dusty referee's changing-room at

Worcester's St George's Lane home. Minutes earlier, John calculated he works a 40-hour week for the club. You can add at least another ten hours if you include travel time from his home in Derby. 'It's a full-time job done on a part-time basis,' he muses. 'It's hard to squeeze those 40 hours in. It pinches time off your family. They would like to see more of me, but they have to accept that football is part of me, really.'

To make matters worse, John is also a full-time college lecturer in Burton. 'I'm probably in the two most stressful jobs you can have and the combination of putting them together makes it doubly worse, I suppose. I'm not sure which is the hardest to handle – players or dissatisfied students!'

The car journeys from Derby to Worcester take an hour and a half each way, which he has to do at least three times a week. There are regular scouting trips on top. 'On Saturday, I'll go out at 10 a.m. and be back at 10 p.m. That's for a home game.'

The obvious question is why do it? 'I wouldn't make regular 140-mile round trips for any other club. Worcester City gave me my chance to get into full-time football. That's the affinity. This club done well by me. I like to think I'm doing well by them.'

Barton's playing career took him from Worcester City to Everton in 1979, then on to Derby County three years later. He returned to non-league football with Kidderminster Harriers, Tamworth and Nuneaton Borough, where he was appointed manager in 1993. He's had three years at Nuneaton, four years at Burton Albion and has been at Worcester for three years so far. There hasn't been too much of an upward curve – it is unlikely John is destined for the Football League.

An intelligent man, he talks touchingly about all his former clubs, large and small. The highlight of his career was playing in Europe for Everton. 'I wouldn't have swapped it for anything. It was every kid's dream. We had Bob Latchford, Colin Todd, Martin Dobson, Dave Thomas, Andy King, George Wood . . . great players.' Now, he's knackered and talking to a scribe who is delaying him from a journey home to his family. A face pops around the door. 'Tea?' 'Yes please,' I reply. 'That's John Newman who used to manage Derby County,' says Barton. 'He helps out sometimes.' Old managers don't die, they just make the tea at non-league clubs.

Worcester City are one of English non-league football's sleeping giants. The club have been keeping their powder dry for a World War One-style big push for promotion towards the Conference from the Dr Martens Premier Division, where they have been trapped for 15 years. When Barton played here, they were the biggest non-league club in the country, attracting big crowds and with a string of FA Cup giant-killings under their belts. Barton feels the frustration of fans who want them to do better, but doesn't understand some of the strange reactions football brings out in people. To take personal stick when doing what is essentially a part-time job is difficult.

'This club has suffered from expectation that hasn't been achieved and couldn't be achieved. The expectation level has been too high. The climate within the game is too aggressive. Football brings out the worst in people. You get spat at, fists punching the air, faces contorted with rage. This is going to sound strange. I don't like it but it doesn't bother me. As long as I'm confident in thinking I'm doing what I can, I'm putting the time into it, then I can live with myself. The person who says they're at their best when the bullets are flying, well, show me someone who says that and I'll show you a liar. A lot of people have had their reputation bitterly hurt by football. The game does hurt you, there's no doubt about that.'

Barton believes there is slightly more managerial security at non-league level – but not much. His job is increasingly complicated by agents, mainly former players seeking to earn from the wages of players who are paid at best a few hundred quid a week at this level. 'I honestly could not see that being as commonplace as it is now when I started in management. It's not the term "agent" that I find irritating but the small word that goes before it – *my* agent. It says something about the ego of a player who wants to use that term "my agent" when you're operating at Dr. Martens Premier level.'

John recalls an agent calling to ask how a client of his was getting on. 'I questioned what concern it was to him. He wanted to negotiate a new contract. I mean, at *our* level? I said, "Isn't it funny how you only ever appear at these times?" He replied "No, I have the best interests of my player at heart." I haven't heard from him since. Never had a call to ask how is so and so doing? Isn't it marvellous how they only call when there are expiry dates coming up on contracts, or when they're looking to move a player on?' It's enough to make you hold your head in your hands on a cold Thursday night.

He has one of the most famous surnames in British football management but Nigel Clough has no intention of following in his father's footsteps – or those of John Barton, his predecessor at Burton Albion, for that matter. Brian Clough's sad association with the bottle, other health problems and 'bung' allegations took the sheen off what was undoubtedly a magnificent career in football management. But the long hours and total commitment of his father to the job are not for Nigel. 'My dad was one of those who worked 100 hours a week. We never saw him so much when we were growing up but that was part of the job at the time. He ran Derby County and Nottingham Forest from top to bottom. One of the attractions of coming here was that it wasn't full time, and you wouldn't be away all day. That was a priority. It wasn't a case of finding a job and getting the family to fit in. It was finding a job to fit in with the family.'

Most of Nigel Clough's playing career was under his father at Nottingham Forest. He had shorter, and less enjoyable, spells at Liverpool and Manchester City. Burton, just promoted to the Nationwide Conference from the Unibond League, is his first sojourn into management. He made a few bob out of football and has one or two other businesses, so he can do most of his work from home. 'You're at the end of the phone but you don't have to physically leave the house. You might be out three, four, five nights a week watching matches – tonight we should have had a reserve game – so you come in early and do your work. The hours still add up, not to the professional level, but they add up.'

Clough's name has been linked with jobs in the full-time game, but for the time being he is content at Burton. I turn up at Eton Park in the middle of the rainstorm from hell. It is a deluge, and Nigel, who is getting out of his car, points to the offices. To shake hands and attempt to exchange pleasantries out here would be madness. 'Just got to make a few phone calls,' he says, as he and club secretary Tony Kirkland make a desperate phone around to let everyone know that the evening's reserve fixture is cancelled. 'It drains really quickly, it will be dry in a couple of hours,' says Nigel, between calls. 'We'll do a bit of training on the edge of the pitch instead.' This is the lovable side of non-league football. All hands to the pump, everyone pitching in. 'It's all part of the job,' explains Nigel, 'you're under no illusions about what the job can hold.'

The management of professional clubs is different to his dad's day. 'The clubs are so big now, with different departments, that I don't think it is feasible or there are characters who can do it now.' At this level of the game, though, Nigel is a proper manager, not a coach. 'A coach goes out on to the pitch and trains the players and deals with the technical side of things. The manager is certainly still applicable because he has to do so many things.'

Like John Barton, he says non-league management is a full-time job done part time. 'You could come here in the daytime and it's deserted because everybody is part time, but there's an awful lot that goes on, more than people imagine. The load gets shared, everybody chips in.'

Clough's team play in the tried, trusted (and successful) family manner. Neat, passing football with lots of movement off the ball, a joy to watch, particularly among the hoofers at this end of the game. His father, who watches Burton occasionally, must be proud.

'Time is precious with the players. You only train once a week if you play a midweek game as well. It is a frustration. You're so busy preparing for the next game you don't get a chance to talk about the last one. We try not to get bogged down with intricate tactics. You just try to instil the basics in them. If you're brought up on certain principles, they stick with you. The other major part of it is getting them to enjoy it because then they will play better. There is no right or wrong way. It's personal choice. We don't always play football. If it needs to go over the stand, that is where we put it.'

More than any other manager in non-league football, Clough's name is inevitably linked with jobs at a higher level. It's the family name, again. 'There's nothing you can do about it whatsoever. Sometimes a reporter from the local paper will ring and say, "I'm sorry but I've got to ask you . . ." I just say, "See you on Saturday." That is all you can say. I have said to the chairman I haven't, and wouldn't, apply for any jobs while I am under contract here, so I don't apply for any.'

The dreaded sack is Nigel's big concern in the game, and the attitude of club chairmen. 'You're not immune from it at this level of the game. Money rules at the moment. With the financial gains everyone is desperate for success, everyone needs it now. But if you look at the teams who have had the managers for the longest time they are the most successful. [The chairmen] pick the manager, so they must be held partly responsible, and if they pick a bad one, then it is up to them to put their hands up and say they made a mistake, but you don't hear too many of them doing that.

'Managers will always have to work for these people – getting the crap end of the stick so to speak. You see someone get the sack and somebody else appointed two days later, and that's not good. Football is a stand-alone sort of business. They sack at will, it's hire and fire. You hope somebody somewhere will see sense and try to get some stability at their club.'

Jake King is a coachaholic. Full-time football to Jake means every waking hour. Not that he sleeps well, either. Jake talks fast, drives fast, does everything, well, fast. There isn't a moment to spare. He squeezes a quart into a pint pot day after day. Unsurprisingly, he has rocketing blood pressure. 'It is going through the roof,' he laughs. You worry for him.

He is the manager of Telford United, who play in the Nationwide Conference. King, a Glaswegian who played in the same school team as Andy Gray, spent most of his career at Shrewsbury Town. He later moved to Wrexham and Cardiff City.

His managerial career with Telford began in 1997. He quickly progressed to league football with Shrewsbury, but was sacked after two years and has had the frustration of seeing his successor benefit from the youth players he developed. King returned to Telford United when their ambitious owner Andy Shaw made the bold decision to go full time in March 2000. Shaw is rebuilding Telford's Bucks Head ground, (and building a hotel on site), but with average gates of 750, maintaining a full-time playing staff has never been financially viable. In October 2001, Shaw announced that the club would revert to part-time from season 2002–03. King was unable to bring in any new faces, which left him with only 12 available players towards the end of the season. Still they finished in the top half of the table.

King works hard for his money. He trains youth and junior teams and has his own club, Shrewsbury Juniors. Every weekday evening, when he isn't coaching, he is out scouting. The long, lonely journeys into mid Wales are a side of the job few fans ever see. He's even picked up a couple of pub players who have progressed to the Football League this way.

The odd thing is that King is financially secure. He bought and sold a couple of restaurants and made a few bob. Cooking, strangely, is his other passion. When he arrives home on Thursday nights, he cooks pasta or bangers and mash followed with bread and butter pudding for his players to munch on Friday lunchtimes. He doesn't have to do this. He enjoys it and believes it helps team spirit if the players spend an hour or so together over a meal.

'Look at me, I'm tired at the moment because I got in at 11.30 last night and I was out at 7.30 this morning. When I finish this interview I'm off again,' he says. With dispirited staff – they were soon to be released at the end of the season – King worked wonders to keep Telford in the top half of the Conference in 2001–02. Vultures were hovering over his players long before the end of the season when their full-time contracts are up and they can leave for free. In the summer of 2002 his side was ripped apart, with his best players leaving for wealthier clubs. It is a painful experience for a man who puts so much into his work. Not that he could easily take to being a couch potato. 'I couldn't sit around all night watching TV. I would go mad.'

King has no truck with 'it's tough at the top' managerial complainants. While in charge at Shrewsbury Town, he went to a LMA meeting and when asked what type of manager he wanted to be replied: 'A lucky one.' Only he didn't use the word 'one'. In particular he has little time for top-name managers who effortlessly glide into top jobs but 'couldn't hold a coaching session if they tried', and insists the higher up the ladder you go, the less coaching you do. 'At this level you have to work harder,' he adds. 'There are people who say, "You couldn't manage at the top level because you never played any higher than the old Second Division." Well, let them come down to our level and see if they could manage here.'

King never lost his appetite for coaching. He spent seven months travelling to Crewe day after day to watch Dario Gradi and observed Howard Wilkinson when he was at Leeds United. He has been to

Ajax, Roma, Porto, Russia and France to ingest the training sessions of top European clubs. To think he does all this to bring it back to Shrewsbury Juniors leaves a warm feeling inside.

He is a big believer in developing young players. At Shrewsbury Town, a club that had been relegated from the Second Division, rather than paying a team of old pros to plod around the park, he worked on the youth team. Having agreed a long-term policy with the chairman, King feels he was prematurely sacked. 'I'm really bitter because the success they've got now is partly because of the things I did. I think if a chairman says he's going to give you five years, then unless you are relegated you should be given five years, because we agreed it would take that long to rebuild the club.'

These are the frustrations of managers who are out there coaching and looking for players day in, day out, night in, night out. They don't get the opportunities that effortlessly fall the way of big-name ex-players. But then there are people working at a level below King who doubtlessly feel he has used his own name as a former Shrewsbury player to become manager of Shropshire's two biggest clubs.

'If anything happened to me and I couldn't be a manager I don't know what I would do, because I would be stuck in every night. I'm used to it and I've done it for years. I've never been motivated by money. I'm motivated by success.'

Not that football management is all about winning. 'At this level you've got to relate to the players. I've had a player here this morning with his head down. He's had a car bill costing him £600, he's only on £200 a week. We've helped him out, because that is what life is all about. Sorting things out for each other.'

The honesty of non-league football is new to Kenny Hibbitt, who had spent the whole of his adult life in full-time professional football as a player, coach and manager until he lost his job as director of football at Cardiff City in 1998. After a break from the game (not always a wise move in management – you soon get forgotten) he relaunched his career at Hednesford in the Dr. Martens Premier Division in the autumn of 2001. He is getting to grips with the realities of life at the grassroots of the game, including the sack.

'I feel as though I'm involved with real honest people now,' Hibbitt told me when we met in February 2002. 'We've had 11 supporters scraping mud off the pitch and putting sand down so we could get the game on. They were filthy. They worked their socks off. That is what football is all about.'

Hibbitt was disillusioned with the direction in which football is heading. His experience at Cardiff didn't help: he was director of football one minute, youth development officer the next. 'That was the first time I lost my enthusiasm since I was a kid. I didn't want to be directly involved. Football as a sport has now turned into a business. The chairmen have got their fingers on the trigger all the time. You lose four or five games on the bounce and irritation sets in. At one time, the chairmen and directors never used to listen to the supporters' opinions. Now the supporters get the managers the sack. They [the chairmen and directors] don't want to take the stick, so they sack the manager. But they never accept that when they appointed these guys, they made the mistake. And when they appoint, they don't give them long enough. It is sad to see some good guys out there, out of work. There are hundreds of great managers around who are not going to get back.'

Hibbitt lives in a charming Cotswold village, the trappings of his years in the game. He played for Wolves, Coventry City and Bristol Rovers, where he went into coaching initially under Bobby Gould and later alongside Gerry Francis. His first chance in management came at Walsall, where he had four turbulent years trying to cope on a tight budget. Then he moved to Cardiff for a yo-yo four-season stint with his differing job titles.

Picture-postcard Gloucestershire is a far cry from his home city of Bradford, where Hibbitt only went to school if it involved PE or sport. He joined his local Football League club, Bradford Park Avenue, in 1966. His first wages were £8 15s 6d. His brother Terry (who died in 1994) joined Leeds United and had a notable career with Newcastle United in the 1970s. Wolves paid £5,000 for Kenny. He couldn't believe that anyone would pay that amount of money for 'a little snotty-nosed kid who'd come out of the backstreets of Bradford. I didn't even know where Wolverhampton was, I just knew it had a First Division club.'

Hibbitt was a committed midfielder who ran his heart out for whichever club he played for. He can't relate to the apparent lack of desire of today's top-flight players. When Kenny played for Wolves he couldn't put his shirt on until he was in the tunnel because he would sweat so much through nerves. His team mate Willie Carr would be physically sick. Football matters. Kenny had palpitations while managing Walsall, and still won't socialise on Saturday evenings if his team lose. 'I don't think they really care enough. I see some managers and players and it doesn't hurt them enough when they've lost.'

After a few years out he has recharged his batteries. Hednesford was a challenge to him. They were relegated from the Conference two seasons ago and Kenny has had to battle hard to keep them in the Dr. Martens Premier Division. It was touch and go for most of the season, but they stayed up thanks to an away win on the final day of the season. Days later he was given the sack. 'I feel like I've been kicked in the teeth,' he told me shortly afterwards. 'I achieved what we set out to do this season – survive – and then plan for next season. I went into a board meeting expecting to talk about a budget and plans for the future and I was sacked. It has been hard to take.'

The experience hasn't dampened his enthusiasm to get back into football at a non-league level. Although working with part-time players has been frustrating (Kenny spent his entire career in the full-time game), they are what he calls 'honest people'.

'Time is so precious at this level. If you over-train them, they have to go to work with aches and strains the next day and that isn't fair. And you can't always get them all together for training anyway. Some are caught on the motorway or stuck at work. It is frustrating, but it does bring a sense of realism. I have got a challenge here at Hednesford. They had only won three out of thirteen before I came. There was no discipline at the club. It was flat – I got it buzzing. It was the hardest challenge I've faced.'

Management at Hednesford was supposed to be a part-time post, and we initially met on a supposed day off. But our conversation was interrupted by a dozen or so phone calls. If he didn't deal with them, things didn't happen. One of his players needed international clearance to play in a trial match in Scotland the following evening. This is the sort of background work the supporters don't see. If you worked at a lathe all day you couldn't do this job. It is time consuming, but Kenny doesn't count the hours.

'I'm at the nitty-gritty end of the game, with the mud and matches called off. It's new to me, but it's great.' At the time of writing, Kenny was looking for a new club. Like all managers in that position he tries to find out what is going on elsewhere. 'Heard any rumours?' he asks me. It's back to the snakes-and-ladders of football management for Kenny Hibbitt.

One of the intriguing aspects of writing a book on football management is the crossover you find between managers, coaches and player. The interconnections in football are fascinating. Links are passed on from one footballing generation to the other; influential characters relay their experiences to younger colleagues, who in turn go on and develop those techniques. Kenny Hibbitt, for example, worked closely with Gerry Francis at Bristol Rovers, who had been a coach with Terry Venables at Crystal Palace. Venables in turn had been a coach with Malcolm Allison – one of the original West Ham academy back in the 1950s.

John McGinlay's career started in the Highland League in Scotland with Elgin City. He moved to Yeovil and Shrewsbury Town. His manager there, Ian McNeil, moved to Millwall and took John with him. Millwall's boss was Bruce Rioch, who is liberally quoted throughout this book. McGinlay followed Rioch to Bolton Wanderers where he enjoyed the best spell of his playing career. Rioch owed much to Frank O'Farrell, Malcolm Allison's old team mate at West Ham in the 1950s. Funny how these things work, isn't it?

McGinlay's managerial career began in January 2001 at Dr. Martens Western Division club Gresley Rovers. Like Rioch, who cleaned the baths at Torquay, and O'Farrell, who pursued players around the country persuading them to join him at Weymouth, McGinlay started at square one. 'If I had waited for a job in the professional game I'd still be waiting now,' he notes. McGinlay is hoping to tread a well-worn path. Martin O'Neill, Ron Atkinson, Howard Wilkinson, Jim Smith and David Pleat are among those to cut their managerial teeth in non-league football.

'I think you're better off doing something rather than nothing. I think at non-league level, if you can progress to the lower end of the

Football League, you are going to come across the same problems – no budget, money is tight, you've got to wheel and deal a bit – that you're going to come across with just a bit more money. It will stand you in good stead.'

McGinlay did a reasonable, if not spectacular, job at Gresley. Steady progress was made in his year and a bit in charge, during which he moved them from the lower half of their league to the top half. He says it has been an eye-opener and good experience.

In the week I completed this book I discovered John had moved to another job a league higher at Ilkeston Town. Steady progress. He is on his way. The long drives from his home in Bolton, when he would ponder over team talks and tactics, have paid off. 'I find the driving gives you time to think about what you're going to do in training or in a match. I think on the way back it can drag – especially if you've been beaten. If you have a midweek away game down in Gloucestershire or somewhere it's a long way back home.'

The hours are likely to be just as lengthy at Ilkeston as they were at Gresley. John drew up a schedule of the week before our conversation:

> Friday night: Left Bolton at 9.30 p.m. Arrived in Burton at 11.15 p.m. Stayed in a hotel.
>
> Saturday morning: Left on the team coach to go to Chippenham at 10.45 a.m, finally got back to Bolton at 10 p.m. Saturday night.
>
> Sunday: Spent three hours on the phone discussing football matters.
>
> Monday: Training night. Leave Bolton at around 3.30 p.m, got back at 11.30 p.m.
>
> Tuesday: Left Bolton at 3.30 p.m, travelled to sign two players on the way in Stoke on Trent. Went down to watch Alfreton v. Belper. Got back to Bolton about 11.30 p.m.
>
> Wednesday: Travel down to Gresley. Leave Bolton at 3.30 p.m. Return at 11.45 p.m.
>
> Friday: All day meeting with the chairman to discuss budgets and the money available for next season. In the evening we have football forum in the social club with supporters. Stay over Friday night.

Saturday: Game at home. Get back about 8.30 p.m. on Saturday.

The total is a 47-hour week for a part-time job. Is it worth it? 'Those are full-time hours. You have to do the hours because you've got to make the calls. You're not doing it for money. The buzz is winning and getting a good squad of players together. I look at the team we've built now and they're good to watch and a good bunch of boys, great characters and it's rewarding because they've come on quite a lot. They've improved as a team. It's my team now – I can't blame someone else. The buck stops with me now.'

Whether McGinlay can progress depends on many factors. Escaping the part-time job done on a full-time basis lifestyle of football's non-league gaffers can be difficult; without the endless hours they put in, non-league football could not survive.

– CHAPTER TWELVE –

From a 'Turnip' to a Swede: International Management and the Continental Coaching Invasion

DURING THE 2002 WORLD CUP, SEVERAL OF THE 44 DESIGNATED cameras placed around each of the grounds focused on the team benches. The demeanour of managers during matches provides an insight for viewers into the trials and tribulations the men in charge of national football teams go through. The story of the World Cup and the pressures managers endure is written on their faces.

Throughout the tournament, England manager Sven-Goran Eriksson stood alone, often physically, maybe even metaphorically. There was no excessive arm-waving, touchline-prowling or fourth official-berating from our Sven. While Eriksson's calm exterior may have belied the fact that inside he was churning with tension, other than the odd rare outburst of emotion he never quite seemed to share the passion of his players and coaches, or the fans. He didn't display any of the mannerisms that are so characteristic of the football-mad nation he was managing. Then again, why would he? He is an outsider looking in.

Eriksson is an enigma. Dubbed 'the Iceman', England's first-ever foreign coach is the epitome of the continental cool guy: studious, multi-lingual, bespectacled, always immaculately suited and booted and, of course, vastly experienced. He is a very un-British football manager; merely the fact of his 'foreign' status made him a mystery to the press when he was appointed in October 2000. Sure, they knew the bare bones – this Swedish coach had managed several top European clubs including Benfica, Roma, Fiorentina, Sampdoria and Lazio in a 20-

year career – but he was an unknown quantity in a country which, until recently at least, did not have a reputation for looking outwards for its football influences. So when Sven took up the reins in January 2001, the British media didn't know how to judge him.

So what led the English FA to appoint its first foreign national team coach? Scepticism about all things across the Channel had melted away during the 1990s. Huge sums of money poured into the leading clubs as a result of their split from the rest of the game to form the Premier League and massive TV deals with Sky were negotiated. Football's broad cross-class popularity and overall gentrification post-Hillsborough (which led to all-seater stadia), with Gazza's tears and Pavarotti's rendition of 'Nessun Dorma' during Italia '90 brought the game's essential theatre to the fore. Nick Hornby's *Fever Pitch* hit the right notes with the previously indifferent chattering classes who had viewed football as a game played – and watched – by oiks.

It was only a matter of time before the PLCs began fishing beyond these shores. On one hand, they were responsible for much of the greed and price-hiking that continues to anger traditional fans who have had to fork out ever-increasing sums to watch football. But, on the other, they brought in chief executives and directors smart enough to headhunt the best players and coaches. And if that meant casting their net beyond the confines of the UK (where returning prodigal sons were traditionally the preferred managerial option) then so be it.

British football had always cast a wary eye across the water. It had its own tried and trusted training methods, its own culture, passed on down the generations. The logic of British football was that the pros knew best. To quote Edward and Tubs from *The League of Gentlemen*, outsiders were 'simply not welcome – there's nothing for you here'. Yet across the English Channel lay a shoal of players, managers and coaches whose outlook and overall professionalism wasn't just different but culturally distinct. By and large (and this is a sweeping generalisation) they were better educated for the job: players in relation to their diet, fitness and technique; managers and coaches as educated sports professionals. That isn't to say such knowledge didn't exist in the UK, but a professional background is more or less guaranteed from those schooled in the top European football countries. British football had succeeded despite its insularity, not because of it.

It is, of course, a two-way street. Occasionally a rare player or coach (Jimmy Hogan in the early part of the century, Vic Buckingham and Ronnie Allen in the post-war era) would feel comfortable coaching on the continent. And throughout the 1980s and early '90s, when the English game had been blighted by hooliganism and dwindling crowds, many top players headed overseas, including Glenn Hoddle, Ian Rush, Mark Hughes, Liam Brady, Ray Wilkins, Graeme Souness, David Platt and Paul Gascoigne. Managers like Bobby Robson (post-England, notably), Roy Hodgson, Terry Venables, Souness and, that most quintessential of English managers, 'Big' Ron Atkinson, had chanced their arm on the continent with varying degrees of success.

But this emigration of British football talent has been insignificant compared to the flood of players and coaches coming into Britain over the past decade. With more than half of all Premiership players now coming from overseas there must be, as the song goes, 'trouble ahead'. Will domestic players in youth development programmes progress to first-team football? And if not, what will the consequences be? Yet there is little doubt that the foreign coaches who have entered British football have raised the standards of the game. Many must have barely believed what they saw when they got here.

Foreign managers are now commonplace (Arsène Wenger, Gérard Houllier, Claudio Ranieri, Jean Tigana, Jozef Venglos, Jan Sorensen, Egil Olsen, Wim Jansen and Dick Advocaat are but a few of those who have contributed to British football). Sven-Goran Eriksson is merely the most high profile. The first foreign manager of an English football club was Danny Bergara, a Uruguayan who played most of his football in Spain but moved to Luton Town in 1974, towards the end of his career. A calf injury finished his playing days but he became a coach, completing his badges in double-quick time. 'It was the only way I got a work permit to stay here,' he said. Bergara was given his full badge and told 'Danny, you've pissed it' long before his course had ended at Lilleshall. 'I was thrilled,' recalls Bergara, who soon carved out a reputation as a youth coach.

Bergara's verdict on the English style of training was damning. 'There was little logic in the training. People didn't know why they were doing certain things. For a country of 55 million people you should have won the World Cup more than once. But you only work on one half of the game – organisation, preparation and tactics – and not enough on skill, technique or fitness.'

Bergara had learnt that football was a game of three verbs: to want, to be able, and to know. 'I was brought up in an environment where the football fever was high. You wanted to play football. To be able to play, you have to be fit to play. Finally, you must know how to play. If you've got all three, you've got a chance. You also need a guy who can improve that game of yours.'

In contrast to Spain, Bergara came across managers and coaches in England who didn't fully appreciate or understand fitness, psychology or medicine. 'It was all tactics and teamwork. How many managers had taken courses in fitness? Now it's different, but back then, most of them didn't have a clue. In Spain, it was part of the overall coaching manual. The technical side was included with the tactical elements in one book. How can you be a doctor without understanding medicine? Unless you've learned how to coach, how can you teach football?'

Bergara, who was an England youth coach, likens developing young footballers to the process of polishing rare diamonds. 'Footballers are exactly the same as diamonds. But we crush them before they are ready to be taken out and shaped. We're trying to shape diamonds that haven't finished their growth – so what happens? They're ruined. You see young kids playing games full of tactics. Let them play, let them dribble. They will learn to enjoy the game. The Gazzas, Georgie Bests and Beckhams of this world, they'll still make it because their technique is good. They can learn the tactical stuff later. That's what they do in Brazil – and there's no shortage of quality players there. We stopped doing that in Uruguay, which is why we went into decline.'

Before he went into league management, Danny worked with the England Under-18s but found himself coaching players whose skill and technique levels were under-developed. 'I would ask them, "How much work do you do on that side of the game?" They would say, 'None – we just play five-a-sides.'''

Five-a-sides. The cornerstone of British football training. Excellent for tight control and neat intricate passing in limited time and space – not to be sniffed at, but surely not the be-all and end-all although the training sessions of majestic European Cup-winning sides like Liverpool and Nottingham Forest consisted mainly of this time-honoured tradition.

Jan Molby, a Danish international who has now carved out his own, albeit so-far lower-league management career in England, joined Liverpool in 1984 from Dutch giants Ajax. What he witnessed wasn't what he was expecting from a club that had won the European Cup four times in the past eight seasons.

'Ajax was a great club for coaching, they probably over-coached us a bit if anything. But they got results and produced some wonderful players,' recalls Molby, whose distinguished career began at Kolding in Denmark. 'When I moved from Denmark to Ajax, it was exactly what I was expecting. I was at a better club and it was hard work every day. I was working with some super players like Johan Cruyff, Marco Van Basten and Ronald Koeman.

'Then you go to Liverpool, who had won four European Cups, and you think this is going to be another step. But it wasn't. There was this big thing about we don't want to over-train, we warm up, we do our five-a-sides and that's it. Nobody ever stayed behind to do extra training, we didn't work on set-pieces. All we did was concentrate on us. I swear we didn't know who we were playing against. We played teams like Austria Vienna in the quarter-final of the European Cup but we wouldn't know anything about them – we would just go out and play. We won 3–0.

'At Ajax we'd have a meeting an hour and a half before games. It was thorough preparation, that was the background I came from. All of a sudden you find this other way where there are no preparations, we just rely on what we are – good footballers. But whoever we played in Europe we would wipe the floor with them.'

Molby is convinced the secret of Liverpool's success did not lie in five-a-sides. 'If you do that type of training for years your touch becomes better but Liverpool handling and picking the best players was the key. That was proved when it started to go downhill. Once the players weren't the best, the club suffered. At Liverpool, I had a lot of respect for people like Joe Fagan and Kenny Dalglish but they weren't coaches, they were managers. There's a massive difference.'

Much has been made of Liverpool's infamous Boot Room – the club's coaching nerve centre where coaches met to discuss managerial matters and, notably, where ideas and opinions were passed down from one generation to the next. 'Obviously that helped,' says Molby. 'The way people were brought into the club and integrated was important. But it has to be down to the amazing ability of the club to keep finding those players. They also had great patience. In the 1970s, when they paid £200,000 or £300,000 for players, which was a lot of money, they were prepared not to include that player for 12 months. That takes something special as well.'

Molby claims Liverpool 'lost it' during football's boom-time in the early 1990s – the era when Graeme Souness came in as manager and attempted to introduce the things he had picked up in his own playing and management career both at home and abroad. His modernisations made sense, but they disrupted the continuity at Anfield and the training ground at Melwood. 'He needed instant success,' recalls Molby, 'because the club had gone 18 months without success which, looking back, was nothing, but at the time, people thought it was huge. So instant answers were what the club went looking for and because of that they went slightly off the rails.'

Molby reckons English managers work too hard on keeping a distance from their players, whereas in Denmark or Holland it's no big deal. 'On the continent, people have a different type of respect for the people they work for. But I think a lot of continental players have respect for themselves. There's not the emphasis on getting players to play for the manager, which is a big thing in this country. Players play for themselves. They have more self-respect. Even if they don't get on with the coach their self-respect sees them through and they still want to do their best. On the continent, coaches have to get a tracksuit on and prove to the players that they're good enough, whereas over here there are still managers who get jobs because of their playing careers. It would never happen in Europe.'

So, while British managers tend to call for more respect than Aretha Franklin, continental managers concentrate on proving themselves. Which brings us back to Sven-Goran Eriksson – who, if rumours are to be believed, hasn't directly taken a training session with the England team yet – bucking the continental emphasis of coaches earning their spurs on the training ground. Perhaps Sven prefers to point to his vast experience and the employment of a coaching team who can do that for him. His role is to oversee things. It makes sense. Typically continental, he is immensely qualified, standing in sharp contrast to his predecessors.

The England manager's post has been described as the second-most important job in the country after the Prime Minister. The decision to award this position to a foreigner took immense courage by the FA. Maybe that's why it happened under a Scots chief executive, Adam Crozier, himself a surprise appointment when he replaced Graham Kelly in late 1999. Crozier, whose own background was in marketing (he joined the FA from advertising giants Saatchi & Saatchi) has rung the changes at the FA. He has streamlined the organisation, swapped Lancaster Gate for Soho Square and rebranded and refocused many of the FA's activities. He has brought in lots of broadly similar 'outsiders' – people with ability rather than a solid time-serving background in football. He has shaken off the FA's dowdy old image and found fresh funding partners (a very new FA word) to come on board.

One of Crozier's most unusual and unexpected acts in his first year in charge was when he walked into the dressing-room toilets at Wembley in order to persuade England coach Kevin Keegan not to quit following England's World Cup defeat by Germany in October 2000. Here, in the crumbling remains of a clapped-out national stadium, Crozier had to convince a football man to the marrow (if not necessarily the most adept coach in the world) to carry on in a job that Keegan admitted was 'maybe beyond him' – a bold admission. Whatever faults Keegan may have, at least he had the humility to acknowledge his limitations. Something new was required. England needed rebuilding – the question was, by whom?

Jimmy Armfield, an FA consultant and former England player, says: 'When you're taking over England, you're not taking over a second-class football nation. You're taking over a soccer-mad nation. It was a question of looking at who was available. They've also got to be able to handle the job, to carry the weight on their shoulders. The expectation of a nation is intense.'

There wasn't an endless queue of likely candidates. Writ large, all of Eriksson's predecessors had faults. Keegan was seen as attack-minded but tactically naïve (indicative, some may say, of his lack of coaching background). Glenn Hoddle had put too much faith in mystics rather than tactics and had to resign in the wake of some ill-advised comments made in a newspaper interview. And the prospect of a return by Terry Venables, who undoubtedly had the coaching nous but had to quit the role to defend court cases, seemed unlikely. Venables had taken over from Graham Taylor, who was seen as a small-time domestic manager out of his depth, vilified as a 'turnip' whose foul-mouthed language aimed at the linesmen in the World Cup qualifier between England and Holland in Rotterdam in 1993 said more about his having agreed to a fly-on-the-wall TV documentary than the real Graham Taylor.

The FA decided to break with tradition and look abroad. They settled on a man who had no international team experience but an impressive track record in European club management in three different countries.

Born in Torsby in Sweden in 1948, Sven-Goran Eriksson had been an undistinguished player for Swedish Second Division side Karlskoga. Like so many managers who turn to coaching at a fairly young age, a knee injury curtailed Eriksson's career and, at 28, he was appointed coach of Swedish Third Division side Degerfors. He guided them to the top flight within three years, then moved onto IFK Gothenburg, taking them to the Swedish championship, two domestic cup titles and the 1982 UEFA Cup final. That same year, he moved to Portuguese giants Benfica where he won championships in successive seasons and, in 1984, switched to Italy to coach Roma and, later, Fiorentina. He returned to Benfica for two years, taking them to the 1990 European Cup final and the 1991 League title. He returned to Italy with Sampdoria (winning the Italian Cup) and Lazio, again winning the Italian Cup, the Cup-Winners' Cup – their first European trophy – and, in 1999–2000, the League and Cup Double.

Although he was forced to resign earlier than expected (he already had the England job) when Lazio went through a poor run of results, Eriksson was released from his contract in January 2001. It wasn't the first time he had considered English management. Eriksson had signed a contract to manage Blackburn Rovers in 1997 but pulled out. He was also linked with Celtic at one point. His record of five championships and assorted European trophies in three different countries was impressive. He was also multi-lingual and a fluent English speaker. He wasn't known for tearing off a volley of four-letter words or stalking the touchline with a menacing scowl on his face. In short, this seemed a man with credentials far ahead of any previous English manager or any domestic candidate standing against him.

Reaction to the historic appointment was mixed. While the tabloids launched into the '20 things you didn't know about Sweden', with IKEA (jokes about whether he would play a flat pack four, etc), ABBA and Ulrika Jonsson (whose reported association with Sven would develop later) frequently mentioned, there was plenty of critical comment elsewhere. The LMA chief executive, John Barnwell, waded in with typical defence of his members, saying it was an 'insult' to English coaches. 'We at the association are not in favour of a foreign coach,' said Barnwell. His opposite number at the Professional Footballers' Association, Gordon Taylor, was similarly defiant: 'There was no consultation with either ourselves or the LMA before this appointment was made, which I do not think is right.'

Even Terry Venables thought the job should go to an English manager: 'If we can't find a young Englishman or two to be groomed, it beggars belief, I can't understand it at all,' he said. 'I'm very English, very loyal and I would want to see an Englishman do the job.' So too did Dennis Mortimer, former Aston Villa captain and now a regional PFA coach. 'Regardless of his results, I think it was wrong of the FA to employ a foreign coach when there are coaches in this country who could do the job. They didn't look at CVs,' added the 1982 European Cup winner.

But when pressed to name names, Mortimer could only muster ex-England full-backs Phil Neal and Mick Mills – good background coaches maybe, but without records in management worthy of leaders of the national team. It was suggested that players might not play for Eriksson, that clubs would be reluctant to release players to the national side (like they had ever shown willing in the past?). In fact, past enmities and strained relations between club managers had caused problems. This was another advantage of bringing in someone from outside. There could be no bad blood between previously competing managers. And there was none of the irritating bias against so-called smaller or unfashionable clubs, whose players had often been overlooked for international duty. Eriksson had the temerity to select one such player in his first squad – Charlton's much-travelled defender Chris Powell. Eriksson simply liked what he saw. Too many of his predecessors had feared a negative reaction.

Eriksson's appointment could have been a disaster. But, polite and personable, he gave likely critics very little to build on. He has been the subject of gentle parody, not least from TV impressionist Alistair McGowan and Radio 4's *Dead Ringers*, but is also admired as an enigma. Because he says so little, people seem to hang on his every word and search for cryptic meanings.

Eriksson has impressed observers with the sheer number of games he watches and has assembled a team of respected coaches who are more than capable of putting experienced internationals through their paces: Steve McClaren, Sammy Lee and Ray Clemence (so much for not developing future England managers). He has also brought in his own people, including assistant Tord Grip and sports psychologist Willi Railo. Eriksson has set an example. 'He brings great dignity to his job,' says Sports Coach UK chief executive John Stevens. 'His dealings with the media are professional, he has been able to motivate pretty demotivated players, he isn't rent-a-quote – he's a coaching role model.'

An impressive string of five consecutive wins for Eriksson won the nation's heart. There was a blip in a home friendly defeat against the usually difficult Dutch, then came the biggie – a do-or-die World Cup qualifying game in Munich in September 2001. Result: Germany 1 England 5. Thereafter Eriksson has walked on water.

Four days after Munich, England put in a distinctly below-par performance but still managed to beat Albania 2–0 at St James' Park to nudge even closer to the World Cup finals. England then very nearly tossed away their advantage by falling behind their final group game at home to Greece, but skipper David Beckham saved the day with that now infamous last-gasp free-kick which gave England an ill-deserved 2–2 draw and a place in the finals in South Korea and Japan. Sven was even hailed as a hero after this performance. Sports psychologist Willi Railo had supposedly helped Beckham when he needed it most. Very little attention was cast upon why psychology hadn't worked for his team mates, who had laboured through the 90 minutes, or why Goldenballs had failed to net just one of so many other set-piece attempts.

Eriksson was even spared the fierce criticism which would have tormented many of his predecessors when England won just one of their next six games leading up to the World Cup finals. But they returned home from Japan as heroes with an estimated 6,000 fans turning up at Heathrow Airport at midnight to welcome their boys back. England had reached the last eight of the tournament, and having beaten old enemy Argentina in the group stage and Denmark in the second phase was seen as enough, despite looking lacklustre against Sweden, Nigeria and especially against eventual winners Brazil.

The manner of the Brazilian defeat raised the first eyebrows about Eriksson's influence; it suggested England have further to go than many had imagined if they are to win the World Cup. Although England had taken a first-half lead, thanks to a Michael Owen goal, the Samba boys equalised in first-half injury-time through Rivaldo. Ronaldinho chipped an early second-half free-kick over a floundering David Seaman's head for the eventual winner.

England's inability to fight back – even after Ronaldinho was controversially sent off minutes after scoring – was alarming. Against a supposed 'flaky' Brazilian defence, they were caught between two stools: neither committed to all-out attack nor crafty enough to carve an opening. In the strength-sapping heat, England's World Cup campaign fizzled out. Late in the game, they didn't resort, as almost every other nation surely would have, to the percentage chance game – looking to pick up scraps from long balls fed in the penalty area. In short, it would appear that for all his grace and composure, one thing Eriksson had not improved was the technical ability of his players. Like every other national team manager, there is a limited amount he could have done in that area; national team managers do not get the players for long enough. The 5–1 thrashing of Germany had been a glint rather than a glow.

Whether England making the quarter-finals of a World Cup in which Senegal, South Korea, Turkey and the USA also reached the same stage is seen as a success long term remains to be seen. As yet, the knives have not been sharpened against Sven-Goran Eriksson. The blank piece of paper upon which the collective British press have yet to write their story of England's first foreign coach has not been written. Even a reported affair with Swedish television presenter Ulrika Jonsson was covered in 'lucky Sven' tones. But, as the previous incumbents found out to their cost, times may change.

Perceptions are all-important. The general feeling is that Eriksson has been a fairly successful England manager; impressive victories over Germany and Argentina would support this view. Defeats by Brazil, Italy and Holland may suggest otherwise.

Graham Taylor's three-year reign as England manager between 1990–93 is generally regarded as a disaster. England didn't do well in the 1992 European Championships and failed to qualify for the 1994 World Cup finals. Against that, Taylor went 12 matches unbeaten at the start of his period in charge (far more than Eriksson) and his win-draw-lose record stands up to scrutiny against all other England managers. Results are always subjective – and there is '30 years of hurt' to consider – but statistics show that most England managers' results have not varied greatly.

Five of England's ten full-time managers (Bobby Robson, Eriksson, Taylor, Don Revie and Venables) have won exactly half of their matches. Walter Winterbottom did slightly better, winning 56 per cent of matches, Ron Greenwood, Glenn Hoddle and Alf Ramsey all won around 60 per cent. Only Kevin Keegan brings up the rear with his 38 per cent win-rate (though his reign was brief and crammed with competitive matches). In terms of draws (and England managers tend to draw between 21 and 25 per cent of games) only Taylor (37 per cent), Keegan (38 per cent) and Venables (44 per cent) bucked the trend. Other than Venables, who only experienced two defeats as England manager, Taylor has the next lowest percentage of defeats – 12.5 per cent. Success or failure, you see, is relative; impressions are all-important.

Despite Taylor's record and the nature of his four defeats: a friendly against Germany; an experimental team fielded in the USA; an unlucky 2–0 defeat against Holland in Rotterdam (famous for Ronald Koeman fouling David Platt with neither a penalty awarded or red card issued); and a defeat by home nation Sweden in the 1992 European Championships, no manager has ever been more pilloried in the press. Taylor is an intelligent, thoughtful man, much more so than the average football manager. He led his Lincoln City players on factory tours to build a bond between players and fans. At Watford, he helped to redefine the link between club and community, introduced the first club chaplain, took Watford from the old Fourth Division to second spot in the First Division and an FA Cup final. He elevated Aston Villa from the Second Division to runners-up spot in the First. He had been the youngest-ever person to complete his full coaching badge at the age of 21 and had coached England junior teams. In 1990, he seemed the obvious choice to replace Bobby Robson. Yet the job almost drove Taylor to kill himself.

'If it hadn't been for my wife and family, I would have been a suicide job by now,' Taylor told a national Sunday newspaper when he resigned as England manager in November 1993. 'If I'd known then what I know now, I would never have taken it. The anguish my family and I have suffered has left me emotionally drained.'

Reflecting some nine years later, Taylor takes a more sanguine view. 'I can look back on 30 years in football management and see it as two years where I had a tough time. When I took over I was the popular choice. I took over what had been a successful England side which had reached the semi-finals of the World Cup in 1990, which is unusual in management because normally you are taking over a side that hasn't done well. I knew I had to change the side because Peter Shilton and Terry Butcher retired, and in three months Bryan Robson had gone too, so I was having to change the side round as well as qualify for the European Championships in Sweden. We went into Sweden in 1992 with only one defeat in 21 games. I was quite happy.'

He was also missing Paul Gasgoigne, England's world-class play-maker. A poor show in Sweden changed things. 'Unfortunately it was a strong championships. There were only eight teams. You had to finish top of your group. We drew with Denmark, drew with France and lost to Sweden after being 1–0 up. We were within 45 minutes of qualifying for a semi-final.' For many fans, Taylor made the fatal error of substituting golden boy Gary Lineker, an experienced international goalscorer, arguably when England needed his talent most.

'I actually gave those people who didn't like me an opportunity to be very critical. I knew I had to then qualify for the World Cup. So the period of coming out of Sweden to November in 1993 when we didn't qualify was very difficult.' England failed – and Taylor was branded as a 'turnip'.

'As much as people refer to *The Sun* and their headline "turnip" and all that sort of thing I have no problems with that. The problems I have are with the media accepting responsibility for what they do. When they caricature you as they did, OK, I can take that. But where are the people who do this when you come up against two 26- or 27-year-old drunken idiots with their sleeves rolled up, tattoos and pints of beer in their hand and think they can talk to you like shit? Where are the media people who have made such personal attacks on you that people read them and think they can talk to you like that? Where is the responsibility of the media then?'

There are many who would say insults come with the territory. This is true: England managers earn good salaries. But Taylor found his family were also pursued by packs of pressmen. 'I was fortunate that my two daughters were grown up and were married so they don't carry my surname, and they were not able to be pinpointed. The biggest problem was my parents, who were elderly and people knew who they were.

'It wasn't what people read about me in the press, it was what was happening to me privately. People would sometimes come up to your house, particularly freelance journalists who were hoping to make some money out of a story, and there were cameras at your house all of the time. After I left the England job I couldn't go home for three days without police protection. People don't know that. The media were camped around my house. You can't do ordinary things. We were in America and we lost to the USA 2–0 and there was a television crew at my parents' house, who were then in their late 70s.

'They knocked on the back door, opened it and walked straight into the kitchen and said: "Well what about your son, now?" I had to stop that. I had to get back and threaten them with legal action. My wife and her mother, who has now passed away, were staying with us while I was in the States. She'd been out doing her ordinary shopping in a supermarket in a wheelchair and there was the media following her around asking her for an interview.'

Who on earth could concentrate on their job with this happening to their family? Instead of addressing the supposed problems with the national team, Taylor had to divert his attention to measures to prevent incidents like this re-occurring. 'The general public don't know that sort of thing is going on when they read the headlines. But the media know it's going on.' This from a manager whose father was a journalist in Scunthorpe. 'I am a strong believer in the freedom of the media. But with any kind of freedom comes responsibility.'

Today, Taylor still carries 'the professional hurt of not qualifying for the World Cup' and the realisation that it didn't work out for him as England manager, a job he had wanted throughout his career. He bounced back to manage Wolves, and Watford again, whom he took from the Second Division to the Premier League (and back down again).

In February 2002, he came out of brief retirement to become manager of Aston Villa for the second time.

'If you let people's comments defeat you then you really are finished. Generally speaking, the media have been very good to me, but there are a handful of people I will never, ever please. They will never have a good word to say about me because that would mean having to admit they had got one or two things wrong themselves.'

Taylor believes coaches are better respected on the continent. 'I can go abroad and the civility and respect I receive as an England manager is so much higher than I get in this country. I remember signing John de Wolf, the Dutch player, for Wolves. He couldn't believe that the manager of a club was addressed by his surname and not as "Mr".'

Taylor may have been out of his depth; he may have lacked the expertise or worldliness to cut it in international football. But did English football really have better candidates to offer when Taylor got the job? If so, why didn't the members of the press who so berated him point out who these people were? And when you judge him on his record, did he really deserve this treatment? Does anyone?

Continental coaches work under similar scrutiny, but do not suffer the same levels of hostility. Unless the status of domestic management in Britain improves it will surely not attract the required level of candidates. That means many more clubs will look abroad, where coaches are both better educated and respected. Dennis Mortimer is saddened by this development because he believes there are good coaches who are not getting their chance. 'I don't want to see more foreign coaches coming into the country. We've got good coaches at a lower level but because their names haven't been in the spotlight like some guys who have played in the Premiership or in top divisions abroad they don't get the chance and they don't get the jobs where the money is and where they can make their mark.'

Even Scotland, a country with an amazing record of producing top coaches and managers, have opted for a foreign manager. In February 2002, Berti Vogts, the former German player and national team coach, replaced Craig Brown, who quit a few months earlier. Brown played for Glasgow Rangers, Dundee and Falkirk and in the same Scottish youth team as Sir Alex Ferguson. His coaching career began as assistant manager at Motherwell, then he was manager of Clyde for ten seasons, taking them from the Scottish Second Division into the First, and developing players like Steve Archibald and Pat Nevin. In 1986, he became assistant national team manager and manager of the Under-21 team. Seven years later, he replaced Andy Roxburgh as national coach.

Like Taylor, his period in charge is widely viewed as one of failure. Yet of his 71 games he lost only nine competitive matches (two against England, two to the Czech Republic, the opening game of the 1998 World Cup against Brazil and other defeats to Morocco, Sweden, Greece and Belgium). Just as England qualified for the World Cup finals with a late, late goal, Scotland let in a goal three minutes into injury time at home to the Belgians. 'It gave them a draw but stopped us qualifying,' recalls Brown. 'A very narrow elimination.' It was the second defeat in his last 12 matches – the other was a friendly against reigning world champions France. 'The perception was that the results were bad or that Scotland were struggling. The only thing that was bad was that we failed to qualify for the World Cup finals. My actual record on paper was reasonably good.'

But, as is so often said, football is played on grass not paper. Despite all the doom and gloom and talk about the pressures of international management, Brown insists it is a great job. 'It's a privilege. You got a tremendous response from the players and fans. Motivation was never a problem. Berti Vogts will get a real good response from the fans, too.'

The public don't see the many hours spent travelling by international managers, whose existence is often nomadic. 'It's not all glamour, because you're in the car or on a plane a lot. You feel you are someone else's property. It's a bit like being in a play. I did miss the day-to-day involvement of coaching a team but I combined the national team manager's job with the technical director's role which meant I was coaching players on courses as well.'

But being an international boss means you cannot switch off – or take holidays. 'I didn't count the hours because my job is my hobby and my hobby is my job. I would sooner go to a game than the theatre. It's your life and it never leaves you. All the time I was Scotland manager, I never had a fortnight's holiday in the summer. It's a distorted type of life but I wouldn't have had it any other way.'

The number of continental managers coming into British football may inhibit the opportunities for domestic coaches. So often, like all other bosses, the 'foreign legion' look to bring in their own backroom staff. But others are shrewder. The two longest-lasting foreign managers in the Premier League are Arsène Wenger at Arsenal and Gérard Houllier at Liverpool. Both have appointed British assistants – Wenger has Pat Rice and Houllier has Phil Thompson (who took over while Houllier was convalescing after suffering a heart attack last season). But they have also brought colleagues from France. Houllier has former French youth team coach Jacques Crevoisier at Anfield, Wenger has former Yugoslav international Boro Primorac with him as first-team coach. Even Eriksson has Tord Grip and Willi Railo.

England's present Under-21 coach is David Platt, who played under Sven at Sampdoria. 'The opportunity came along and the answer was "Yes",' says Platt. 'I miss the day-to-day stuff but you have to ask yourself, "Will I get this opportunity again," so it's worth missing out on some things to get the other.' Platt sees no point in waiting around in league management. Despite his minimal league experience, he has been tipped as a future England manager. 'As an England Under-21 manager, I went into it young but, to me, it doesn't matter what age you are, the important thing is you earn respect. I can't go in there and demand it.'

That is the same for all managers – and arguably the foreign coaches in British football will have to work even harder to gain their respect. After all, unless they plied their trade here first they cannot rely on tried and trusted former player links which buys so many managers precious time. Perceived continental charm will only last so long.

Frenchmen Wenger and Houllier have untypical football backgrounds. Wenger graduated from the University of Strasbourg with an economics degree while Houllier was a student teacher in Liverpool in the late 1960s and stood on the Kop to watch matches. French football gave them the chance to divert from their original career paths, but if they'd been British this would have been virtually impossible. It's unlikely the game would have accepted them.

Whether the likes of Houllier and Wenger remain the exception to the rule in British football remains to be seen. There is much talk of a domestic coaching culture being developed within a new framework of courses being shaped under the FA's technical director Howard Wilkinson. Unless the British, and more specifically the English game, sharpens up its act, it seems that clubs will continue to look to the continent for both players and managers.

– CHAPTER THIRTEEN –

Gearing Up the Gaffers of Tomorrow

> You can't be a professional unless you have a dedicated body of
> knowledge, unless you have a ladder of qualifications which
> you have to go up, unless you have a professional/ethical basis.
>
> Howard Wilkinson

IF, AS THE STATS SUGGEST, YOU'RE ONLY LIKELY TO BE IN A LEAGUE
manager's job for 18 months, it's probably best to get yourself geared
up. And fast. Chapter Seven put the case for clubs to appoint qualified
managers above ex-players, who use their popularity to get managerial
jobs rather than any proven ability to coach. There is overwhelming
support for the introduction of mandatory coaching qualifications.
Only those tired-eyed professionals who fear the game will be
mysteriously overrun by 'schoolteachers', and club directors, who
reckon it might cost them a few bob, are against it. The question is,
how should we gear up the gaffers of the future?

History has shown that it is impossible to prevent managers from
delving into other aspects of the business, and at lower and non-
league clubs this is essential anyway. So do we need something more
than just coaching qualifications? Also, how do we develop a
coaching strategy that isn't piecemeal, that doesn't work in isolation
from events in other countries and other sports, that is a beacon for
other sports – who don't have have the benefit of football's immense
finances – to follow?

In 2003, all clubs entering the Champions League will need to have
a coach or manager on their staff who has a UEFA Pro coaching licence

– or else. This is the top coaching award you can get. It is recognised around the world and has been standardised so it means the same in different countries across Europe. It carries weight. In most countries you won't stand a chance of getting a top job unless you have either a Pro licence or the next level down, the UEFA A licence. But it is new to England. We, as ever, are playing catch-up.

But coaching is only part of the story. Would-be managers need to prepare in a variety of ways given the current climate and rapid turnover. So many disappear without trace or after one or two attempts at being a boss. Where do they go?

Like a World War One army captain, about to send the clean-limbed, fresh-faced boys over the top into a hail of fire across No Man's Land, you almost feel like giving Corporals Moyes, Cotterill and Co. a tin helmet, a swig of army rum and a firm 'good luck old chap, you'll need it' handshake. Oh, and don't dilly-dally on the way . . . These keen-eyed up-and-coming managers need more than the misguided faith of those off to 'hammer the Bosch'. Unless they have a Baldrickesque 'cunning plan', you fear they will be cut to ribbons by enemy artillery – the massed ranks of the press corps and those cruel snipers, who carp and cower from the side. Managers need guts and a fair go, but they also need education, education, education.

So how do we go about it? There is genuine optimism in the country at the moment because of the great strides being made since Howard Wilkinson went to the FA as technical director in 1997. He has, in some ways, cemented the classic divide that has hampered the training of coaches and managers in England since time immemorial.

In earlier chapters I explained how and why Britain lags far behind most of the other major countries in Europe. But separating the British nations for a moment, even Scotland, with its limited financial resources and Auld Firm polarisation, has a healthy track record in coach education. For example, it developed its own version of the UEFA Pro licence well ahead of England. In March 2002, Scotland had 42 Pro licence coaches. Unless they were trained elsewhere, England has none. England's first batch will qualify in the summer of 2002. Some of them have already been sacked by their clubs!

We are miles behind Europe's leading football countries. We are 57 years and counting behind Germany, who have 53,000 UEFA certified coaches compared to less than 3,000 in England. Mandatory qualifications were introduced in Germany after World War Two and a national coaching centre was developed at Cologne University. In Italy, prospective Serie A managers have to sit a one-year university course. Holland's coaching system is based on Germany and France, who have 17,000 UEFA coaches and a national football centre at Clairefontaine, near Paris.

Coaching development has been held back by enmity between the professional game (motto: we're pros – we know best) and the perceived amateur academics at the FA. There is belligerence on both sides.

One of the ludicrous old pro's myths is that there is too much coaching going on. The game, somehow, coaches the supposed 'natural' talent out of players. What rot. Coaching can, equally, coax the talent out of players – a point that is often ignored. As for 'natural talent', clubs can no longer whistle down a mine and up pops a centre-forward. And children don't hone superb skills by dribbling a pine cone down cobbled streets anymore. The game *has* to be coached.

The divide between the pro game and amateur academics is quite sad. The FA didn't even have a coaching department until after World War Two. Walter Winterbottom was the first head coach and made great strides. In 1963 he handed the baton to Allen Wade. Winterbottom, for all his charm, was viewed by some elements of the professional game as 'a teacher'. Wade is a former part-time Notts County player and PE teacher who became a trainer at Loughborough University. He established a network of regional coaches, including several who went on to become top managerial names like Howard Wilkinson, Bobby Robson, Dave Sexton and Terry Venables. That was the success. His failure, he says, of his 20 years in charge was 'a lack of authority to compel clubs to employ qualified coaches'. He blames this on 'the cronyism among club directors and chairmen who prefer to appoint successful players, who then bring in their own friends as coaches rather than qualified staff. Walter Winterbottom, myself and my successor all failed in getting things changed,' Wade explained.

Winterbottom introduced two professional coaching courses, the preliminary badge and the full badge, which were one-week courses and have now been renamed in line with UEFA standardisation (the

UEFA A and UEFA B licence). Wade managed to get the full badge extended to a two-week course – still miles behind the other top European countries, but progress.

You might think the professional clubs, so resistant to change, so wary of 'teachers and scout masters', might have gloried in the ease with which its community could become qualified. Yet they even objected to this basic requirement becoming mandatory. They simply drew on their cigarettes and muttered 'no chance'. We're pros – we know best. Now run along.

Armed with a technical department consisting only of a director, an assistant, eight regional coaches and ten administrative staff, Wade wasn't able to wield enough political power on the FA Council, or any of the notorious committees. He left in 1982 after he had 'lost' both the war and the will. 'I wanted England to follow Germany's lead in developing coaching education; the others didn't.'

The 'others' were the committee men from the professional game. 'I was an embarrassment to them. We couldn't get the clubs to agree on professional coaching. Money was behind it. The clubs have the money and influence on the committees. I wanted to introduce mandatory qualifications that might have cost them some small sums. It was important to set a role model throughout all levels of sport. It is ridiculous that clubs don't treat their managers as professionals and don't ask for qualifications when they employ managers. Because no one has given them an exact role or asked them to stick to a coaching role they make one up for themselves.'

Sadly, while all this in-fighting went on, English football was shifting through its sacking gears. More bosses were getting the boot than ever. Few standards were being set, bosses were openly being tapped up to replace one another, former 'names' continued to get jobs because they couldn't think of anything better to do. Coaching equalled boring.

Players objected to going on FA courses because they weren't taught by their own kith and kin. Dennis Mortimer, the former captain of 1982 European Cup-winners Aston Villa and now a PFA regional coach, explains. 'The FA coaches weren't professional footballers in any way, shape or form. They went to college or university and became coaches by working for the FA. It's not to say they weren't good at coaching and getting the message across. They were very good, but the pros resented the fact that they had never played the game.'

Frank Clark, the former Newcastle and Nottingham Forest player, who went on to manage Leyton Orient, Forest and Man City, doesn't agree with Wade's assumption that he was unpopular with the pros. 'Allen Wade was well thought of by the professional game. He was a terrific coach. It was Charles Hughes, his successor, who was the problem. He was an academic who lived in an ivory tower and was reluctant to come out of it. A number of the courses ran by the FA fell by the wayside because no one would take them up.'

Hughes is a much-maligned character. He did not speak to journalists, reputedly not even to the FA's own press office if he could avoid it. He was seen as an FA timeserver, awkward, aloof and out of touch – someone who actually enjoyed the FA's internal politicking. Fleetingly, he was pilloried as a national laughing stock when he released his coaching manual, *The Winning Formula – Soccer Skills and Tactics*, in 1990. Wrongly, it was viewed as an advocacy of the crude long-ball game popularised by Wimbledon, Sheffield United, Cambridge and Watford in the 1980s. But Wimbledon's Crazy Gang antics had as much to do with thrusting elbows into faces and grabbing goolies as it did with long passes. Subtle it wasn't. The game's purists panned this style of football and its limited use of skill. They were looking for a scapegoat and couldn't believe their luck when an apparent blazered boffin from the FA strode over the horizon clutching his life's work to his chest. Hughes might have been able to work the committee corridors of Lancaster Gate but his antennae regarding the wider public was way off beam.

This wasn't surprising. Hughes had seemingly spent the best part of his 25 years at the FA (ever since he had been recruited by Wade from Loughborough in 1964) tucked away in a darkened room nerdishly watching 16mm film footage of old matches. Nice work if you can get it. Rather than concentrate on sublime skill, Hughes counted the number of passes that led to goals. It told him that 87 per cent of goals came from five passes or less. Better still, that the way to cut down on the needless tip-tapping of possession football was to hoist the ball into the opposition penalty area as quickly as possible.

Hughes did not think there might conceivably be mitigating circumstances to goals being scored with a small number of passes. Maybe lots of seemingly unproductive 'possession football' – a phrase Hughes spits across the pages of *The Winning Formula* – would lure defenders out of position? Neither did he consider that this desperate search for a calculable winning strategy was a waste of his time, and that of his PA, Mandy Primus, who had to patiently take shorthand notes as Hughes, eyes propped open with matchsticks, gazed at the screen.

Hughes comes to his conclusion with a depressing joylessness. His *Winning Formula* is obsessed with a mantra that five or less passes leading to a goal equals good, six or more equals bad. Football was, said Hughes, 'long on opinion, short on facts'. And his facts proved that there was such a thing as a winning formula. Your opinion counted for nothing.

Hughes recommended whacking the final ball into the opposition's final third and urged attacking teams to shoot on sight. Teams who had ten shots on goal in a match, he reasoned, inevitably scored more goals. There was no subtle analysis, few shades of grey. That would win you matches. The records prove it. Hughes wasn't bothered about the quality of opportunities – that a team might only need three quality chances to score, say, three goals, or that endless attempts to shoot from all angles would inevitably produce weaker efforts. That the director of coaching in England, at a time when there was widespread concern about the wider effects of the long-ball game and the technical deficiencies in the English game, did not recognise that this would be routed in the media is deeply disturbing.

Hughes was unrepentant. Even those exponents of possession football, the 1970 World Cup-winners Brazil, scored two-thirds of their goals in five passes or less, he reasoned, pointing out that four out of the five goals scored in the Mexico final were from moves involving five or less passes. The exception, and Hughes was well up for it now, was the final goal of the game, Brazil's fourth, which Hughes describes as 'a goal scored in the dying minutes against a dispirited side'.

These words are barely comprehensible to any fan of the beautiful game. Yes, he was talking about *that* goal. You know the one. You've probably seen it tens of times, scored by, arguably, the greatest side of all time. The one that starts with a defender (a central defender, mind) dribbling the ball around a few players. There's a lay-off, a delicious long ball curled down the left, a neat swivel inside and another lay-off to Pelé, who nonchalantly stops the action and, without looking, rolls the ball out to the right edge of the penalty area where the overlapping full-back Carlos Alberto races in to lash the ball hard and low into the net. Football doesn't get any better than that.

Everything that is wonderful about football, and the Brazilians in particular, is encapsulated in those mouth-watering moments. As ten-year-old boys, we'd spend our summer holidays trying to replicate what we'd seen on our TV screens. Our imagination was fired by skill, not by 'lumping it'. We played football all day, joyously. Twenty years later the supposed top coach in the country dismisses it as 'a late goal against a dispirited side'. Incredible. Hughes' analysis in *The Winning Formula* dismisses the notion that the Italians might actually have been 'dispirited' because they couldn't get the ball off a more technically efficient team. What a soulless way to view football.

Allen Wade, while accepting that Hughes 'maybe expressed it a bit too keenly', leaps to his former colleague's rescue: 'He espoused a version of football I would recommend,' suggesting that the modern-day Arsenal and Manchester United sides also play fast attacking football. 'Charles was vilified in the press because they were looking for someone to blame for the perceived lack of skills around.'

Maybe, but his words exposed the bunker mentality inside the FA. The pro game had had enough. Three of the interviewees for this book are so disgusted with *The Winning Formula*, which is an FA textbook, that they refused to 'waste their time' talking about it. The players no longer trusted the FA to turn them into coaches. In 1996, the year Hughes left the FA, the PFA stepped into the breach. They set up their own coaching department to deliver coaching courses to professional players.

Joe Joyce is the current head of the PFA coaching department and one of seven regional coaches spread across England. A former Barnsley, Scunthorpe and Carlisle United player, Joe's imagination was fired by Ian Evans, a coach at Barnsley. Joyce is a big believer in theory being passed through generations of footballers. Evans played under Terry Venables at Selhurst Park, as did Peter Taylor. Venables had worked under Malcolm Allison and so it spiralled back to the West Ham academy of the 1950s and Walter Winterbottom's seminal influence. Mick Wadsworth and Mervyn Day, who had been managed by Ron Greenwood and Howard Wilkinson, are other inspirations.

The PFA educate an estimated 600 players a season. They run three courses – the coaching certificate, which is part of a course academy scholars are expected to take (allowing them to coach Under-14s), and the UEFA A and B licences. The B licence and coaching certificate are run as an independent franchise by the PFA. The more detailed A licence is a residential course comprising of two two-week elements, each one costing £2,000 (though the PFA pay two-thirds of their members' fees). It takes a year to complete and is operated in conjunction with the FA.

'It is very expensive, but these are potentially very good coaches and they are committed to getting the qualification,' says Joyce, who claims a whole generation of players went unqualified because they wouldn't take the FA-run courses. 'The creation of our department was to encourage them back into the network. The FA staff at the time came from an education and academic background rather than a football background. They didn't like the style of play. It seemed too rigid and very direct.'

Joyce doesn't share the grudges some of his profession hold against Charles Hughes, but acknowledges something had to change. 'You've got two cultures clashing there. If you've got an academic trying to tell you how to play as a back four having had no experience themselves then players found that difficult, just as an English literature teacher would find it difficult if a player was trying to tell him what Chaucer was trying to bring out in his work. It's not to say they didn't understand the nature of the game, but they came to loggerheads sometimes.'

Without a mandate there was no incentive for players to take qualifications. 'Senior players, who had a good name as a player, almost seemed guaranteed to walk into a manager's or coach's job. I think you've got to be more forward thinking than that,' says Joyce, who believes there is still a problem with top-name players. 'Stuart Pearce (who managed Nottingham Forest briefly), at 34, was a classic example. He wasn't prepared and wasn't successful. So now he knows he needs to be qualified because he knows what his shortfalls are.'

The PFA have had an input into the development of the English UEFA Pro licence. There is a lot more jaw-jaw than war-war since Howard Wilkinson took over as technical director at the FA. Joyce says players on this élite course are developing a true English coaching culture. 'It is very much a think tank. They're on the course together, they speak to each other, and they cross-fertilise ideas among each other so it is breeding a coaching culture. If we can develop this pool of top coaches then it can only benefit the game overall.'

Time, then, to meet the man charged with overall responsibility for the Pro licence and many other coaching developments – Howard Wilkinson. The public image of Wilkinson is largely negative. Words like dull, dour, boring and methodical are often used to describe him. He is seen as a tracksuit tactician, obsessed with coaching minutiae and training ground chores. You don't expect him to be engrossing company – but that's precisely what he is.

We met in a Derbyshire hotel far away from prying eyes, a bustling office and the hubbub of the football world. Howard was relaxed, open, honest, articulate and in no particular hurry. This was not what I expected. We literally had a fireside chat.

Howard's own story, touched upon elsewhere in this book, is worth recapping. He started his playing career with Sheffield Wednesday, moved to Brighton and Hove Albion for four years but found the life of a professional footballer unfulfilling. He quit the professional game (having had his coaching appetite whetted by Steve Burtenshaw, who taught the preliminary badge to Brighton's players), to study for a PE degree in Sheffield. He played, coached and later managed non-league Boston United part time while studying for his degree, introducing some of the theory he was learning at college, often from other sports and subjects like physiology, diet, fitness and psychology, into the sceptical world of football. A deep thinker and a natural disciplinarian, Wilkinson took to teaching tactics with ease. Thorough preparation and practice made perfect. Boston were successful and Wilkinson managed the England semi-professional team (the pick of the country's non-league players). He became an FA regional coach and eventually an England Under-21 coach.

His first sojourn into professional management came at Notts County, where he had been assistant to gap-toothed legend Jimmy Sirrell. Under Wilkinson, County went up into the First Division in 1981, for the first time in 55 years. Amazingly, they stayed there for three seasons. In 1983, he moved to Sheffield Wednesday, winning promotion in his first of five seasons at Hillsborough. He left in 1988 to pick up the potentially poisoned chalice at Leeds United, who were struggling near the foot of the Second Division. Again, he took them up in his first season and two years later they won the First Division championship. He was sacked by Leeds in September 1996 and took up his current post at the FA shortly after, where he has also managed the England Under-18s, Under-21s and, temporarily on two occasions, the full national side. He is chairman of the LMA.

Wilkinson has the respect of all parties. The professional game recognise he was a player and a hugely successful manager. He is also an academic. He understands and empathises with both sides and can talk freely and knowledgeably about all aspects of football. He can see the shortcomings of the 'we're pros – we know best' stance, and football's age-old suspicion of sports science and academic principles. Equally, he knows you can't talk down to professional sportsmen. They have been there and done it.

He pulls no punches when it comes to the need to train managers for the job. 'You can't be a professional unless you have a dedicated body of knowledge, unless you have a ladder of qualifications which you have to go up, unless you have a professional/ethical basis. You wouldn't send your children to a school which had unqualified teachers, you wouldn't send them to a hospital which had unqualified doctors. People say, "I played for 15 to 20 years, that means I know most of what there is to know about the job." Well, I say to them, "I know lots of people who have driven cars around for 20 years. I wouldn't say they were good drivers or can teach other people to drive."

'We will never have the stability and standards we require if we have this workforce which has no boundaries. If you can recruit a manager from anywhere it's going nowhere. One of the benefits of qualification is that it limits the workforce available. At the very least, it proves you are interested in doing the job and have the staying power to do the qualifications. If someone says "I love the job" but packs it in halfway through, I would question how much you really do love the job. It is a filtering process.'

Wilkinson has needed to win political support within the FA, but doesn't spend every waking hour lobbying the committee and the FA Council. 'It has been difficult to make changes because of the lack of respect within the professional game for the FA's technical department. I had to learn the politics of getting people to agree with you. Most of the crucial decisions require rubber stamps. There have been one or two we haven't been able to get through, but eight out of ten isn't bad. It would be a problem if every time you suggested something you lost.'

Wilkinson remembers the problems his predecessors had – in particular Allen Wade. 'Allen Wade was far thinking. A prophet in his own land. But it was like watching someone walking into a tunnel. There's light at the end but it's full of cobwebs, and the further he goes in the more these cobwebs surround him. While he can see the light and he can see the way forward, he can't get there.'

The cobwebs, claims Wilkinson, were the committee structure within the FA and the prejudice existing outside it, 'the professional game which dismissed a lot of wider ideas purely out of ignorance'. The sort of people who attack Wilkinson's predecessors in a vague belief that coaching per se ruins supposed 'natural' talent.

'Over a five-year period, I've managed 37 games with the Under-18s, Under-21s and the senior team. We've conceded one goal off set-pieces. Is it because I've been lucky, or because the way I see critical issues in set-pieces must be right?

'There is a need in football to reduce everything to the lowest or shortest common denominator. Everything is pigeon-holed. So coaching, training, practising, rehearsal equals boring, kills flair. But that is the antithesis of the process. What is it that makes the good golfer of today, like Tiger Woods, drive as straight and long as he does, but then be able to produce the miracle recovery shot? Are they saying, "Yes, but Woods practises, he's different"? What is it with snooker players? What is it with basketball players? Preparation, practice and training done properly, and properly organised, actually liberates people to use flair.

'The more successful a unit is, the more opportunities the unit has got to exploit situations and to do it with a flourish. It puts layers onto your understanding. When you do something for a long time the thinking says "Now I understand how to do that". They can then say, "I think there's a better way of doing it." It's fundamental to the production of players.'

Wilkinson is, above all, a long-term planner. Everything he has set out to do links into one cohesive plan: many elements for the improved quality of coaching of young players are laid out in 'A Charter for Quality'. His other plans include the development of players and coaches to international level and the building of the national football centre near Burton-upon-Trent.

Designing the English version of the UEFA Pro licence, the highest coaching course for those managers expecting to coach in the Premiership or top European leagues, has been another of Wilkinson's key tasks. 'When we sat down to discuss how we were going to deliver the Pro licence with my staff I made it clear that it should deal with the problems you encounter. It's got to deal with practical situations.'

The Pro licence is a 240-hour-long course. It can take six months or six years to complete. 'Countries do it differently. In Germany people go to Cologne University for 13 weeks. In Italy it takes six months. Ours is unique. It's a one-year course with work experience type stuff, distance learning, using the Internet, DVDs, CD Roms and audio tapes.'

It has been put together this way because English football is playing catch-up. 'We've had to operate within the historical context in which we exist. The people we want to have the Pro licence are already managing. We can't do a conventional course because they couldn't take the time off work. In Italy you take the licence ahead of coaching a club team.'

Eleven managers started the inaugural licence in July 2001. They qualified in summer 2002. Then another batch began – including England Under-21 boss David Platt (who had just completed his A licence) and England women's coach, Hope Powell. The aim is to develop enough Pro licence coaches so that Premiership clubs will be able to appoint only those managers with this advanced qualification.

'We want to end up with a group of students who haven't yet been given the job of running a first team.'

Wilkinson says there are few objections among the Premiership clubs to bringing English football in line with most top European countries by introducing mandatory qualifications for anyone looking to manage a club. The Football League may also agree, but may favour a lower level of qualification.

Eleven coaches took the inaugural Pro licence course, which began with sessions by Fabio Capello and Sir Alex Ferguson, Ipswich Town chairman David Sheepshanks and sports psychologist (and now assistant manager at Middlesbrough), Bill Beswick. Three Premiership club coaches: Chris Houghton, Sammy Lee and Mervyn Day; three First Division managers: Dave Jones, Terry Burton and Dario Gradi; one Second Division manager: Lawrie Sanchez, and one Third Division manager: Steve Cotterill are on the course. A further three, Alan Smith, Stewart Houston and Noel Blake, all lost their jobs within the first few months of the course. It was ever thus!

Pro licence students learn a wide range of skills from coaching to man management, diet and fitness to physiology and psychology; communication, planning and evaluation. Wilkinson hopes it will also help managers to concentrate on doing what they do best – coaching – rather than delving into other aspects of the business.

'The clubs want it. The PLC clubs want clearly defined areas of responsibility. They have got to have accountability. There cannot be any doubt as to who is responsible for what. That is not only professionally desirable but is becoming legally obligatory. The PLCs cannot be vague in transfers, there is too much at stake.'

Despite the fact that managers are involved in all sorts of decisions, duties and responsibilities at clubs, they didn't have a collective group to represent their interests until relatively recently, when the LMA was formed from an idea by then England manager, Graham Taylor, in 1992.

'I don't see the LMA as a trade union, but I do see it as an organisation where it can be involved in negotiations about the future of the game or changes in the game,' says Taylor. 'We never had a voice before. When you've only got 92 managers at any one time you can't be a trade union going into a situation where you would threaten this or that – but you can have professionalism, status and a standing about you – that makes people think well of you.'

The LMA was, for example, involved in designing the Pro licence course (how could it not when its chairman, Wilkinson, is the FA's technical director?). In May 2002 the Association launched its own business management course with the help of the Footballers' Further Education and Vocational Training Society.

'It's called a Certificate of Applied Management,' says John Barnwell, the LMA's chief executive. 'It's designed for future managers. We're saying that to work in the professional game you should have the advanced coaching licence, which should be mandatory, and if you are looking to *manage* you should take the Certificate of Applied Management, which is specifically geared to football.

'It is business oriented to give you an insight into what the chief executive, financial director and marketing director do because that impacts upon your job. The dressing-room might be your inner sanctum, but you must also have some knowledge of the outside area of the football club.'

The certificate consists of a summer school, five one-day seminars and distance learning aids, and is taught by the University of Warwick. It is financed by the LMA, the PFA, the FA and the Premier and Football League. Wales manager, Mark Hughes, was among those who enrolled for the first course. It will also teach bosses how to manage people, personal effectiveness, business planning, strategy and marketing. In short, the sort of skills you would need if you wanted to manage in any other working environment, but which football clubs, despite their huge profile, have traditionally ignored.

'The days of "no comment" are long gone,' says John Barnwell of managers' relationship with the media. 'Minutes after the game has finished the manager has another career and he has to learn that career. He will be judged on what he says during that five-minute interview. So he has to have some skills to handle it. The likes of Houllier, Wenger and Eriksson handle it better than the domestic managers because they've been through an education process.'

The days of learning the ropes lower down and working your way up are likely to be on the way out. Some might say that football management is a bit like ski jumping – the only way to really understand is to experience it. Ian Atkins, now at Oxford United, is in favour of the Pro licence but is unhappy that it is by invitation only. 'If you aren't invited, you can't take it. Who are the people they are inviting? Their friends, who probably haven't achieved anything.'

Ray Graydon, the former Walsall manager, now at Bristol Rovers, also has his doubts. 'I've been invited by Howard Wilkinson onto the Pro licence list but I'm saying where are the Glenn Hoddles on that list? I got my full badge some time ago and I've upgraded it to the UEFA qualification. But we have two past England managers who haven't got the A licence. How can that be right? All the people doing it are guys like me. I want to do it, and I believe in it, but it should be for everyone. The guys who are on the course at the moment are at the bottom of the ladder wanting to go into the Premiership. The Lawrie Sanchezs and Steve Cotterills of this world are earning peanuts in comparison to the other guys who won't take it.'

David Sheepshanks, who is on the FA's international committee, believes clubs should educate all of their staff, starting at the top. 'Both myself and the Ipswich manager George Burley take training courses each year, as do all members of the club staff, to improve our understanding of the business. Football managers should be no exception.'

Sheepshanks is a forward-thinking chairman; he is determined to change the gaffer's lot and to raise standards throughout clubs. The long-term future of the gaffer is at stake.

– CHAPTER FOURTEEN –

I Will Survive: Does The Gaffer Have a Future?

Most managers have been in a situation where they are one defeat away from the sack.

Frank O'Farrell

IN JANUARY 1990, WITH MANCHESTER UNITED'S TITLE HOPES once again fading to dust, Alex Ferguson took his team to Nottingham Forest for an FA Cup tie. He was under pressure – on the ropes. The knives were out for Ferguson, who hadn't won anything in four seasons at Old Trafford. Had United lost, speculation was rife that he would lose his job. The City Ground was Ferguson's last chance saloon. United won 1–0.

So who saved Fergie? Bryan 'Captain Marvel' Robson? The mercurial Mark Hughes? Mike Phelan? No; it was Mark Robins, a 20-year-old fair-haired striker from United's youth team. A smartly taken chance at the Trent End by a soon-to-be-forgotten United starlet settled an awkward away tie and kept Ferguson in the manager's chair. They came through two entertaining semi-final games against Oldham Athletic to reach the final, where they beat Crystal Palace, again over two matches. But it could all have been so different, not just for Ferguson but for Manchester United.

This is the knife edge that football managers live on. Football is a results-based business. Managers are powerless to dictate matters once their players cross the white line. They can encourage and cajole; they can attempt to extract the maximum effort from their players, they can shout themselves hoarse and wave their arms about in an animated fashion. They can bring on substitutes, berate referees, but ultimately their jobs, their futures, are decided by the performance of their players. This powerlessness, felt by people who are, quite often, control freaks by nature, haunts many a manager. Their careers are in the hands of others.

This precarious occupation requires a particular breed of person. When the flak – or at least the spittle, hurled programmes and verbal abuse – is flying, you need to be strong to survive, to have balls of steel. For all of English football's attempts to create a continental milieu in the Premiership with its plethora of international players and coaches, for all its corporatism, slick marketing and £800 season tickets, the prevailing climate is basically the same. What do we want? Results. When do we want them? NOW! It would be wildly optimistic to expect this to change. Time waits for no man, and it taps its wrist impatiently at football's gaffers.

Football management in Britain has traditionally attracted a certain type of person: ebullient, strong, hard-faced; characteristics construed to show they can cope with the rigours of management. The job particularly suits ex-defenders or midfield grafters. But is the death knell ringing for the old-style gaffers, people like Bruce Rioch, who cheerfully describes himself as 'a dinosaur', or dugout doyens like Jim Smith, who started at Boston more than 30 years ago and has jokingly had 'more clubs than Jack Nicklaus'. He was sacked twice in 2001–02, but when you've managed as many clubs as he has the sack loses its fear. He's already back in management at Portsmouth

Is football going all touchy-feely? Gary Megson brought the players' wives and girlfriends into the West Brom dressing-room before their final match of the 2001–02 season against Crystal Palace, when a win would send them up into the Premiership and told them 'This is who you're playing for.' The missus doing a team talk – whatever next?

And then there is the appliance of sports science. The old days and ways of hands-on management are on the way out. Most of the younger managers I have interviewed for this book are open to new ideas. They are not afraid, for example, to utilise the expertise of a team of sports specialists to get the best out of their players. They understand there is more to motivation than throwing the teacups around. Mark McGhee at Millwall, for example, spends a six-figure sum a year on diet and nutrition, ensuring his players' body weight is less than ten per cent fat. 'In the past there was a fear factor when it came to sports science,' says McGhee. 'At Millwall we employ a company to work with the players' physiology, diet, vitamin and mineral intake and to taper their training towards performance. The result is players are fitter now.'

At Cheltenham Town, Steve Cotterill (a widely tipped managerial star), who moved on to First Division Stoke City in May 2002, spent more money on the quality of their pitch than any individual player. 'How can they improve as players if they can't pass the ball to one another?' he reasons. Cotterill is appalled by the ambivalence fellow league clubs show towards the surface they play on.

'No one has any excuses for not playing good football on our pitch,' Cotterill told me while managing Cheltenham. 'I think you've got to create an environment where players want to come every day, want to train, want to play, want to work, so it is not a chore.' Cotterill even researched the exact sub soil of Cheltenham's playing area and the type of turf they need. Many older managers would balk at this sort of thorough preparation – but they aren't being tipped for the top, like Cotterill.

David Moyes, appointed as manager of Everton in March 2002, uses a psychologist to help his players. 'I'm always looking for something new. It might be better fitness, better dietary information, psychology – something to give you an edge. As a coach you need imagination or else your players can become stale and so you need to seek something to fire their imagination and offer them something fresh.'

This type of up-and-coming manager is mad keen for it. There is a look of hunger for success in the eyes of people like Moyes, Cotterill and Nigel Clough, even Ian Atkins, who ought to be worn out by the basement battles he has waged at three clubs near the foot of the Third Division. These are the newer breed of boss, replacing the old-style gaffers. There are no magic sponges, no bully-beef dinners or physical threats to underachieving players.

But is everyone getting a fair crack of the whip? There is talk of a supposed managerial merry-go-round – if so, there seem to be a lot of people who fall off – but is everyone given the chance to leap aboard? Flair players are often viewed as flaky, less likely to be able to cope with the tough rigours of management. And where are Britain's black managers?

At the time of writing – and I make no apologies if I am not up to date now, given the rapid turnover of managers – there are just three black football managers among the 92 Premiership/Football League clubs. Of those, Jean Tigana is French, while Carlton Palmer and Andy Preece, at Stockport and Bury respectively, are in their first managerial jobs. Garry Thompson, Gary Bennett and Noel Blake were black managerial victims of season 2001–02, but even if you total them together to make the most optimistic figure of six black managers of the 92 English League managers, it is still only half of the 12 per cent of black players currently in the game. Where are they?

'Black managers are conspicuous by their absence,' says Piara Power, of the football anti-racism campaign, Kick It Out. 'For the Gullits, Tiganas and John Barnes of this world, whose playing ability might get them a job, it isn't an issue, but for those black managers who are qualified but don't get the chance or don't have a big name, race is a problem.

'Club chairmen aren't prepared to give black players a chance because they want to associate themselves with popular players, or people who tend to reflect something about the town, and that usually means they want a white manager. It leaves a question-mark about the way the game selects its coaches and managers. There is a generalised idea that lower down the Football League the role of the manager is much more important as a media contact and as someone who has respect within the club and the wider community. It is an impresario role and chairmen are less likely to give that to a black person.'

It is a chicken and egg situation. Are black candidates not getting jobs because there is racism in boardrooms, or because not enough black players are taking coaching qualifications and/or applying for jobs? It seems there are too few role models for them to follow. 'Some coaches are concerned about their progress,' says Power. Chris Ramsey is the highest-qualified black coach in England, but has been working in the United States because he couldn't find a good job in English football after he was sacked from Luton, along with another black manager, Ricky Hill. Ramsey also coached the England Under-18s and was a regional FA coach for the South-east.

When you've got just two black British managers it is difficult for black players to have someone to follow,' says Joe Joyce, head of the

PFA's coaching department. 'We have identified that we do need more black players on coaching courses and we're getting a forum together for black coaches to speak to black players to show them the benefits of taking courses.'

Brendan Batson, the PFA's former vice-chairman, now managing director at West Brom and one of the first black British footballers to play in the First Division, whose own manager at West Brom and Cambridge United, Ron Atkinson, accused him of 'having a chip on his shoulder', believes there is a resistance from some black players to taking up management positions. 'They don't see it as a career progression,' admits Batson, who views this as a misconception and believes that the 'glass ceiling' has been broken. 'The opportunities are there. It is a level playing field, it's up to the players to get qualified and put their names forward.'

Like Piara Power, Batson believes racism still exists at football club boardroom level. 'There is a feeling that it is still there and there's nothing to suggest it has changed. But we're drawing from a small potential pool of players. What we have to make sure is they [black players] get their coaching qualifications so they won't be disqualified on those grounds. We did get Ruud Gullit's name mentioned for the England post when Glenn Hoddle got it. Now that would have been unheard of a few years ago, a black person being considered for the England job, so things are changing.'

Batson supports a fresh approach to management. As a young player at Arsenal, when Bertie Mee was manager, he recalls meditating in a field as mental preparation for training. They did aerobics too, long before lycra had been invented. 'I was sitting on the training ground and being told to open my mind and take myself somewhere pleasant and have positive thoughts. It was quite interesting really. Bertie was fantastic.'

Mee was an unusual choice when selected as Arsenal manager in 1966, because he had been one of the club's physiotherapists. 'He was from an untypical football background and was open-minded,' recalls Batson. 'He had an inquisitive mind. He didn't coach at all, but managed to instil in players an ethos that you are playing for a club which looks after its players.

'His motto was: "Remember where you are, who you are and who you represent." His philosophy was we will provide you with the best of everything – the best training facilities, the best travel, best diet, best medical attention.'

Football managers who don't have a conventional playing background – like Mee – are rare. It is difficult, nigh on impossible, for someone who didn't play the game to become a manager. The previous chapter pointed to the acrimony between the professional game and the supposed amateurs who coach the game. If the pro game won't accept outsiders as coach educators, then they stand little chance of becoming a manager. With more specialists employed by clubs in a variety of roles, who is to say this might not change in the future?

Traditionally, it has been difficult enough for players who couldn't fall back on a notable playing career to break into top-flight management. People like Graham Taylor, David Pleat, Dave Bassett, Howard Wilkinson and Jim Smith, have all shown it is possible. But these are still in the minority of British football management. Most gaffers are ex-players, usually at their former clubs. Continental managers like Sven-Goran Eriksson and Gerard Houllier have built careers without anyone referring to their playing days. They see themselves primarily as coaches.

Everton manager Dave Moyes is similar. The Glaswegian had an unremarkable, nomadic playing career beginning with a handful of appearances for Celtic, before moving on south to Cambridge United, Bristol City, Shrewsbury Town, back north to Dunfermline and Hamilton, finally ending his career at Preston North End, where he became manager in January 1998. 'I am a coach. I'm happiest when I'm on the training ground, when it's not too cold and you can stand around and talk about things and help the young lads and work to give them something new.'

We met when he was at Preston, weeks before joining Everton, in PNE's boardroom. Endearingly, his two young children were with him. Mum had 'flu, so Dave was keeping them clear of the house. Not many managers would do this; the lads might think them cissy. They ran merrily around this notoriously friendly club while Dave and I chatted about his background.

Coaching is in the blood. His father ran the Drumchapel Amateurs in Glasgow, a club Alex Ferguson played for, and from the age of six, Davie would go to games with his father. He took up coaching to improve his game. 'I qualified when I was 21 or 22 in Scotland,' he recalls. 'I started very young. I've recently completed the Pro licence course so I've got the full set.'

As a player he would mimic the manager's job by going on scouting missions. 'When I came here as a player everybody knew I hoped to someday be a coach. I used to go on scouting trips at whichever club I was at. Football was my hobby. When I was at Celtic I would go and watch Rangers, Clydebank or Partick Thistle. When I was at Cambridge I would watch Arsenal and Spurs or Norwich and Ipswich. I would always ask the secretary, "Any chance of getting me a ticket to watch these games?" It's something I've always enjoyed.'

Moyes is comfortable with the modern-day coach's role – the chief executive or director of football handling the business side of things: contracts, transfers etc; freeing him to do what he does best, coach and scout. The modern-day media demands at Premiership Everton will be a step up from First Division Preston North End, but Moyes is tipped by many to do well. He might not have a big name but he has pedigree and enthusiasm. For gaffers who hope to survive these are much-needed ingredients.

Managers are also role models. Their mannerisms are likely to be copied on playing fields every Sunday morning. Just go and look sometime. John Stevens, chief executive of Sports Coach UK, believes the gaffers of the future need to present themselves in a better light than many of their predecessors.

'Someone like Sven-Goran Eriksson brings great dignity to his job,' observes Stevens. 'His dealings with the media are professional. He isn't rent-a-quote, he's a coaching role model. You see people on TV who are highly paid, supposedly professional, sports coaches – top football managers – and the way they go about their job portrays a certain image and you then see that image being aped, because imitation is often where most people start in this game. I see practices copied every Sunday morning but I also see coaching behaviour mimicked.'

If you're going to copy anyone, copy good people. Ray Graydon, the new manager of Bristol Rovers, who was sacked by Walsall in January 2002, has never lost his enthusiasm. You virtually have to pin Ray to the floor. We met at a motorway service station. He has been a coach for 20 years and loves it. He can't wait to step back into it, but at the time was taking a break. He isn't a born gaffer – he is happy to be either a coach or manager, comfortable in either role. He was 50 years old when he got his first chance as a manager at Walsall, and although most people would be angry at losing their job in mid-season at a small club who weren't expected to do anything but struggle in Division One, Ray isn't bitter.

'I had served a long managerial apprenticeship. I knew what I wanted to do and how I would do things . . . I could do so much more than a player who has just finished his career. In terms of transfers I probably took in £1 million and spent around £200,000. So I was pleased about that. I won two promotions and had one relegation. I had a burning ambition to be a footballer – but I didn't have the same desire to be a manager. It was more important for me to be happy in my job.'

The fans at Walsall called him 'Sir Ray'. Graydon was certainly noble in the way he handled his dismissal. 'There wasn't the resource to spend lots of money so I knew the situation. And when the chairman called me in and said it was time to move on, I told him there was no bitterness. I had four fantastic years and I could hold my head up high. I said to him: 'Nothing could take away the fantastic time I had here and you and I will remain friends.' They settled my contract straightaway. I'm not bitter about anything. He has to answer to his board and the fans. I think I did okay. I can look anyone in the face and say I left the club in better shape than when I arrived and that's all you can promise.'

Graydon is one of the game's nice guys. You can see the desire in his eyes to get back into football. After our interview he showed me an illicit short cut home. 'Follow me until I turn right . . . I'm going to buy my wife some flowers, because I'm a soppy git.' I did the same. And have many other Fridays since.

Not all managers get their contracts paid up as swiftly as Graydon did at Walsall. It is a big bugbear of the job. The LMA are keen to get the Sports Minister to put pressure on the Football League clubs to agree to settlements within a month of the manager leaving and before they can appoint a successor. This system is already operating in the Premiership. However, while people have sympathy for managers who are left waiting months, maybe years for these payments (and clubs are often quick to claim compensation if a manager leaves for another job), this is likely to fall on deaf ears at struggling clubs, who are staving off relegation and liquidation.

'At the moment a huge success at many clubs is survival,' says Steve Coppell, the former manager of Brentford (he quit in June 2002). 'Bank managers are more important to football clubs than football managers these days, where paying the wages is a massive achievement at many clubs, who exist on poor gates . . . But supporters don't want to hear that.'

So will that make clubs more cautious in sacking managers in the future? 'I think football clubs will learn to be more patient with their managers when they see that the clubs who are successful are those who give their manager time,' says Peter Taylor, the former England Under-21 coach. 'It has to be the way forward.'

Mark McGhee says the sack is 'part and parcel' of the job. 'Football is a dynamic, volatile environment. If you look at the majority of sackings there are understandable circumstances that dictate events. The media and the fans don't see what goes on behind closed doors. Every case is different. People point to the clubs who have managers for a long period of time and say they must be successful, but employing someone for a long period of time could be a disaster. You have to judge each individual case.'

McGhee believes the future of management has to be to ease the manager's heavy workload. 'At Millwall, the chairman negotiates all the contracts and handles the transfers. There is good communication between myself and the chairman. We are a team and we share the responsibilities. It frees my time to work with the players. I think we have to get away from this culture of blame – looking for a simple figurehead to blame if things go wrong. There is more to it than that – but it is understandable the fans will always want someone to blame, and that, I guess, will always be the manager.'

Football management is an enigmatic profession. One generation replaces the next. The ways of Stan Cullis and Matt Busby were different to those of Malcolm Allison, with his fedora, cigar and bottle of Moet, and the ever-ready wit of Tommy Docherty. George Graham and Terry Venables are different to David Moyes, Steve Cotterill and the other younger managers.

No one really expects the sack race to disappear – but their ways will change. Some, of course, just keep on going. Bobby Robson, for example, at 67, is still creating wonderful, entertaining sides. Alex Ferguson, too. These men are married to the job. There really is no substitute for an ageing ex-player.

'I miss it,' says John Barnwell, with a strange pregnant pause. He subconsciously curls his lip round his teeth. 'Yes, I do. There is nothing like putting a team together, improving a player and getting results. But I made a decision to leave and I've kept to it.'

The 'crack' of the dressing-room, the nurturing and coaxing the best out of players, the assembling of a winning team, the unearthing and 'polishing' of rough diamonds: these are the reasons people become football gaffers – to stay in the sack race. They are a breed apart.

Football clubs are essentially dream factories. Inside the confines of the grounds are found hopes and ambitions, real or unreal, massive expectations, anticipation, inspired beliefs, a sense of community, of belonging, of togetherness. Players, directors, fans, the press, everyone attached to football feels it – but no one more than the gaffer.

It seems incomprehensible that British football clubs could ever be run by inconspicuous head coaches in charge of groups of anonymous sports specialists. Football will always needs its leaders and, conversely, its fall guys. The role may soften, coaches may need to be qualified, they may change to being called 'head coach' . . . but they will still be gaffers.

Howard Wilkinson, a deep-thinking man, not given to over-emotion or animation, believes sacking the manager is part of football's 'eco-system'. 'The short tenure of football club coaches compared to elsewhere in the normal world will never go away. It's part of the football business. Football, because of its profile, its popularity and the fans' involvement, needs victims. We have to accept as coaches in the bigger picture we are the most painless victim. It's difficult to get rid of the players, it's difficult to get rid of the directors. At the end of the day the public sees you as the villain of the piece.

'One of the problems is unrealistic ambitions and expectations. No one asks "Where is our true position, where are we entitled to finish?" But if you take the dream away, what is left?' Not a lot.

Bibliography

The Book of Football (The Amalgamated Press, London, 1906)

Butler, Bryon, *The Official History of the Football Association* (Queen Anne Press, London, 1991)

Campbell, Denis, May, Peter, and Shields, Andrew, *The Lad Done Bad – Scandal, Sex and Sleaze in English Football* (Penguin Books, London, 1996)

Crick, Michael, *The Boss: The Many Sides of Alex Ferguson* (Simon & Schuster, London, 2002)

Clark, Frank, *Kicking With Both Feet* (Headline, London, 1999)

Clough, Brian, and Sadler, John, *Clough: The Autobiography* (Corgi, London, 1994)

Conn, David, *The Football Business: Fair Game in the 1990s* (Mainstream, Edinburgh, 1997)

Dunphy, Eamon, *A Strange Kind of Glory: Matt Busby and Manchester United* (Heinemann, London, 1991)

Edworthy, Niall, *The Second Most Important Job in the Country* (Virgin, London, 1999)

Ferguson, Alex, with McIlvanney, Hugh, *Managing My Life: My Autobiography* (Hodder & Stoughton, London, 1999)

The Football Association Coaching Manual (Evans, London, 1936)

The Football Association Handbook (season 2001–02)

The FA Premier League Handbook (season 2001–02)

The Football League Handbook (season 2001–02)

Gibson, Alfred, and Pickford, William, *Association Football And The Men Who Made It* (The Caxton Publishing Co, London 1905)

Higg, Tony, and MacDonald, Tony, *West Ham United Who's Who*

(Independent Sports Publications, London, 1991)

Holden, Jim, *Stan Cullis: The Iron Manager* (The Breedon Book Pub. Co, Derby, 2000)

Hughes, Charles, *The Winning Formula* (Collins, London, 1990)

Koning, Ruud H., 'An econometric evaluation of the firing of a coach on team performance', SOM Research Report No. 00F40, Department of Econometrics, University of Groningen, Netherlands

O'Leary, David, *Leeds United On Trial* (Little, Brown, London, 2002)

Matthews, Stanley, *The Way It Was* (Headline, London, 2000)

Meisl, Willy, *Soccer Revolution* (Phoenix Sports Books, London, 1955)

Morris, Peter, *West Bromwich Albion* (Heinemann, London, 1965)

Mourant, Andrew, *Don Revie, Portrait of a Footballing Enigma* (Mainstream, Edinburgh, 1990)

Novick, Jeremy, *In A League Of Their Own: Football's Maverick Managers* (Mainstream, Edinburgh, 1995)

Pawson, Tony, *The Football Manager* (Methuen, London, 1973)

Robson, Bobby and Harris, Bob, *Against The Odds: An Autobiography* (Stanley Paul, London, 1990)

Rollin, Glenda and Jack (eds), *The Rothmans Football Yearbook 2001–02* (Headline, London, 2001)

Rollin, Jack *The Guinness Football Factbook* (Guinness, Middlesex, 1993)

Smith, Jim and Dawson, Mark, *Bald Eagle* (Mainstream, Edinburgh, 1990)

Soar, Phil and Tyler, Martin, *Arsenal: The Official Centenary History* (Hamlyn, London, 1986)

Tibballs, Geoff, *Do I Not Like That* (Virgin, London, 1995)

Turner, Dennis and White, Alex, *The Breedon Book of Football Managers* (Breedon Pub Co Derby, 1993)

Walvin, James, *The People's Game* (Mainstream, Edinburgh, 1994)

Sources

Jimmy Armfield
Ian Atkins
John Barnwell
John Barton
Brendan Batson
Danny Bergara
Rob Bradley
Craig Brown
Callowbrook Swifts (Nigel
  Brindley)
Frank Clark
Nigel Clough
Steve Coppell
Steve Cotterill
Andrew Cullis
Tommy Docherty
Dr Dorian Dugmore
John Duncan
Chris Evans
Ray Graydon

Kenny Hibbitt
Joe Joyce
Jake King
Mark McGhee
John McGinlay
Jan Molby
Dennis Mortimer
David Moyes
Frank O'Farrell
David Platt
Piara Power
Bruce Rioch
David Sheepshanks
John Steven
Peter Taylor
Paul Thompson
Allen Wade
Howard Wilkinson
Andy Williamson

Index

2001–02 season, review 13–27

agents 119–20, 127–8, 129, 130–2, 167–8
Allison, M. 73–4
appointments, basis of 96, 104, 109, 116–17, 213, 215
Armfield, J. 65–6, 184
Arsenal 57–8, 102, 126, 132–3
assistants, sackings of 96, 97, 98
Atkins, I. 14, 15, 33–4, 116, 209

Barnwell, J. 9, 81–2, 88–90, 151–5, 208, 219
Barton, J. 165–8
Bassett, D. 91, 155–6
Bassett, W.I. 50–1, 52–3
Batson, B. 214
Bergara, D. 10, 134–9, 180–1
Best, G. 85, 141
Birmingham City 22, 38–9, 78, 84
black managers 213–14
Bradley, R. 100–1, 144–5
Brown, C. 112, 117–18, 158, 192–3
Bruce, S. 22
Bungs' Inquiry 119, 127–31
Burley, G. 103
Busby, M. 58–9, 67, 69–72, 85–6, 140–2

chairmen/boards 14, 134, 143–4, 170, 173
relationship with managers 137–43, 145–9

Chapman, H. 57–8, 121
Charlton, B. 141–2
Chelsea 84–5
Clark, F. 37–8, 99–100, 116–17, 139–40
Clough, B. 37–8, 123, 125, 129–30, 168
Clough, N. 165, 168–70
coaching 10–11, 106–7, 112, 197–201, 205–6
history/development of 49–55, 58, 61, 62–3, 65–6, 74
coaching qualifications 23–4, 109, 195–8, 202, 206–7
attitudes to 104–5, 111, 113–15, 202–3, 209
mandatory 24, 110, 115–17, 118, 198, 207
Colchester United 33–4
continuity, benefits of 98, 101–3
contracts
managers 30, 89–90, 217–18
players 48–9, 80–1, 132–3, 147–8, 164–5
Coppell, S. 14, 34–5, 96, 114, 143, 158, 218
corruption/dishonesty 119–21, 122–5, 127–31, 133
Cotterill, S. 157, 159, 160, 212
Coventry City 95
Crewe Alexandra 101, 102
Crystal Palace 22, 34–5, 98–9
Cullis, S. 9–10, 67–9, 72, 75–9, 84

development of

football/management 43–59, 120
current trends/future 11, 211–15, 216, 217–19
1950s ('golden age') 60–74
1960s 79–87
Docherty, T. 48–9, 82, 84–5, 124–5, 139
Dugmore, Dr D. 156, 157, 161–3

England (national team) 61–2, 63–4, 86, 108, 178–9, 184–91
Eriksson, S.-G. 26, 112, 178–9, 183, 185–8
Evans, C. 97–8, 116

FA (Football Association) 49–50, 61, 62–3, 109, 184, 201
fans 16, 27, 41–2, 100, 144
Fenton, R. 127, 128, 129–30
Ferguson, Alex 15, 101–2, 112, 210
Finney, T. 64, 66
foreign coaches/managers 10, 178–9, 180, 183, 186, 192, 193–4
Francis, T. 14, 22, 39

'gaffer', use of term 28–9
Gradi, D. 101, 102
Graham, G. 85, 125, 126, 128
Graydon, R. 37, 96–7, 158, 159, 209, 216–17

health issues/problems 25, 65, 66, 113, 150–63
Hibbitt, K. 114, 131–2, 165, 172–5

Houllier, G. 25, 155, 194
Hughes, C. 199–201, 202

international management
    25–6, 61, 184–93, 194
Ipswich Town 47–8, 102, 103
Ireland, J. 76, 77–8

job descriptions, lack of 30,
    36, 144, 147
Jones, D. 138
Joyce, J. 201–3, 213–14

Keegan, K. 95, 107–9, 113,
    184, 189
King, J. 170–2
Koning, R.H. 93

Leeds United 16–18, 39, 40,
    121–2, 204
Leicester City 91, 94
Lincoln City 41, 100–01, 144
Liverpool 71, 83, 102, 182–3
LMA (League Managers
    Association) 15, 88–9,
    156, 186, 207–8
loyalty 21–2, 83, 101–3

management qualifications
    204–5, 208
    see also coaching
    qualifications
Manchester City 58–9, 95,
    99–100, 108, 139–40
Manchester United 67,
    69–72, 85–6, 124–5, 131,
    140–3, 210
    match fixing 122, 123
Matthews, S. 54, 61–2
McGhee, M. 157–8, 211–12,
    218
McGinlay, J. 165, 175–7
Mee, B. 214–15
Megson, G. 12, 20–1, 145–6,
    148, 149, 211
Meisl, W. 56–7, 58, 65
Molby, J. 36, 158, 182–3
Mortimer, D. 55, 109, 186,
    198–9
Moyes, D. 27, 38–9, 117, 158,
    212, 215–16

new managers, difficulties
    30–2, 33–5
Newcastle United 107, 108

non-league management
    164–77
Nottingham Forest 102, 125,
    129–30

O'Farrell, F 30–31, 32, 72–3,
    74, 82–3, 140–43
O'Leary, D. 17–18
ownership issues, clubs
    143–5

PFA (Professional
    Footballers' Association)
    15, 80, 201–2
Platt, D. 24, 109–12, 113,
    194, 206
pressure, effects of 25,
    150–51, 155–6, 161–2

racism 15, 213, 214
re-employment, after
    resignation/sacking 21,
    89, 97, 139, 140
resignations 21, 90–91
Revie, D. 121–3
Rioch, B. 30–2, 35–6, 39,
    132–3, 159, 160–61
role of managers 20, 29–42,
    114–15, 132, 134, 146–8,
    160
    development of 47–9, 51,
    60, 79–80, 82, 86–7
Rous, S. 49, 50, 61, 62

sackings
    effects of 87, 91–6, 98–100
    reasons for 11, 15–16, 89,
    93, 95–6, 134
    statistics 14, 83–4, 88, 90
Scotland
    coaching 26–7, 117–18,
    196
    national team 192–3
Shankly, B. 71
Sheepshanks, D. 47–8, 103,
    209
Sheffield United 18–19
Sheringham, T. 127, 128–9
Smith, J. 14, 211
Souness, G. 183
Stevens, J. 112–13, 114–15,
    216
Stock, A. 11–12, 31, 37
Stockport County 10, 136–9
Strachan, G. 14, 95

Swindon Town 123–4

tactics, football 56–8, 69, 73,
    86, 199–201
Taylor, G. 41–2, 117, 185,
    189–92, 207–8
Taylor, P. 16, 22–3, 94, 157,
    218
television 13, 86–7
Telford United 170, 171
tenure, managers 14, 83–4,
    90, 99, 219
Thompson, P. 19–21, 145–9
Tottenham Hotspur 126–7,
    129
training methods 50, 51–5,
    69, 73, 106–7, 180–82
transfers 80, 81, 119–20,
    127–31, 132

Venables, T. 85, 125–7, 129,
    184–5, 189

Wade, A. 74, 117, 197–8,
    199, 205
wages 49, 80–1, 82–3, 84, 85,
    109
Walsall 96–7, 217
Warnock, N. 18–19
Watford 41–2
Wenger, A. 194
West Bromwich Albion
    18–21, 30, 48, 145–6,
    148, 149
West Ham United 72–3, 83,
    102, 103
Wilkinson, H. 30, 39–40, 54,
    86, 132, 196, 203–7, 219
Winterbottom, W. 49, 62–6,
    74, 197
Wolverhampton Wanderers
    9–10, 67, 68–9, 75–9,
    97–8, 152–4
Worcester City 165–7
working hours 24–5, 29, 35,
    158, 159, 168
    non-league management
    165–6, 168, 174–5, 176–7
World Cup 58, 61, 63–4, 86,
    187–8, 193

youth development 97–8,
    115–16, 164–5